The Keekin-Gless

The Keekin-Gless

An Anthology of Poetry and Prose from Perth & Kinross

Edited by

Robert Alan Jamieson (1995)
and
Carl MacDougall (1999)

William Soutar Fellows

and
an essay on the literary traditions of Perth & Kinross

Perth & Kinross Libraries
1999

in memoriam:
T.S. Law
Alex Galloway

edited by
Robert Alan Jamieson and Carl MacDougall

ISBN 0 905452 23 2

Published by
Perth and Kinross Libraries
1999

Subsidised by the Scottish Arts Council

Printed by
Cordfall Ltd
0141 572 0878

Front Cover
'Perthshire Landscape' by John Duncan Fergusson (1922)
© The Fergusson Gallery, Perth and Kinross Council, Scotland

The Keekin-Gless

William Soutar

Lassie at the keekin-gless
ye arena there yoursel';
Owre ilka shüther is a face
That comes to keek as weel.

Lassie at the keekin-gless
Ye aye maun look on three:
The dead face, and the livin face,
And the ane that is to be.

(1941)

Acknowledgements

Thanks are due to the many folk who've helped make this publication possible: but especially to Jim Guthrie, Mike Moir and the library staff, Joy Hendry, John Law, Murdo Macdonald, Stuart McHardy, Gordon Beange, Joan McEwen, Sheila and Andrew Douglas and The Scots Language Society, Lynn Baxter, Jim Finnie, Margaret Gillies Brown, Willie Davidson and the Perthshire Writers Group, Louise Moran and Dunkeld & Birnam Writers, Jane Higgins and Blairgowrie & Rattray Writers Group, the Mither Tongue, the University of the Third Age, and all the writers who submitted material. Most of all, thanks to the Soutar family whose hospitality the William Soutar Fellow continues to enjoy, and to the Jamieson family, whose patience I try.

Robin Bell's poems are from *Scanning The Forth Bridge* (1995), published by Peterloo Poets; George Gunn's 'Nine Lyrics from Strathmore' are from *Sting* (1991), published by Chapman; Ian Abbott's collection *Avoiding the Gods* is published by Chapman; Margaret Gillies Brown's 'Parachutes' and 'Buchanty Spout, October' are from *Footsteps of the Goddess* (1994), published by Akros.

Research for 'Literary Figures in Perth & Kinross' made use of a number of sources, but special mention is due to *Fair Upon Tay: a Tayside anthology*, edited by Sheila Douglas, published by the Scots Language Resource Centre, A. K. Bell Library, Perth; *The MacMillan Companion to Scottish Literature*, edited by Trevor Royle, published by MacMillan; *Encyclopaedia Britannica*, 11th edition, which belonged to William Soutar and which was returned to the Soutar Hoose in 1988 by Alex Galloway, to whom Soutar had given it before his death in 1943.

Robert Alan Jamieson

General Introduction

The best laid schemes o' mice an' men
Gang aft a-gley,
And lea'e us nought but grief and pain
For promis'd joy.

So writes the National Bard, oft quoted with approbation as a universal truth – and of course there's verity within it. But what it fails to tell us is that often schemes are not so well-laid and that the force which overturns them sometimes opens up new possibilities, quite unforeseen – that joy can be the issue of the unexpected, as well as grief and pain. The anthology you are now reading arose out of such a circumstance, my original schemes having gone happily a-gley, leading to the production of the book you now have in your hand.

For this scheme started out not as one but as three. Firstly, my personal researches into the literary traditions of Perth and Kinross since I took up the William Soutar Fellowship in September 1993; secondly, a project involving writers' groups and individual writers to produce a portrait of the area through poetry and prose sketches; and thirdly, the 'Perthshire in Bloom' creative writing competition organised by the Leisure and Recreation department of Perth and Kinross District Council, which I judged in conjunction with Lynn Baxter of Perth Community Arts and Jim Finnie of Leisure and Recreation.

These three initiatives started out quite separately, but as they progressed I began to see how mutually informative they were. The historical dimension to literature in the area actually helped contextualise much of the work being produced by the writers of today, while the 'Perthshire in Bloom' competition, organised on a four part basis introduced a seasonal dimension to the portrait of the area which I had not initially envisaged. Allied to this was the fact that in response to my appeal for writing about the area, I received pieces which were set in the past and therefore didn't fit with the plan, which was to sketch the contemporary scene – but were nevertheless well-written and deserved to be published, even if they didn't fit with my rubric.

So, in the spirit of adaptability which has served folk so well throughout the ages of human existence, I set aside my not-so-best-laid schemes and began to consider how this circumstance might be utilised to benefit all concerned. I think that the outcome is a most interesting publication which maps the territory, of literature in relation to Perth and Kinross, quite effectively. It brings together past, present and – in the writing of the children included – the future. It outlines how the landscape has affected the work folk do, and how that work has moulded the culture. And by juxtaposing the bright voices of childern with the reminiscences of older people, by contrasting celebrations of the seasons with darker tales of homelessness, adjustment to personal loss and abuse, by setting the city of Perth in the context of the country around it, something of the fullness of life as lived in Perth and Kinross is captured. And perhaps most importantly of all, it shows how the local area is connected into the national scene – and indeed, the international.

Having adapted my plans and settled on a structure, the question was then, what to call it – the child needed a name. As always, this is a difficult process which, if one is honest, is often fairly arbitrary. I considered a number of possibilities, and finally, in exasperation, I asked the spirit of my patron for assistance. I picked up Dr. Aitken's selected poems of William Soutar and opened it – hopefully – at random. The poem which met my eye was one my mind hadn't registered before, although I must have read it once at least. At first glance I thought it wouldn't do, but when I read it through, I saw the connection – the keekin-gless, or mirror, was a metaphor for the function of literature in reflecting the world back at itself, so that we may see ourselves as others see us. Literature, indeed all art, has the capacity to do just that. And in this poem of Soutar's, had he not identified exactly the three aspects of past, present and future, 'the dead face, and the livin face, And the ane that is to be'?

So I offer you this keekin-gless, with three faces in it, and hope that you'll look long into the light that it reflects on Perth and Kinross.

RAJ

Literary Figures in Perth & Kinross

Chronological List

Ossian (3rd century?)
Andrew of Wyntoun (c.1355-1442)
Gavin Douglas (c.1474-1522)
John Gaw (d.1533)
James MacGregor (d.1551)
The Wedderburn brothers: James (d.1553), John (d.1556) Robert (d.1557)
Alexander Scott (c.1515-83)
John Stewart of Baldynneis (1539-1606)
James Tyrie (1543-97)
George Bannatyne (1545-1608)
James Crichton of Cluny (1560-1582)
Sir David Murray (1567-1629)
David Malloch (c.1705-65)
Dughall Bochanan (1716-68)
Adam Ferguson (1723-1816)
Donnchadh Ban mac an t-Saoir (1724-1812)
Jeremiah Stone (1727-1756)
Michael Bruce (1746-67)
Robert Burns (1759-96)
Carolina Oliphant (1766-1845)
Walter Scott (1771-1832)
George Gilfillan (1813-78)
Robert Nicholl (1814-37)
John Ruskin (1819-1900)
David Pae (1828-84)
James Logie Robertson (Hugh Haliburton) (1846-1922)
John Watson (Ian MacLaren) (1850-1907)
Patrick Geddes (1854-1932)
William Archer (1856-1924)
John Davidson (1857-1909)
Mary Findlater (1865-1963)
Jane Findlater (1866-1946)
Beatrix Potter (1866-1943)
John Buchan (1875-1940)
Christopher Grieve (Hugh MacDiarmid) (1892-1978)
Naomi Mitchison (b. 1897-1999)
William Soutar (1898-1943)
Ewan MacColl (1915-1989)
Hamish Henderson (b. 1919)
Atholl Cameron (1917-1992)
James Kennaway (1928-1968)
Ian Abbot (1944-1989)

An Historical Narrative

Robert Alan Jamieson

The first literary connection with the area is through the semi-mythical figure of **Ossian**, the son of Fingal, thought by some to have been a 3rd century Celtic warrior and poet. Ossian's very existence has been challenged by some scholars and while Perthshire can point towards a great stone in the Sma Glen as "Ossian's Grave", it should be noted that County Antrim in Northern Ireland also boasts of an "Ossian's Grave". In fact the historical data is so uncertain that it is best to pass over the matter until a later period in history, when his figure emerges from the Dark Age mists to inspire writers of the Romantic period.

Setting aside Ossian for the moment, perhaps the first figure of note is **Andrew of Wyntoun**, (c.1355-1422), who was Prior of St. Serf's Inch in Loch Leven from 1395 until 1413. These were years of struggle in Scotland, as various noble families vied for control and external forces continued to threaten Scottish independence. At the behest of his patron Sir John Wemyss, Andrew wrote *An Orygynale Chronykil of Scotland*, a history of the country from the Creation onwards. It may well have been designed as an early exercise in political propaganda, as the author is keen to assert the nature of Scottish independence, yet the chronicle is an important source for information on earlier eras of Scottish history.

One of the results of the turmoil of this period was the imprisonment of young **King James I** (1394-1437) in England for eighteen years. James was influenced by the ways of the English court, where the work of the poets Chaucer and Lydgate enjoyed popularity.

When he returned to Scotland in 1424, James set about taking control of the kingdom by whatever means was necessary. Perthshire was central in this and at first the king's greatest ally was Walter Stewart, earl of Atholl, Caithness and Strathearn. But James alienated many of the nobles by his excessive demands and, famously, he met his end in Perth when murdered at Blackfriars, with the earl of Atholl implicated. The news of his assassination spread across Europe and versions of the story were written in France and Italy. In England the poet John Shirley (c.1366-1456) translated 'The Dethe of the King of Scottis' from Latin, the best account of the murder extant.

In 1783 William Tytler discovered and published *The Kingis Quair*, a Scots poem of 197 stanzas written in rhyme-royal by King James I, telling the story of his love for Lady Joan Beaufort. Other poems have been attributed to him, including 'Christis Kirk on the Green' and 'The Ballad of Good Counsel'.

A member of one of the great families in Scotland in the medieval world, **Gavin Douglas** (c.1474-1522) was the son of the 5th earl of Angus. He attended the University of St. Andrews and may have studied in Paris subsequently, but it is with his appointment to the Deanery of Dunkeld that he comes within our focus here. After a period as Provost of the Collegiate Church of St. Giles in Edinburgh, Douglas returned as Bishop of Dunkeld in 1515. The site of his house in Perth is marked by a plaque in St. John Street, opposite the Salutation Hotel. The house itself was demolished in 1821.

Douglas is often described as one of the Scottish Chaucerians, along with Henryson and Dunbar. His use of Middle Scots as a medium for his compositions helped to extend the literary frontiers of that language, and he is remembered particularly for his translation of Virgil, *The XIII Bukes of the Eneados of the Famous Poet Virgile Translated out of Latyne Versis into Scottis Meter*. His description of a northern winter's day from the Prologue to Book VII may strike a chord even today, especially in mind of his residence in Perth:

> The soyl ysowpit into watir wak
> The firmament ourcast with rokis blak,
> The grond fadyt, and fawch wolx all the feildis,
> Montane toppis slekit with snaw ourheildis;
> On raggit rolkis of hard harsk quhyn stane
> With frosyn cauld clynty clewis schane.
> Bewte was lost, and barrand schew the landis,
> With frostis hair ourfret the feldis standis.
> Seir bittir bubbis and the schowris snell
> Semyt on the sward a symylitude of hell,
> Reducyng to our mynd, in every sted,
> Gousty schaddois of eild and grisly ded.
> Thik drumly skuggis dyrknyt so the hevyn,
> Dym skyis oft furth warpit feirfull levyn,
> Flaggis of fire, and mony felloun flaw,
> Scharpe soppys of sleit and of the snyppand snaw.
> The dolly dichis war all donk and wait,
> The law valle flodderit all with spait,
> The plane stretis and every hie way
> Full of floschis, dubbis, myre and clay.

In a rough translation this reads:

> The soil soaked into watery mush/ The firmament overcast with black clouds/ The ground faded, the fields all paled/ Mountain tops slick with snow were covered/ On ragged crags of hard harsh rock whinstone/ With frozen fronts cold flinty cliffs shone/ Beauty was lost, and barren showed the lands/ With frosty hair over all the fields stand/ Waves of bitter blasts and showers sharp/ Seemed on the sward a similitude of hell/ Bringing to our mind, in every stead/ Ghostly shadows of old age and death/ Thick gloomy shapes darkened so the heaven/ Dim skies oft threw forth fearful lightning/ Flashes of fire, and many a fell quall/ Sharp sops of sleet and of the sniping snow/ The doleful ditches were all dank and wet/ The low vale flooded all with spate/ The flat streets and every highway/ Full of muddy puddles, mire and clay.

It is not too fanciful to imagine this scene being composed in the old town of Perth with its flat street plan, and where people know from all too recent experience about 'the low vale flooded all with spate'. But of course the winter's harshness is balanced by the beauty of the Tay in summer and a poem attributed to **King James IV** (1473-1513) describes these equally as clearly:

> When Tayis Bank was blumyt brycht with blossumes brycht and bred,
> By that river that ran doun rycht undir the ryss I red;
> The merle meltit with all her mycht and mirth in mornyng maid,
> Throw solace, sound and semely sicht alswyth a sang I said.

Again in rough translation:

> When Tay's bank was blooming bright with blossums bright and broad/ By that river that ran down right through the reeds I rode/ The blackbird whistled with all her might and mirth in morning made/ Through solace, sound and seemly sight right out a song I said.

This is the opening stanza of 'Tayis Bank, or Lord Drummond's Beautiful daughter', a poem of fifteen quattrains reproduced in full in P.W. Drummond's *Perthshire in Bygone Days* (1879). The 'beautiful daughter' of the title was Margaret Drummond (d.1501) who was wooed by the king and apparently became his fiance, though they never married. James IV had a number of mistresses and children by some of them.

After the battle of Flodden in 1513 at which James IV was killed, Gavin Douglas' work as poet seems to have been suspended in favour of political manouvering. With Scotland under the regency of the Duke of Albany, the Douglas family were vying for power and Gavin Douglas was imprisoned in St. Andrews for a time before being exiled in London, where he died of plague in September 1522.

Around this time, **James MacGregor**, best known as the Dean of Lismore, succeeded to the hereditary post of Vicar of Fortingall in Glen Lyon. MacGregor's outstanding contribution to Scottish Gaelic literature remained little known until after the Ossianic controversy of the 18th century, when the 'translations' of the Badenoch schoolteacher James Macpherson became the fashion of literary Europe following the publication of his *Fingal, an ancient Epic Poem, in six books, together with several other poems composed by Ossian, the son of Fingal, translated from the Gaelic Language by James Macpherson* (1761). These prose poems which Macpherson claimed to be English versions of a great Highland epic, composed by a 3rd century warrior-bard, were greeted with enthusiasm in Edinburgh, but challenged by the London club headed by Dr. Johnson as forgeries. The provenance of these Ossianic poems become a *cause celebre* throughout Scotland and Ireland for a century and more to follow.

James MacGregor, Dean of Lismore and vicar of Fortingall, whose work might have spared some of Macpherson's blushes had it come to light sooner, died in 1551. The reemergence of the texts written down by MacGregor and his brother Duncan in the early 16th century in *The Book of The Dean of Lismore* helped validate some of Macpherson's material. It comprises 88 poems, reckoned mostly to have been composed in the early 14th century by clan bards, and includes praise poems, love songs, satires and laments as well as the Ossianic poems celebrating the Fenian heroes.

It is interesting to note that in 1732 soldiers building the Wade Road from Crieff to Dalnacardoch shifted the great boulder in the Sma' Glen known as Clach Ossian, and found a stone coffin containing burnt bones. These were carried away by a procession of some eighty locals led by a piper, venerating the remains as those of Ossian himself, and were deposited under a great cairn atop the western side of Glen Almond, where they would never more be disturbed by man.

Although it seems that the remains were most probably prehistoric, we can imagine the story of the rediscovery of Ossian's bones being carried northwards by the roadmen, into Badenoch where the young Macpherson was born in 1736 – literally, a rolling away of the stone which led to the resurrection of the poetic spirit hailed throughout Europe as the 'Northern Homer'. Burns and Wordsworth have been among the pilgrims who have gone to pay homage in the Sma' Glen.

It might also be mentioned here, although out of step with our chronology, that Ossian's Cave at the Hermitage near Dunkeld postdates Macpherson, although is a magnificent tribute to the popularity of the Romantic myth right into in the 19th century, and that one of the first appearances of translations from the Gaelic were by **Jeremiah Stone** whose poem 'Alvin, or the Daughter of Mey', with some others, appeared in *The Scots Magazine* in 1756. Stone had started life as a pedlar laddie, but through his own efforts rose to be schoolmaster in Dunkeld, where he died at the age of 29.

Another poet and churchman, **Alexander Scott** (c1515-83) was made Canon of Inchaffray in Strathearn and later acquired further estates in the area. His poems fall into two rough categories: courtly love lyrics and others preaching morals, with the exception of 'The Justing and Debait up at the drum betwix William Adamsone and John Sym' which is a pastiche of the more earthy folk tradition. Thirty six of Scott's poems were preserved in the manuscripts collected by **George Bannatyne** (1545-1600), the son of a lawyer from Kirkton of Newtyle in nearby Forfarshire. Besides Scott's work these priceless manuscripts running to over 500 pages were responsible for preserving the works of William Dunbar, Robert Henryson and Sir David Lyndsay, along with many lesser writers. They were held in the family of Bannatyne's daughter until 1724, when the then owner Lord Hyndeford allowed parts to be published in *The Evergreen*, a two volume collection of early and Middle Scots poetry compiled by Allan Ramsay.

It was at St. John's in Perth in 1559 that John Knox delivered the sermon which may be said to have precipitated the Reformation in Scotland, but even before that we find a Perth-born divine disputing the proper path for the Church to take. **John Gaw** (d.1533), whose treatise 'The Richt Vay to the Kingdoms of Heuine' is one of the few religious works written in Scots during the Reformation period, studied in Denmark and Germany.

Later, and in opposition to Knox over the indivisibility of the Church, another son of Perth **James Tyrie** (1543-97) published 'The Refutation of ane answer made by Schir John Knox to ane letter send be James Tyrie', again in Scots. Tyrie was educated in St. Andrews and Louvain, France. He entered the Jesuit College at Clermont, and later became its Rector.

Whether by coincidence or not, the writers aforementioned have mostly been churchmen, while those immediately to follow are of a new breed – the courtier poets. It may be that the Reformation meant that matters of religious concern so overtook the clergy that none had time for simple poetry. It may be that the emergence of the Renaissance had redefined the proper skills for a courtier to acquire. Added to this, the gradual introduction of printing changed the status of literature. Of course these events are not distinct from one another, but are contiguous, as will be seen.

A contemporary of Alexander Scott's who owned land at Baldynneis near Dunning, **John Stewart** (1539-1606) was a distant cousin of James VI, of whose 'Castalian Band' of poets Stewart was leading member. This group, which included Alexander Montgomerie and William Fowler, was formed after the king's imprisonment by the Scottish nobles following the Raid of Ruthven in 1582. Its aim was to encourage a literary revival, and the young king himself laid down the ground rules in his essay, a 'Schort Treatise conteining some Reulis and Cautelis to be obseruit and eschewit in Scottis Poesie', a serious attempt to introduce the Renaissance into Scotland's literature. Stewart's poems and sonnets appeared in *Rapsodies of the Author's Youthfull Brains* (1556) but his most successful work was a translation of Ariosto's 'Orlando Furioso'.

However, the strains of such a dictatorial approach soon told. Montgomerie was banished for his religious beliefs, and when the court favourite 'the Master of Gray' fell from grace, John Stewart of Baldynneis went with him. He spent his last years in Strathearn, where he died three years after the removal of the court to London in 1603 following the Union of the Crowns. With the court went the patronage on which James VI's Renaissance experiment depended.

Short-lived but greatly admired, **James Crichton of Cluny** is a shadowy but exotic figure, the very essence of a Renaissance man. By some accounts he was born on August 19th 1560 at Cluny although others suggest his birthplace as Eliock in Dumfriesshire. He was an outstanding student at St. Andrews University, where his physical strength and beauty made him a favourite. By 1577 he was in Paris, where certain legends grew up around him. He is described as 'displaying a considerable Classical knowledge', 'a good linguist', 'a ready and versatile writer of verse' and, above all, as having 'an astounding memory'. His biographer Sir Thomas Urquart states that in Paris Crichton held dispute in the college of Navarre, on any subject and in twelve languages, and that the next day he won a tilting match at the Louvre.

By 1579 we find him in Italy, addressing the Senate and Doge in Genoa; in 1580, Venice, where a handbill advertising his skills gives a short summary of his appearance and skills: 'he speaks ten languages, has a command of philosophy, theology, mathematics; he improvises Latin verses in all metres and on all subjects, has all Aristotle and his commentators at his fingers' ends; is of the most beautiful appearance, a soldier from top to toe, &c.'

In Venice he defeated all disputants except Mazzoni and was followed around by an admiring crowd wherever he went. From here he moved on to Padua in triumph and continued his success in Latin debate. Urquhart states that he then went to Mantua where he was employed as tutor to the young Prince, and that he was killed by his pupil in a street quarrel in 1582, although this has been challenged.

So little work by this amazing youth (let it not be forgotten that he was barely twenty-one years old) remains extant that it difficult to judge his abilities as a writer. His fame rests more on Urquhart's hagiography than the rather dull, learned disquisitions published bearing his name. It is possible that Crichton's art was dependent more on his quick-minded and beautiful presence than his skills as a writer.

The third of these courtier poets is **Sir David Murray**, born in Abercairney in 1567. He first appears in records as Comptroller of the Royal Household and a Gentleman of the Bedchamber to the son of James VI, Prince Henry, and for his services to the Crown he was awarded a state pension and granted the lands of Gorthy, where he died in 1629. His poems were published by the Bannatyne Club in 1823 and include sonnets *Coelia* (1611), a long poem *The Tragicall Death of Sophonisba* (1611), a metrical version of Psalm CIV (1615), and *The Complaint of the Shepherd Harpatus* (1620).

In the seventeenth century there occurs a lull in literary activity not only in the area we are concerned with, but in Scotland generally, rivven by war and religious dispute, deprived of King and court as it was. As Agnes Mure Mackenzie writes in *Scottish Literature to 1714*:

> The "literary" poetic tradition of Scotland had ended in blood by the middle century, not to revive again for a long time; and for the last hundred years it had run thin enough, though the stream is "Helicon the clere well." Parallel with it, however, for its last century and a half, and outliving it, is another growing stronger as that weakens, since on it the Reformation had slower effect. This is the tradition of "popular" or "folk" verse, which after it first shows is never quite cut off, surviving underground through the Valley of Dry Bones, to emerge again in the fulness of time and inspire some of the greatest things of the eighteenth-century Risorgimento — to be the seed of Burns, and transmuted, of some of the finest things in Scott.

According to Mrs. Mackenzie, it is with **James Graham, Marquis of Montrose** (1612-50) that this "literary" poetic tradition dies in mid-seventeenth century Scotland:

> . . . almost the last serious verse of our literature, for two full generations, is the lament for him (King Charles I) by his great servant Montrose, a strange fierce thing, only too passionate to be grotesque in its image, a cry from the soul of a man who had the strength to storm Corryarrick in deep winter, will to fire a dead-beat army in the retreat from Dundee, but swooned headlong at the news of his master's death.

The Graham family held lands in Perthshire and one of the family seats was at Aberuthven near Auchterarder, where the young James Graham spent part of his youth. As a boy he wrote poetry, though he was reticent about showing it to anyone. Following the death of his father, he became the 5th Earl of Montrose in

1626. He was educated at St. Andrews and travelled abroad. When the religious tensions broke into political action in 1637, he was one of the four noblemen who drew up the National Covenant, and in 1638 he suppressed opposition to the popular cause in the north-east. In 1639, following the signing of the Treaty of Berwick, he became disaffected from the Covenanting cause, opposing the power-base of Argyll. He was cited in Parliament as communicating with King Charles I, and imprisoned for five months in Edinburgh Castle, after which he retired from public life in Oxford.

In 1644, he reentered Scotland as the king's lieutenant-general and met with a force of 1200 Scoto-Irish auxiliaries at Blair Atholl. With these and the support of the clans, despite being poorly equipped, his army routed Lord Elcho's forces near Perth, at the Battle of Tippermuir on September 1st, 1644. After long campaigns northwards through Buchan, Moray, Badenoch and Lochaber, his famous victory at Kilsyth and defeat at Philliphaugh near Selkirk, he returned to Atholl to try to raise another Highland army. Unsuccessful, in 1646 he sailed for Norway and rounded the North Sea to Germany, the Low Countries and Paris. After the execution of Charles I, Montrose swore to avenge his death and attempted to return to Scotland through Orkney into Caithness. He and his small army were shipwrecked and what few survived this disaster were cut to remnants at Invercharron in Ross-shire. Afterwards Montrose lived as a fugitive in the wilds of Sutherland, till he was surrendered by MacLeod of Assynt, into whose protection he had entrusted himself. He was taken to Edinburgh and hung, drawn and quartered in the High Street on May 21st, 1650. Eleven years later, his remains were gathered from the airts and buried in St. Giles – all bar his heart, which has its own romantic tale. In 1888 a stately monument was erected in there.

Montrose was a man whose remarkable deeds inspired respect even among those whose beliefs placed them on the other side of the religious divide. Biographies of this heroic figure have been written by John Buchan and Margaret Irwin, among others. Of his poetry, little now remains.

The death of Montrose marks the end of a certain literary tradition, but as has been pointed out, another begins to emerge from 'underground' to take its place – a tradition belonging to the world of the 'folk', rather than the aristocracy or the church.

The first signs of this 'underground' oral tradition transferring from the spoken to the written had already taken place, with the aforementioned *Book of the Dean of Lismore* in the Gaelic world, and in Scots through the work of the **Wedderburns** of Dundee – three brothers of the sixteenth century, James (d.1553), John (d.1556) and Robert (d.1557) who collected sacred and secular songs and ballads together in *Ane compendious Book of Godlie Psalms and Spirituall Songs collected out of the sundrie partes of the Scriptures with sundrie of other ballads changed out of prophane sangis for avoyding of sinne and harlotrie with the augmentatioun of sundrie gude and godlie Ballais not contend in the first editioun* (1567 – the first edition is lost). Let any publisher try to fit that title on the spine of a book! Commonly known as *The Gude and Godlie Ballads.* this book contained evidence of the ballad tradition without leaving much for the reader to enjoy after they had been 'changed out of prophane sangis'.

However, by the early eighteenth century, the oral tradition was beginning to merge with the literary. Ballads such as 'The Gaberlunzie Man', 'Edward, Edward', and 'The Twa Corbies' clearly belonged deep in Scottish culture, whether oral or literate, and their influence spread through Scottish literature increasingly. Allan Ramsay, who helped revive the earlier literary tradition in *The Evergreen*, also assisted the emergence of the oral through *The Tea Table Miscellany: a Collection of Choice Songs, Scots and English* (1724 and 25; 27; 32; 37). Although many of the songs were Anglicised to suit genteel taste, *The Tea Table Miscellany* helped spark patriotric interest in the ballads and the folk tradition – and literary figures from this area were involved in this resurgence.

David Malloch, who changed his surname to Mallet after he arrived in London so dropping a consonant alien to the Southron tongue, was born near Bridge of Earn sometime around 1705. He was the son of a farmer and attended the High School in Edinburgh where he befriended James Thomson, later author of *The Seasons*. Malloch began publishing poems in Edinburgh as early as 1720, and a ballad of his entitled 'William and Margaret' appeared in Ramsay's *Tea Table Miscellany*. He was afterwards private tutor to the Duke of Montrose's sons and travelled on the continent, before taking his MA at Oxford. In London he befriended Alexander Pope, then at the height of his popularity, and through this connection he was made private secretary to the Prince of Wales. After Pope's death, however, he vilified the poet's memory and earned considerable notoriety. He was satirised as 'Moloch' by John Denis and Dr. Johnson in his dictionary gave the meaning of 'alias' as 'otherwise, as Mallet *alias* Malloch, that is otherwise Malloch.' He had become, in effect, a professional writer, whose pen could be bought. It was a pathway trod by any number of writers in London seeking patronage.

Malloch's works included plays produced by his friend David Garrick at Drury Lane, a life of Francis Bacon, a memoir of Lord Bollingbroke, and co-authorship of the patriotic song now such a fixture at the Last Night of the Proms, 'Rule Brittannia'. He is now best remembered as the author of ballads and songs, an edition of which was published in 1857.

If Malloch was a man on the make who put his literary skills to work in the political mill to the detriment of his poetry, **Donnchadh Ban mac an t-Saoir (Duncan Ban MacIntyre)** (1724-1821) was the exact opposite. Born March 20th 1724 and raised in Glen Orchy on the border between Perthshire and Argyll, his early working life was spent as gamekeeper and forester there. His first contact with the world of literature seems to have been through the Rev. James Stewart of Killin. The publication of Alasdair Mac Mhaighstir Alasdair's *Ais-eiridh na Sean Cháin Albannaich* (1751) caused an upsurge of interest in Gaelic writing, partly because it was so controversial in its favouring of the Jacobite and nationalist cause, and Donnchadh Ban may have been influenced by its appearance. Whatever, being illiterate, his own poetry was written down for him by the Rev. Stewart's son John, who prepared a volume for the press, and shortly before their publication in 1768, the poet moved to Edinburgh. Here he worked as a sedan chair man – the equivalent then of a taxi-driver – and served in the City Guard. Despite the publication of his poetry, it seems he did not meet with the literary establishment of the enlightenment city and we are left to wonder what a fraction of the patronage lavished on Malloch might have meant to him as a writer.

Donnchadh Ban mac an t-Saoir's nature poetry is reckoned to be in the highest rank of Gaelic writing, and even in translation his extraordinary talents are obvious. His long poem 'Moladh Beinn Dobhrainn' (Praise of Ben Dorain) is a remarkable work which imitates the complex structure of the classic Pibroch or *ceol mor*, and has been translated into English by both Hugh MacDiarmid and Iain Crichton Smith.

A second Perthshire Gaelic poet of this period whose life is connected with Donnchadh Ban is *Dughall Bochanan (Dugald Buchanan)* (1716-68), a relative of Rob Roy MacGregor, who was born at Ardoch in Strathyre and educated at the parish school, after which he became tutor to a neighbouring family. From there he went to Stirling for two years further education and then on to Edinburgh. At the age of eighteen he was apprenticed to a carpenter in Kippen, but returned to his father's farm in Ardoch after he was married. In 1753 he was appointed as teacher to Kinloch Rannoch and subsequently became catechist there.

In 1767, along with the same Rev. Stewart of Killin, he was appointed to supervise the printing of the Gaelic New Testament in Edinburgh. The first edition of his 'songs' were published at this time. While in Edinburgh he attended classes at the University in philosophy, astronomy and anatomy and met, amongst others, David Hume with whom he had a famous encounter. Hume quoted Shakespeare, *The Tempest*, Act IV Scene 1 148-158, and asserted that in his opinion it had no equal. Buchanan in reponse quoted Revelation XX 11-13, 'the solemn grandeur of which Hume admitted'.

Two years later Buchanan went back to Kinloch Rannoch to attend to his family who were ill with a fever, and caught the infection. He died, aged 52, and was buried with great pomp. In 1785 a monument was erected at Kinloch Rannoch by public subscription.

Buchanan's work is full of religious fervour, as might be expected, and was extremely popular in its day. The editor of the 1913 edition of *The Spiritual Songs of Dugald Buchanan*, Rev. Donald MacLean asserts that "what the sublime conceptions of Milton and John Bunyan were to the devout thought of England, those of the sacred bard of Rannoch have been to Gaelic Scotland . . . no Gaelic book has been printed so frequently as these poems".

Like Donnchadh Ban mac an t-Saoir, the 'Gentle Poet of Lochleven' **Michael Bruce** (1746-1767) knew the natural world well. Born at Kinnesswood on March 27th, Bruce was the son of a weaver. His father Alexander was a member of the Secessionist Church with a great love of the folk tradition and son followed father in his interests. Encouraged in every way by his parents, he gained an education beyond the expectation of a lad beginning life in his social position. A gifted child, after attending the village school, a small legacy and donations from neighbours allowed him to enroll at the University of Edinburgh. He then taught for a time at Gairney Bridge near Kinross, where he joined the Burger Synod Theological Hall with the intention of becoming a minister. While teaching near Tillycoultry he fell ill with consumption and returned to Kinross, where he died on July 5th 1767.

Michael Bruce's poetry was collected by a college friend, John Logan, and published in 1770. As a boy, Michael would be sent to keep an eye on the flocks in the Lomond Hills and it was here that he developed the love of nature evident in his writing. The poem 'Lochleven' recalls these childhood days, but his best known work is 'Ode to a Cuckoo' which remained popular long after his death. Edmund Burke described it as 'the most beautiful lyric in our langauge'. A controversy broke out when Logan claimed that the ode was in fact his own work, and not Bruce's, but this claim has since been discounted, though Logan may have had an editorial hand in the poem.

Eleven editions of the work of Michael Bruce have appeared over the years and his 'Gospel Sonnets' are still sung in churches around Scotland. The Michael Bruce Memorial Trust maintains the poet's cottage at Kinnesswood and every year a memorial service is held at Portmoak Parish Church. In 1991 a national poetry prize bearing his name was established.

The emergence of the folk tradition into literature during the eighteenth century is probably best evidenced by the great and enduring popularity of **Robert Burns** (1759-96), who rhymed his way through Perthshire in August 1787, on his third tour of the Highlands. Burns, who enumerated Macpherson's Ossian among his favourite authors, visited the 'grave' of the 'Northern Homer' in the Sma' Glen. He composed 'The Birks of Aberfeldy' while standing by the Falls of Moness, left a permanent reminder of his visit in The Kenmore Hotel in the form of a handwritten verse above the mantlepiece which the visitor can still see, passed on to Birnam and Dunkeld where he met the great fiddler Niel Gow and again paid homage to Ossian at the Hermitage. Then on he travelled round Loch Tummel to Killiecrankie and Blair Atholl, where he was entertained by the Duke and Duchess. By the falls of Bruar, he composed alfresco again and on he went northwards, effusing emotion, charming folk and gentry alike, composing and posing.

One further piece of Burnsiana is worthy of mention here – it was in the house in Sciennes, Edinburgh belonging to **Adam Ferguson** (1723-1816), the Scottish philosopher born at Logierait and educated at Perth Academy, that the twelve year old Walter Scott met with Rab, soon after his first dramatic entry into Edinburgh society as the author of *Poems, chiefly in the Scottish Dialect*. Ferguson held the Chair of Natural Philosophy at Edinburgh University and was a central figure in enlightenment Edinburgh. In 1792, he brought **Walter Scott** (1771-1832) northwards, through the Trossachs and into eastern Perthshire where they stayed at Craig Hall near Rattray and Meigle in Strathmore, a journey which effected the genesis of the ballad *The Lady of the Lake* (1810), set as it is around Loch Katrine and Glenartney near Comrie.

In later years, near the end of his life, Scott again used the Perthshire area as a setting for *The Fair Maid of Perth* (1828), a story set in the late 14th century which makes use of local history. The Fair Maid's House still stands in the centre of the old town today and there is a seated sculpture of the Fair Maid by David Annand in the pedestrianised High Street.

Burns had many followers spring forth in his wake. There are three worth noting in this context. **Carolina Oliphant**, best known as Lady Nairne, was born at Gask in Strathearn on August 16th 1766, into a family which had settled in Perthshire as early as the 13th century. She was the third daughter of Laurence Oliphant, one of the staunchest supporters of the Jacobite cause, and was named Carolina in memory of Prince Charles Edward. She was a strikingly beautiful girl and her pleasing ways led to her being called the 'Flower of Strathearn'. She married her cousin Major

William Murray Nairne in 1806 and became Baroness Nairne after his forfeited family estate was returned to him in 1824. They lived in Edinburgh until his death in 1830, when she moved to Enniskerry, Co. Wicklow in Ireland. In later years she travelled in Europe, before returning to Gask where she died on 26th October 1545.

From an early age she had loved the songs of Robert Burns, and began writing songs herself with the intention of bringing out a collection of national airs set to appropriate words. To the traditional lyrics she added many of her own composition. Her eighty-seven songs were first published in *The Scottish Minstrel* (1821-24) and posthumously as *Lays from Strathearn*. Some are bowdlerisations of bawdy favourites. Many were in support of the Jacobite cause, such as 'Will ye no come back again?', 'Bonnie Charlie's noo awa' and 'Charlie is my darling'. Others were drawn from contemporary life, like 'Caller Herrin', or were patriotic lyrics like 'The Land of The Leal'. One of the best known and most anthologised is 'The Laird o Cockpen', which is worth reproducing here as it underlines how the ballad tradition had encroached into even the mind of a 'blue-blooded lady of impeccable background' as Agnes Mure Mackenzie calls her. Also, it could be argued that the 'penniless lass wi a lang pedigree' may have some autobiographical resonance:

> The Laird o Cockpen he's proud an' he's great,
> His mind is ta'en up wi' the things o the state;
> He wanted a wife his braw house tae keep,
> But favour wi' wooin was fashious tae seek.
>
> Doon by the dyke-side a lady did dwell,
> At his table-head he thocht she'd look 'well;
> McLeish's ae dochter, o Clavers-ha Lee,
> A penniless lass wi a lang pedigree.
>
> Hi wig was weel pouther'd, as gude as when new;
> His waistcoat was white, his coat it was blue;
> He put on a ring, a word, an' cocked hat
> An wha could refuse the Laird wi' a' that?
>
> He took his grey mare, he rade cannilie,
> An rapped at the yett o' Clavers-ha Lee,
> 'Gae tell Mistress Jean to come speedily ben,—
> She's wanted to speak wi' the Laird o Cockpen.'
>
> Mistress Jean she wis makin' the elder-flow'r wine;
> 'An' what brings the Laird at sic a like time?'
> She put aff her apron, an' on her silk goon,
> Her mutch wi' red ribbons, an' gaed awa doon.
>
> An' when she cam' ben he bowèd fu' low,
> An' what was his errand he soon let her know;
> Amazed was the laird when the lady said 'Na!'
> An wi a laigh curtsie she turned awa'!
>
> Dumbfounder'd was he, but nae sigh did he gi'e,
> He mounted his more an' he rode cannilie,

An' often he thocht, as he ga'ed through the glen,
'She's daft tae refuse the Laird o Cockpen!'

There is something in the very name 'The Laird o Cockpen', strengthened by its repetition, which works to great effect in this lyric, underlining the pomposity and blinkered self-regard of a man who cannot imagine that the fault may be his. The 'Flower of Stratheam' obviously had an ironic sense of humour

Like Lady Nairne, **Robert Nicholl** can be considered 'in the Bums School', as Charles Kingsley suggested in 1851. Nicholl was once known as 'Scotland's Second Burns', which may have helped him at the time, but hasn't preserved his memory. In fact, his life seems to have been ill-starred from the start.

He was born at Tullybelton on the 7th of January 1814, where his father was a farmer. Before the boy was five years old, his father went bankrupt and Robert was denied an education. He was apprenticed to a wine-merchant and grocer in Perth at sixteen, began contributing to *Johnstone's Magazine*, but found his apprenticeship cancelled in 1833. He went to Edinburgh but found no work. He opened a circulating library in Dundee and in 1836 became editor of the *Leeds Times*. His opinions were forthrightly radical but in his political eagerness he overstretched himself and suffered a physical breakdown. He resigned his editorship and died on December 7th 1837, not twenty-four years old, at a friend's house in Edinburgh.

A volume of his poems, entitled simply *Works*, appeared in 1835, and in 1844 a posthumous edition, *Poems and Lyrics* with a memoir by Mrs. C. I. Johnstone. His lyrics in Scots are described as 'simple in feeling and expression, genuine folk-songs,' designed as a compliment, which shows to what extent literature and the folk tradition had intertwined.

This trend towards an interest in the homegrown showed itself in Perthshire through the work of men like **George Penny**, a radical journalist whose gossipy *Traditions of Perth* was published in 1836, and **Robert Ford**, song-collector and author of *The Harp of Perthshire*. The city of Perth grew rapidly in the early nineteenth century and the coming of the railways in 1847 heralded a new era, not just for Perth, but for the Highlands beyond: the era of 'Balmorality', as some have called it, when Queen Victoria and Prince Albert established a fashion for all things Scottish. Perth station was a nexus for travel, with seven lines converging here when the Glen Farg route to Edinburgh was opened. The stop-over of the Royal party on their regular path northwards became a feature of Perth life.

A writer whose life bridges the period between Baroness Nairne and the Victorian age is **George Gilfillan**, who is best known for his life of Burns. As a minister in the Secession church, his interest in Burns might seem a surprising one. In fact, with Gilfillan we see an classic post-Reformation Scottish conflict between the churchman and the literary man. Gilfillan was born in Comrie on January 30th 1813 and grew up there, where his father was also a Secession minister. He studied at Glasgow University and then was ordained pastor of a church in School Wynd, Dundee. In 1839 he published a volume of discourses, and then a sermon on 'Hades' which was criticised by his co-presbyters and withdrawn from circulation. He began contributing a series of literary portraits to the *Dumfries Herald*, which led in 1846 to the publication of his highly popular

Gallery of Literary Portraits. In 1851, there appeared his most successful work, in which he attempted to unify the two great forces in his life: *The Bards of the Bible*, a work intended as a 'poem on the Bible', more rhapsodic than critical. In 1856, he published his life of Burns.

His intended masterwork, however, was a long poem over thirty years in the making, called simply *Night*, which was a disappointing failure when it finally appeared in 1867. Later works included a life of Walter Scott (1870), a book of local interest, *Comrie and its environs* (1872) and a memoir of James Thomson (1874). A year before he died in August 1878 at Arnhalt near Brechin, Gilfillan published his revised edition of Burns' life. As a preacher and lecturer, George Gilfillan gathered large crowds, but never a literary reputation commensurate with those successes.

The conflict between religion and literature in the eighteenth century surfaces again and again. In his outstanding *Popular Literature in Victorian Scotland* (1986), William Donaldson outlines the essence of the problem:

> Fiction was at the centre of the struggle for control of the popular imagination in nineteenth century Scotland, but the evangelicals' use of it was always uneasy. One wing of the movement mounted a sustained attack upon the very idea of popular fiction for upwards of half a century, and the controversy broke out anew during the 1850s and 1860s when the problem assumed vastly greater proportions with the advent of a large scale press. One anxious reader of the Edinburgh *Christian Advocate* wrote to enquire whether a Christian could buy, sell, or read popular fiction without hazard to the soul. He received a disconcerting reply:
>
> FICTITIOUS READING – QUERY AND REPLY
>
> We are not sufficiently acquainted with these publications to pronounce judgement upon them so fully as our correspondent may desire: but we can say this much, that such numbers of them as we have seen we could not with a good heart read. Apart from the time wasted in their perusal, we believe the tendency of such exciting stories as form their principal attraction will be exceedingly vicious. They are mental narcotics which intoxicate the mind to as deadly an issue as man can reach. Who knows the habitual reader of such love and murder fictions, to be also a hearer and doer of the word of God? Who that knows God will say they are fit reading for either saint or sinner? We know not.

Granted Donaldson is talking about serialised fiction in newspapers, rather than so-called 'serious' literature. But when we recall that Dickens' work was serialised in just this way, we see the potential conflict for a man of the cloth with literary ambitions. Thanks to these researches, we are able to see more clearly the reasons behind the splits that took place in the established Church of Scotland in the nineteenth century and how they affected the evolution of our literature during that time. Indeed, Donaldson has turned up a new name in the history, one **David Pae** (1626-84) who was born in Buchanty in Glenalmond, though his mother moved away soon afterwards to her own family in Coldingham, Berwickshire, when his father, a miller, was killed.

Pae was well-educated and was apprenticed to the bookseller and publisher Thomas Grant in Edinburgh. Here he discovered the theatre and became editor of a theatrical review. In the 1850s, with the very foundations of religion in Scotland shaking, he joined a group of liberal evangelicals who disavowed the established doctrine regarding redemption. Unlimited atonement, the idea that Christ died for everybody, not merely a few Elect, lay at the heart of this movement. Pae believed, along with other Millenarians, that the end of the world was literally a few years away – he even published his belief in the popular press.

Nevertheless the Millenarians were committed, to differing degrees, to social improvement. David Pae, writing as always anonymously, began publishing fiction with the express purpose of changing the reader's attitude to life the production of reading material which bore all the outward signs of cheap sensational fiction, but which had a moral purpose. The end of *Jessie Melville or the Double Sacrifice* makes this clear:

> Our whole and only aim, dear reader, has not been to amuse you. We had a much higher object in view, and fondly trust it will not be altogether unattained. Our design was to inculculate the great and noble duty of self-sacrifice – to show it adhered to in perhaps the most difficult of all circumstances; and to show that, when faithfully maintained, it brings sooner or later an abundant reward. Every one of us is called upon in our different spheres to exercise this duty to a greater or less degree, but alas! many of us shun and shrink from it. What is the cause of much of the social disorder which exists around us but our neglect of self-sacrifice?

And so it goes on. Unwittingly, David Pae had struck on a perfect formula. His own desire to mix Dickensian tales of lost inheritance and social deprivation with moral teachings seemed to find on echo in Scotland generally. Now the reading of popular fiction, as well as the writing of it, could be justified by all. *Jessie Melville* caused great excitement when it appeared, and from then on, for twenty years, Pae produced 'on average two substantial serial novels annually which were initially published either in the *People's Journal* or in the *People's Friend*, whose editor he became in 1870.' Stories which entered into the heart of social deprivation in the new urban Scotland, which are evidence that Scottish fiction did not split into simply two veins, one retrospective focusing on a rural world long lost, the other stories of adventure coursing the breadth of the British Empire. David Pae became, according to Donaldson, the most widely read author in Victorian Scotland.

If Pae has only the most tenuous connection with Perthshire, there are parallels between his desire 'to instruct as well as to amuse' with a writer whose Perthshire origins are certain. Indeed, it was two lines from one of Lady Nairne's songs, 'There grows a bonnie brier bush in our kailyard/ And white are the blossoms in our kailyard,' that **Ian MacLaren** took as the epigraph to his first book of stories, which in turn led to the term 'Kailyard' as applied to a whole school of Scottish fiction around the turn of the 19th century.

Ian MacLaren was the *nom de plume* of John Watson, who was born in Essex on November 3rd 1850 where his father was a Receiver of Taxes. The family moved to Perth in 1854 when Watson senior was posted there, where they lived in Marshall Place beside the South Inch. Young John attended Perth Academy and spent holidays with his mother's family, who farmed near Blairgowrie. When his father was transferred to Stirling in 1862, he enrolled at Stirling High School, and afterwards studied Divinity at the University of Edinburgh, becoming a minister in the Free Church. He spent four years in the parish of Logiealmond, before moving to take up a charge in Glasgow and subsequently in Sefton Park, Liverpool. He died while on a lecture tour of America on May 6th 1907.

Many of Watson's publications were theological, several of them contending radical positions, but it was the name of Ian MacLaren that rose to fame with the publication of *Beside the Bonnie Brier Bush* (1894), a collection of stories set in the fictional Drumtochty and modelled on the Perthshire villages that he knew so well. Further volumes in similar vein followed, including *The Days of Auld Lang Syne* (1895); *A Doctor of the Old School* (1895); *Kate Carnegie and other stories* (1896); *Afterwards* (1899). The following extract from 'Cunning Speech of Drumtochty' gives a sense of the flavour of his work, with its quietly patriotic understatement:

> Jamie was the cynic of the glen – who had pricked many a wind bag – and there was a general feeling that his meeting with Mr. Hopps would not be devoid of interest. When he showed himself anxious to learn next Sabbath, any man outside Drumtochty might have been deceived, for Jamie could withdraw every sign of intelligence from his face, as when shutters close upon a shop window. Our visitor fell at once into the trap, and made things plain to the meanest capacity, until Jamie elicted from the guileless Southron that he had never heard of the Act of Union; that Adam Smith was a new book he hoped to buy; that he did not know the difference between an Arminian and a Calvinist, and that he supposed the Confession of Faith was invented in Edinburgh. This in the briefest space of time, and by way of information to Drumtochty. Jamie was making for general literature, and still had agriculture in reserve, when Drumsheugh intervened in the humanity of his heart.
>
> "A' dinna like tae interrupt yir conversation, Maister Hopps, but it's no verra safe for ye tae be stannin' here sae long. Oor air hes a bit nip in't, and is mair searchin than doon Sooth. Jamie'll be speirin' a' mornin gin ye'ill answer him, but a'm thinkin ye'ill be warmer in the kirk."
>
> And Drumsheugh escorted Mr. Hopps to cover, who began to suspect that he had been turned inside out, and found wanting.
>
> Drumtochty had listened with huge delight, but without a trace of expression, and, on Mr. Hopps reaching shelter, three boxes were offered Jamie. The group was still lost in admiration when Drumsheugh returned from his errand of mercy.

"Sall, ye've dune the job this time, Jamb. Ye're an awfu' creetic. Yon man'ill keep a quiet cheep till he gets Sooth. It passes me hoo a body wi' sae little in him hes the face tae open his mooth."

"Ye did it weel Jamie," Domsie added, "a clean furrow free end tae end."

"Toots, fouk, yir makin' over muckle o' it. It wes licht grund, no worth puttin' in a ploo."

Throughout MacLaren's work, like Pae's, is the concern that his writing should not merely amuse, but educate the reader in spiritual matters. In their day, his books were widely read and appreciated by an international readership, who recognised and affirmed the qualities of the characters MacLaren loved to draw.

The work of the poet **James Logie Robertson** (1846-1922) who also wrote under the pseudonym of 'Hugh Haliburton', shares some of the characteristics of MacLaren's prose writings. Robertson was born at Milnathort on September 18th 1846, and became a pupil teacher at Haddington, before matriculating at Edinburgh University. His working life was spent as a teacher in Edinburgh, latterly at Edinburgh Ladies College (Mary Erskine's). His early work was published under his own name, but in 1882 he invented his alter ego 'Hugh Haliburton', whose *Horace in Homespun: a Series of Scottish Pastorals* (1882) written in Scots, was extremely popular. Further titles followed: *For Puir Auld Scotland's Sake* (1887); *In Scotland's Fields* (1890); *Ochil Idylls* (1891) and *Furth in Field* (1894).

Through his sweet odes to nature and eulogies on the beauty of the Ochils, J.L. Robertson's work anticipated the revival of Scots language poetry which was to take place in the early 20th century. Robertson was a committed and well-loved teacher who edited editions of the work of William Dunbar, Allan Ramsay, Robert Burns, Allan Cunningham and Thomas Campbell.

The 'Kailyard' school was not without its critics, and there were writers who deliberately challenged the easy, insular world it portrayed. One of these was **John Davidson** (1857-1909) who was born at Barrhead in Renfrewshire, the son of a minister of the Evangelical Union. At thirteen he went to work in a sugar-factory in Greenock, before returning to his former school as a pupil teacher. From there he went to Edinburgh University and into teaching. His connection with this locality came when he was appointed to first Perth Academy in 1878 and then Morrison's Academy in Crieff. Here he was the most popular of all the masters, and took a stand against what he saw as the cruelty with which the pupils were treated. He attempted to organise his fellow teachers to overturn the system, but failed. He resigned and went on a dramatic and musical tour of Perthshire and the Glasgow area with his most ardent supporter among the staff, John Barlas, but this too failed and he was soon back at the chalk-face. However one of his most striking stories, 'The Schoolboy's Tragedy', tells the tale of a pupil being systematically destroyed by a vindictive master.

Determined to follow a literary vocation, Davidson had already published three poetic, fantastical plays and in 1890 he moved to London when his prose-romance *Perfervid* appeared. This portrait of small town Scottish life undoubtedly owes much to his time in Perthshire, and has been called 'one of the most fascinating and original stories of "young blood" and child adventure ever written.' But neither it nor a sequel *The Great Men* (1891) caught the public eye, whatever their merits, and Davidson subsisted as a journalist.

However in 1893 he found success with a volume of poetry, *Fleet Street Eclogues* which immediately placed him firmly in the new generation of poets. Further prose works followed: *Baptist Lake* (1894), very much a critique of the Kailyard view of rural Scottish life; *Earl Lavender* (1895); *A Random Itinerary* (1894), but it was as a poet that he began to make his name. In particular, his use of the ballad in *Ballads & Songs* (1894), *New Ballads* (1896) and *The Last Ballad* (1898) modernised the old form to suit the taste of the period.

During this time both he and his old Crieff colleague John Barlas contributed to *The Yellow Book* (1894-7), a short-lived but notorious publication devoted to literature and art, which was in the avant-garde of the 'Decadent' movement and had Aubrey Beardsley as art editor. *The Yellow Book* also published Henry James, Edmund Gosse and Arnold Bennett, and featured artists like Walter Sickert and Wilson Steer.

Davidson's later work became more and more didactic as he moved away from lyric poetry, attempting to use scientific terminology to produce a poetry of ideas. He was awarded a Civil Pension in 1906 and moved to Penzance in Cornwall a year later, where he disappeared under suspicious circumstances on March 23rd 1909. His body was recovered from the sea six months later.

Davidson's work was highly influential and two of this century's greatest poets acknowledge a debt to him. T.S. Eliot wrote that Davidson's use of colloquial speech in his ballads helped formulate 'The Wasteland' while Hugh MacDiarmid admired the adventurous spirit of his later work – techniques which MacDiarmid himself employed in poems such as 'On A Raised Beach'.

While Davidson was working in London in the 1890s, publishing in *The Yellow Book*, the Perth Academy educated polymath **Patrick Geddes** (1854-1932) was leading a new wave of Scottish culture in Edinburgh; William Power describes Geddes as 'the greatest dream-builder and generator of ideas Scotland has ever known'. His family had come to live in a cottage on Kinnoull Hill in 1856, where Geddes grew up, and those early years by the Tay shaped his thinking for the rest of his life. His boyhood rambles over Kinnoull Hill led to an abiding interest in the natural world, while the views of the city of Perth and Strathearn, Strathmore and Strathtay helped shape his holistic approach to town planning, which emphasised the need to see the city not in isolation but as the product of the region around it. His reputation rests on his achievements in fields other than literature – though he certainly tried his hand at poetry – but his importance to Scottish culture generally, and literature specifically, is once again being recognised. To quote Israel Zanguill, writing in 1895:

> Patrick Geddes is the key to Northern life and letters. *The Evergreen*
> was not established as an antidote to the *Yellow Book*, though it might
> well seem a colour counter-symbol – the green of spring set against
> the yellow of decadent leaves. It is, indeed, an antidote, but
> undesigned else had not yellow figured so profusely on the cover. *The*
> *Evergreen* of today professes to be inspired by *The Evergreen* which
> Allan Ramsay published in 1724, to stimulate return to local and

national tradition and living nature; Patrick Geddes and Colleagues, who publish it and other books – on a new system of giving the author all the profits, as certified by a chartered accountant – inherit Ramsay's old home; that is to say, they are located in a sort of University settlement known as Ramsay Garden.

The Evergreen appeared only four times as a quarterly, yet it established Geddes as 'a leader of the Celtic Renascence, and not just in Scotland, for Geddes was able to bring together work from, in particular, Ireland and Brittany,' as Murdo Macdonald writes. And it was an essay in *The Evergreen*, 'Scots Renaissance', which first used the term as something applying to contemporary society – a phrase readily adopted and altered to suit the purposes of Hugh MacDiarmid's revivalist trumpeting in the 1920s.

Geddes also connects with another figure of the late 19th century whose reputation is international – John Ruskin (1819-1900). Although he was born in London where his father was a successful wine merchant, Ruskin was, according to one biographer Frederic Harrison, 'a Scot of the Scots, his father and mother being grandchildren of one John Ruskin of Edinburgh. Both parents and he himself passed much of their early life in Scotland, where he had many Scotch cousins, and whence he ultimately took a Scotch wife. He talked with a Lowland accent, and his dominant tone of mind was a mysterious amalgam of John Knox, Carlyle, and Walter Scott.'

Ruskin's grandfather had a house at Rose Terrace in Perth, where the boy John spent some time. His autobiographical *Praeterita* recounts how as a child he would gaze at the eddies of the Tay 'clear-brown over the pebbles' when staying with his aunt and cousins. Later in life, less happily, Bowerswell House on the other side of the river was the scene of his unconsummated marriage to local beauty Effie Gray, subsequently the wife of the Pre-Raphaelite painter John Everett Millais.

A child prodigy, Harrison records an early poem written when Ruskin was seven – juvenilia most interesting locally because of its subject:

> Glen of Glenfarg, thy beauteous rill,
> Streaming through thy mountains high,
> Onward pressing, onwards still,
> Hardly seeing the blue sky.
>
> Mountain streams, press on your way,
> And run into the stream below;
> Never stop like idle clay,—
> Hear the sheep and cattle low.
>
> Those dropping waters that come from the rocks,
> And many a hole, like the haunt of a fox;
> That silvery stream that runs bobbling along,
> Making a murmuring dancing song.

And this from the hand of a boy who was to grow to be 'the writer of the Victorian era who poured forth the greatest mass of literature upon the greatest variety of subjects, about whom most was written in his own lifetime in Europe and America'!

While a student at Christ Church, Oxford, Ruskin won the Newdigate prize and in his youth he considered himself a poet. But soon after graduating he met Turner and realised that his immediate task was to rescue this great painter from neglect. This championing led to *Modern Painters* (1843-50), developing into a spiritual history of Europe with diversions into various fashionable phases and tastes. Ruskin's 'function' was decided, as 'interpreter' rather than practitioner. His inquiries spread from natural beauty and its representation, to architecture, economics, to lectures on the respective duties of men and women, on war, on work and trade and so on. In 1870 he was elected first Slade professor of Art in Oxford, but his later years were difficult ones, as he became more and more isolated in his thinking. Ruskin was greatly admired in his day, particularly by the young Patrick Geddes (who published a book on Ruskin), and we may see the older man's influence in the breadth of the fields which Geddes himself was engaged in.

A contemporary of Geddes's at Perth Academy, **William Archer** was born in Perth on September 23rd 1856 and went on to study for the bar in Edinburgh. But his interest in theatre drew him away from the law and he worked for the *Edinburgh Evening News* as drama critic before moving to London, where he wrote for a number of newspapers. Although his own plays were successful in his lifetime, most notably *The Green Goddess* which opened in New York in 1923 and transferred later to London, he is best remembered for his work as the first English translator of the great Norwegian playwright Henrik Ibsen. Archer's wife being Norwegian, he was often in that country and so identified Ibsen's talent at an early point.

As a theorist on stagecraft, Archer was greatly respected and his *Masks or Faces* (1898) and *Playmaking* (1912) remained standard works for many years. Along with Harvey Granville Barker, whose plays were recently revived at the Edinburgh International Festival, William Archer was one of the moving forces towards the establishment of a national theatre in England. He died in London in 1924.

Contrary to the very public profiles of Geddes, Ruskin and Archer, **Mary** and **Jane Findlater** were more retiring. They were sisters, the daughters of a Free Kirk minister, and lifelong companions. Both were born at Lochearnhead – Mary on March 26th 1865, and Jane on November 4th 1866 – where they were educated at home. After the death of their father in 1886 they had to move to Prestonpans, until the success of Jane's first novel, *The Green Graves of Balgowrie* (1896), enabled them to go to Devon where they lived till the outbreak of WWI. They spent the war in London, but returned afterwards to Comrie, where they settled for the remainder of their lives. Jane died in 1946, but Mary lived on alone to the ripe old age of ninety-eight.

The Findlater sisters wrote many books. Jane's other works are *Daughter of Strife* (1897); *Rachel* (1899); *The Story of a Mother* (1902); *Stones from a Glass House* (1894); *All that Happened in a Week* (1905); *The Ladder to the Stars* (1906); *Seven Scots Stories* (1912) and *A Grass Widow* (1921), while Mary's publications are *Songs and Sonnets* (1895); *Over the Hills* (1907); *Betty Musgrave* (1899); *A*

Narrow Way (1901); *The Rose of Joy* (1903); *A Blind Bird's Nest* (1907) and *Tents of a Night* (1914). In addition, they co-authored *Tales that are Told* (1901), *Crossrigs* (1908); *Penny Moneypenny* (1911); *Content with flies* (1916); *Seen and Heard Before and After 1914* (1916) and *Beneath the Visiting Moon* (1923). They are best known for the joint work, *Crossriggs*, a humorous tale of Victorian Scotland's village life with a range of interesting characters centred around the heroine, Alexandra Hope. The following extract is from the opening chapter of this novel:

> The village of Crossriggs, you know, stands on the top of a long ridge of land. On one side, very far away, lies the sea; on the other, a line of low blue hills. But much prosaic country comes between. There are flat, fat fields, divided by thorn hedges and long straight roads, with now and then a row of cottages. It is a rich, unromantic bit of agricultural country, full of food and prosperity. Lot might have chosen it for his share had he stood on the ridge and cast his eyes over the fertile land.
>
> The village is only a single street ending in an old market-place, in the centre of which still stands an ancient stone-cross. A row of tall lime trees on either side or the street make it almost like an avenue, because the houses stand well back, so that the line stretches on unbroken to the ancient cross in the Square. In winter, those trees show a network of bare branches; green they are in spring, and in summer the scent of their blossom makes the whole air sweet. Then one by one they turn a gracious green colour that adds a spurious cheerfulness even to sodden November days.
>
> There are some commodious old houses in Crossriggs, built for people of local importance in the days before the cities had sucked the country dry; for even here people came and went, so that many of the houses had changed owners several times. Some had sunk, and some had risen in the world by putting out a bow window, or removing old garden walls to make room for a new iron railing. But the house that had once been the Manse remained much the same always – no bow-windows or iron railings there. A tall man (and the Maitlands were all tall men) had to stoop his head to enter the low doorway – an open door it had always ken to rich and poor alike. The square hall was half-dark and paved with black and white flags; the sitting rooms, low-roofed and sunny, wore always the same air of happy frugality with their sun-burnt hangings and simple, straight-legged furniture. There was no attempt at decoration for decoration's sake, only an effect which was the outcome of austere refinement in the midst of plenty.

In this introductory passage, the reader can surely identify Strathearn and the happy youth of these two sisters of the manse, before their father's death. This mood of gladness emanates from *Crossriggs* and the Victorian world they describe charms the reader throughout, as surely as a visit to Crieff today recalls just that period. A joint biography, *The Findlater Sisters: Literature and Friendship* by Eric Mackenzie appeared in 1964.

Like Ruskin, another Victorian visitor to the area whose reputation is international – despite her retiring personality – **Helen Beatrix Potter** (1866-1943) is now commemorated at Birnam by a garden devoted to her well-loved creations. Born in Kensington to wealthy parents and educated at home like the Findlater girls, she was a lonely, reclusive child. On her trips north to Perthshire, she was befriended by Charlie Macintosh, the Dunkeld postman and an amateur naturalist, who helped inspire in Beatrix a love of nature. As a young woman she did serious work in dissecting, drawing and classifying funghi, but in a letter to her former governess in 1893 she began *The Tale of Peter Rabbit*. She illustrated and published the story privately in 1901, but it was with the appearance of *Squirrel Nutkin* in 1903 that she found success. She settled in the Lake District and produced a series of books in similar vein, ending with *Johnny Town-Mouse* in 1918. In later years she devoted herself to farming and to the newly established National Trust. Her diary, written in a secret code so elaborate that it was not deciphered till long after her death, was published in 1963.

Like the Findlater sisters, **John Buchan** was the child of a Free Kirk minister, and was born in Perth on August 26th 1875. The family moved soon afterwards to Pathhead in Fife, then Glasgow, finally settling in Peebles, so Buchan's remembrance of Perth can only have been subliminal. Yet like his great early influence Robert Louis Stevenson, he had a knowledge of the breadth of Scotland which allowed his adventure stories to sprawl across the landscape. For instance, in *Huntingtower* he makes use of local placenames without confining his narrative and the setting for *Witchwood*, Woodilee, though more likely in the area around Falkirk, has certain parallels with the Thrums of Barrie's *The Little Minister* and a scent of Perthshire about it too. But Buchan's main contribution to the literary tradition around Perth is perhaps an coincidental one, through the medium of Hugh Macdiarmid, and affecting the quintessential Perth poet, **Willie Soutar**.

Soutar was born in Perth on April 26th 1898, at the end of the Victorian age. He was the only son of John and Margaret Soutar, members of the Auld Lichts congregation so fondly characterised by J.M. Barrie. Soutar senior came from Spittalfield near Caputh, served his apprenticeship in Perth and became a master carpenter. In partnership he established a firm well respected throughout the area.

Young Willie was a lively youth, excelling at sports and schoolwork. He attended Perth Academy, where he was a prize-winning student, before joining the Navy straight from school in 1915. He served on the convoys protecting shipping in the Atlantic. In 1917, he contracted a mysterious illness while at sea, apparently the result of food-poisoning.

After the war, he continued with his education at the University of Edinburgh, initially in the faculty of medicine. His interests were literary, however, and he transferred to an English course. While a student, he published his first volume of verse and made contact with Chris Grieve (Hugh MacDiarmid), then in Montrose and attempting to spur the Scottish Renaissance into action. Soutar formed a friendship with MacDiarmid which was to last throughout his life – MacDiarmid edited his *Collected Poems* (1948) – and at the older man's suggestion Soutar read John Buchan's anthology of Scots poetry *The Northern Muse* (1924) and afterwards started to write in his native Scots as well as in English.

Sadly, the illness which had first surfaced during the latter part of the war recurred in his final year at university and Soutar was forced to return home to Perth, where he became increasingly incapacitated. The illness was ultimately diagnosed as ankylosing spondulitis, an infection causing ossification of the spinal vertebrae, by then so far progressed as to be untreatable.

From 1930, William Soutar was unable to leave his room in the new house which his father and partner had built on the outskirts of the town. His parents did everything they could to enhance the quality of his life and Soutar's room became a visiting place for the leading Scottish writers of the period, including Hugh MacDiarmid, who was a patient in Murray Royal Infirmary after falling seriously ill in Shetland in 1937, Helen B. Cruickshank and Neil M. Gunn. In later years many younger writers came to see him, such as George Bruce, William Montgomerie, Douglas Young, Tom Scott, and a young Perth man, **Alexander Galloway**, who was a regular visitor during the last years of Soutar's life. The friendly atmosphere of these meetings, by no means the pontificating of a more established writer to younger aspirants, is captured in Soutar's diary of October 11th, 1940:

> Alex Galloway called: rather an amusing incident. Alex confessed that he could not rightly understand my poem, 'The Mystery', in the current number of *The Adelphi*; and on attempting to analyse it I discovered that it couldn't be done — so we left it wholly justified to its title.

Galloway has published two collections of poetry himself, the first while Soutar was still alive in 1942, *War Poems in Scots*. A second volume *The Lasting Vision* (1957) consists of poetry in English. The closing poem in this book is a fine elegy, in which the spirit of Soutar seems to reside:

On Seeing the Face of a Dead Man

This face, in death, hallows an autumn dawn,
An autumn dawn when all the air is still,
And light flows gently through each vale and hill.

Purging eternity for our life's prime,
A sovereignty of grace gives back to time
That which was in us when at birth love found
Our birth-place holy ground.

It seems a morning glory of the soul:
As if his spirit, all erect, had seen
Love beckoning where love had ever been.

Integrity, moulded by joy and care,
Dies not in sorrow's house; but ponders there
The hope of immortality whose grace
Is Jesus in man's face.

Beyond all hate and fear, and grief and pain,
A world of grace and peace comforts the sense
Of mystery—man's abiding Whither? Whence?

Here is a morning sanctified by truth,
That cannot change yet must redeem life's ruth,
Giving to life that trust whose likeness lies,
Love-drawn, in an infant's eyes.

This face, in death, mirrors a morning's calm
When all the air is still, and light flows on,
Master of shadow and the night that's gone.

Of course, not all of Soutar's visitors came to talk about poetry. As his diaries show, he was often forced to listen to the bores of the town, who saw themselves as taking pity on the poor invalid. These scenes are vividly brought to life in Joy Hendry's play about Soutar, *Gang Doun Wi a Sang* (1988), the script of which was recently published.

From his still centre, William Soutar sent out his writing out into the world, gaining a reputation as perhaps the best loved Scots poet of his generation – the natural inheritor to Burns, in that his verse lends itself to music so well. Many of his lyrics hove been set by composers such as Elizabeth McIven, Ranald Stevenson, and James MacMillan.

Soutar died on October 15th 1943, leaving behind a mass of papers including detailed diaries of his years struggling against illness. These are a marvellous testament to human endurance and were published in a shortened version as *Diaries of a Dying Man* (1954) edited by the poet and scholar Alexander Scott, who also wrote a biography, *Still Life* (1958). William Soutar's volumes of poetry were published in limited private editions during his lifetime, and these are now highly prized. A new selection of his work edited by Dr. W.R. Aitken was published in 1988.

When John Soutar died in 1958, he left the house in Wilson Street, Perth to the Town Council, on condition that the poet's room should be open to anyone wishing to see it. In 1988, due largely to the efforts of Joy Hendry, John Law and Jim Guthrie, a Creative Writing Fellowship jointly funded by Perth and Kinross Council and the Scottish Arts Council was established at the house, which continues to promote the work of this remarkable man, as well as to promote literature in the community.

The short life of Soutar is brought home to us when we consider that **Naomi Mitchison**, born the year before him in 1897, continues to be in the forefront of literature at the time of writing. Her publications are so numerous that to list and comment on them all would take up a whole book – they are almost as many as the years of her long life.

Born in Edinburgh, she is the daughter of John Scott Haldane, an eminent physiologist and one of a distinguished Scottish family of intellectuals. Her childhood was spent partly in Oxford where she went to school and partly in Perthshire on the family estates, her beloved 'Cloan', near Auchterarder. She married Dick Mitchison in 1916, a Labour MP from 1945 until 1964 when he was made a life peer. Together they had five children.

Mitchison's novel *The Conquered* appeared in 1923, the first of a series published during the 1920s which drew on her study of myth, history and the Classical world and culminated in the epic *The Corn King and the Spring Queen* (1931). During this time she and her family lived in London, where she moved in the literary circles of the period, befriending among others Aldous Huxley, E. M. Forster, Stevie Smith, the young W.H. Auden and Wyndham Lewis, who painted her portrait. Her historical novels established her as a writer of real ability, able to infuse the past with life and fully-rounded characters, although there were some like W. H. Auden who felt that her settings were less than satisfactory. In a 1931 letter to her he writes:

> I liked *The Corn King* very much indeed. I do wish though you would
> do a contemporary setting sometime. What is this curious
> psychological sturk of yours against it? I always feel in reading your
> work that you are only using those silly old Greeks as a symbol.

Auden was for a time a teacher in Helensburgh and Mitchison attempted to introduce him to some people in Scotland. But Wystan wasn't entirely enthusiastic:

> I don't think any of the Scottish nationalists are any use. MacDiarmid
> is such a fearful intellectual snob and prig.

Whether or not there was conflict of loyalites for Mitchison around this time is unclear, but the 1930s saw a change of direction both in her work and in her life. The political turmoil of the period meant she felt forced to leave the distant past to address present concerns in her writing, and after the death of her father in 1936, followed soon after by both her husband's parents, she and her family moved to Carradale, Argyll in 1937, where she has lived ever since. At the same time the ties were "snapping between me and Cloan" with the death of her aunt.

The move to Scotland and the departure of their literary friends Huxley and Auden for America at the outbreak of the Second World War heralded a third phase in Mitchison's writing – a Scottish phase, best illustrated by the novel *The Bull Calves* (1947) which deals with the historical Haldane family in Perthshire immediately after the 1745 rebellion.

In recent years, she has turned her hand to science fiction, books about Africa, biography and poetry. In Carradale, and in Scotland generally, she has played a prominent role in public affairs for over half a century. Naomi Mitchison died in January 1999.

If Soutar is a poet whose life and work is marked by his WW1 experiences, the work of **Hamish Henderson**, who was born on November 11th 1919 in Blairgowrie and spent his early years in Glenshee, was similarly shaped by WW2. He was educated at Dulwich College and Downing College, Cambridge. His skill as a linguist led to him serving as an intelligence officer with the Highland Division in North Africa and later in Italy, experiences which gave rise to *Ballads of World War Two* (1947), the prize-winning *Elegies for the Dead in Cyrenaica* (1948) and numerous translations from Italian including the work of Montale, Quasimodo,

Gatto and Ungaretto. He has also edited *Antonio Gramschi: Letters from Prison* (1974), a ground-breaking work in political science.

He joined the School of Scottish Studies in Edinburgh at its inception in 1951, where he worked as a research fellow collecting songs and stories. His work in publicising the proud traditions of the travelling folk is rightly renowned, and his meeting with the ballad singer Jeannie Robertson, one of the great tales of 20th century Scottish culture. In recent years Hamish Henderson has become something of a cultural icon in Scotland himself, and his many songs are sung in ceilidhs and gatherings across the country. *Freedom Come All Ye*, a song expressing his most deeply held social and political feelings, has become a standard for the new wave of Scottish cultural activists.

The publication of a collection of Henderson's varied prose writings *Alias MacAlias* (1993) drew together many of the threads of his diffuse and influential work, while a volume of his letters *The Armstrong Nose* was published in June 1995.

A rough contemporary of Henderson's who shores his Perthshire origins and his love of the folk tradition is **Ewen MacColl** (1915-1989, born at Auchterarder on January 25th 1915. MacColl worked in Glasgow Unity Theatre before taking up a post at the Theatre Workshop in London. His documentary ballad-opera *Johnny Noble*, set during the Spanish Civil War and World War II, tells the story of the love between an out of work seaman and his girl Mary, showing how his political awareness develops as a result of his frustrating attempts to make his way in life. MacColl's work in the folk revival on the 1950s is legendary and his *Folk Songs and Ballads of Scotland* (1965) cleared away much of the confusion over the origins of the songs included.

Athole Christina Cameron (1917-1992) was born on January 13th in Glasgow. Her father was a WW1 veteran traumatised by his experiences and the family moved to Glen Lyon where Athole's mother became the breadwinner, as teacher in the local school. It was here in the heart of the Highlands that Athole grew up. A bright girl, she attended Perth Academy and studied at Dundee College of Education, before becoming a primary school teacher herself. She worked in a number of Perthshire schools including Dunbarney at Bridge of Earn, and was latterly head teacher at Howgate Primary in Midlothian.

Athole Cameron was a committed Scottish Nationalist and stood for parliament three times. Her love of Scottish landscape and history emanate from her writing, as in the following poem, where the very brevity of the verse echoes how few are the traces that now remain of the life which preceded the Clearances:

Song for Roro in Glenlyon

This was a town: pause where the stones are scattered
A town where men were glad, a town where nobody mattered.

This was a town, and now is a field of sheep.
Go on your ways, the hills have a tale to keep.

A tale of laughter and life, and grazing sheep and cattle,
Of men who warred with beasts, and did not win the battle.

She was also a stalwart of Perth Theatre, backstage and front of house, and her own play *The Eve of St. Paul*, based on an incident in Perth in 1544, was given a public reading at the Traverse Theatre in Edinburgh.

Athole Cameron died on 6th May, 1992. Her prose and poetry had appeared in many magazines during her lifetime, though never in book form. To rectify this, Midlothian Libraries published a selection of her work and letters in 1995, entitled *A Tartan Chameleon*.

Like Ewen MacColl, **James Kennaway** (1928-1968) was born in Auchterarder, on June 5th 1928. He was the son of a doctor and a solicitor and was educated at Glenalmond College. After serving with the Gordon Highlanders in Germany, he read philosophy, politics and economics at Trinity College, Oxford.

His first novel, *Tunes of Glory* (1956), describes the conflict between two men who are competing for the colonelship of a Highland regiment – Jock Sinclair, a hero of the desert campaigns who has risen through the ranks, and Basil Barrow, who has come from a privileged background through Oxford and Sandhurst, and spent World War II as a prisoner in Japanese camps.

This was followed by *Household Ghosts* (1961), which also has a Scottish setting. This tale of an aristocratic family in decline centres on the destructive force of the complex relationships between Mary Ferguson, her brother Henry ("Pink"), her husband Stephen Cameron and lover David Dow.

Kennaway made his home in London where he worked as a publisher and moved away from Scottish themes in his later novels, *The Bells of Shoreditch* (1963), *The Mind Benders* (1963), *Some Gorgeous Accident* (1967), *The Cost of Living Like This* (1969), which confirmed him as a leading talent in his generation. His novels lent themselves to screen production, with the film version of *Tunes of Glory* starring Alec Guinness particularly successful.

James Kennaway was tragically killed in a car crash when only forty. A further novel, *Silence* (1972), and *The Dollar Bottom and Taylor's Finest Hour*, ed. Trevor Royle (1981) appeared posthumously. Related works are J. & S Kennaway: *The Kennaway Papers* (1981) and Trevor Royle: *James Kennaway: A Biography* (1983).

Sharing the tragic fate of Kennaway, but without any of the social privileges he enjoyed, is **Ian Abbot**, a poet born in Perth in 1944. Abbot was raised in a tenement in the city, where his father was a housepainter. He left Perth Academy without qualifications at the age of fifteen. Where Kennaway's career soared southwards, Abbot worked for a while for Tay Salmon Fisheries, and as a psychiatric nurse, before going to study medicine at Edinburgh University. This was not a successful move, and though he transferred to Stirling and a Psychology degree, he decided that an academic life was not for him. He moved northwards, to Whitebridge outside Inverness, where worked as an agricultural labourer, fencing out in the wilds of the Monadhliath mountains. His one published collection of poetry *Avoiding the Gods* shows a mature talent and a rigorous mind at work, focused on the life he sees around him. In an interview with Colin Nicolson in *Poem, Purpose and Place* (1992), Ian Abbot characterises the landscape he has chosen to live in and his reponse to it:

> There's a very strong sense of historical deprivation there in the
> Highlands. You can see it every day, using your eyes, working; the way

the culture has evolved and been beaten down over the years. And so I find I need, I suppose, to do something about this. To record it at least, to try to capture the smell of it; and to try to influence people's minds and feeling. Because the culture's quite unique, you know, and there are enough remnants of that culture there in the Highlands to make it worth recording.

Avoiding the Gods is a fine collection of poetry, reminiscent of the work of Norman MacCaig but with a harder edge. It does indeed 'smell' of the Highlands, as Abbot desired. It is sadly tantalising that the great promise shown in that one book was so suddenly erased by his death in a car accident in 1989. It would be only fair to his memory if his presently unpublished work is one day released in a second collection, as there could be no better tribute. In the absence of an unpublished poem, I end this essay with a poem from *Avoiding the Gods*, reproduced by kind permission of Joy Hendry at Chapman.

Landscape of a Highland Gentleman

A dried-up river bed,
the mind of this old man
spreads the bone-white of its boulders in the sun.

He has forgotten, now, how once
these gulleys wrestled with the fever of the spate,
how suddenly in spring
the banks blazed into green, and how
the drinking deer
printed the sand with their perfect arrowheads.

Now he sighs, turns over, shuts his eyes
on that ravine of polished stones. he listens
for the wind's dry rabble, for the quiet
sift of pebbles.
He will close his ears
to the corrie's fistful of silence.

POSTSCRIPT:

This brief survey has outlined a field of interest, rather than defined it. There is much more research still to be done – already I'm aware of omissions such as Fred Urquhart and Stuart MacGregor – but what should be clear already is that there is no moat surrounding the territory, keeping 'local writing' in and 'literary types' out – the term 'literature' as I've used it implies no value judgement, it refers only to language which is written rather than spoken.

Looking at the writers mentioned earlier, we may identify certain groupings: the early High Churchmen like Gavin Douglas; the Renaissance-influenced courtiers; the 18th century, often radical, folk poets, both Gaelic and Scots; the 19th century evangelicals like Pae and MacLaren; the reformers like Ruskin and Geddes; the turn of the century writers who moved easily between England, Scotland and the rest of the Empire, including John Davidson who links to the Scottish Renaissance of MacDiarmid and Soutar, from whom the Folk Revival developed through the work of people like Hamish Henderson and Ewan MacColl. And of course the story doesn't stop there. Contemporary writers like Robin Bell, Joy Hendry, John Herdman, Sheila Douglas and Margaret Gillies Brown would have their place in any full account. But it is difficult to fully assess the work of writers who are still highly active, so these and others are excluded from this survey but included in the 'Almanac' of writing to follow.

The writers mentioned above are mostly ones you would expect to find in a literary study of Scotland, whose work has been recognised on a national level. Beyond that are many whose work, for one reason or another, hasn't been brought to the attention of an audience outwith Perth and Kinross itself – writers whose published work is no longer easily found, whose lives have not been written, whose names are often forgotten even locally, yet who in their own lifetimes were well known and well loved. A quick search through the shelves in the local section of the A.K. Bell library will reveal a long list of names not appearing in any literary companion, for instance:

Alexander Campbell: born near Lochearnhead, 1764, a friend of Burns, Scott and David Allan. A confirmed Jacobite, he contributed to *Albyn's Anthology*. He saw himself as a second Admirable Crichton and latterly lived in Rome. P.W. Drummond describes him as "a dreamer of Celtic grandeur". He was the author of 'Row Weel, my boatie, row weel'.

James Sim: he was author of 'Lassie wi the Yellow Coatie' and his poems published in book form in 1811.

David Drummond (1774-1804): born in Crieff, he went to Calcutta in 1812, leaving his poems with a bookseller to be printed; he was author of 'The Bonnie Lass o Levenside', a popular ballad.

Charlie Spence (1779-1869): born in Glendoick, he was a stonemason to trade and author of many popular poems published in the local press, including 'The Faithful Swain'.

Christian Gray, resident at Aberalgie c. 1800 – 1830?. Blind from an early age, her works were published twice, in 1809 &1821.

David Webster: born in Dunblane, he became a weaver in Paisley, and joined the Radical movement. He published his works in 1835 and is best known as the author of 'Tak it, man, tak it'.

Rev. David Malcolm: born in Madderty, he established a school at Crieff; Malcolm published *The Sorrows of Love* (1807 & 1820).

James Beattie: (1796-1838): a stonemason in Errol, known as the "Leetown poet". His poems were published in Perth, no date.

William Nicholl: (1817-1855): born at Tullybelton, he was the younger brother of Robert Nicholl, whom he outllived.

Andrew Sharpe: a shoemaker at Bridgend, Kinnoull, his works were published in Perth in 1820.

Caroline Oliphant: a niece of Baroness Nairne (1814-37), she followed her more famous aunt in her compositions.

Helen Duncan: born 1827 at Kirkstyle, Kinfauns, she was a child prodigy who left the area to travel as lady's maid in 1844. She died in 1856 and afterwards friends and family published *The Posthumous Works of Helen Duncan* (Perth,1857).

James Stewart: born in Perth, he was a shoemaker at Dunkeld, best known as the author of 'The Tailor of Monzie'. His poems were published in 1857.

Rev. John Anderson of Kinnoull, author of *Pleasures of Home* (no date), *A Legend of Glencoe* (1853), *Autumn Leaves* (1893) etc.

Henry Dryerre: author of *Love Idylls: Ballads & other poems* published in Blairgowrie (1884).

These are some of the names remaining to be investigated, and that's without looking at more recent times, or considering that Perth was a main centre for Gaelic publishing until the early 20th century.

So clearly Perth and Kinross has a distinctive literature, especially if we compare it with, say, that of urban Glasgow or the English Midlands – the literature of a heavy industrial base is bound to differ from that of a largely rural community. There are certain threads running through our narrative more or less continuously – the importance of the Church, of the folk or ballad tradition, and of the landscape itself as an inspiration. And when we look at the linguistic picture, with the comparatively recent retreat of the Gaelic, the yet strong Scots tradition, and the opening up of the area to English in the 150 years since the coming of the railway, we begin to get a sense of the broad range of the factors at play.

I hope that this introduction will aid the reader's appreciation of the work contained in the 'almanac' that follows by setting the work of contemporary writers in context, and that the anthology itself will show how literature in Perth and Kinross continues to thrive – that has certainly been my experience.

Place-Work-Folk

An Almanac
of Poetry and Prose
from Perth & Kinross

One of Patrick Geddes' deceptively simple devices for thinking is the three interacting categories of 'Place, Work and Folk'. This analytical framework is derived from the thinking of French sociological pioneer Frederic Le Play (1806-1882), who was one the first to recognise the importance of sociology and its effect on economics. Whereas Le Play used the words *Lieu, Travail, Famille*, Geddes introduces the much more flexible 'folk' for 'family', which indicates a wider supportive community, synergistic and cooperative, as against a smaller kinship group.

Murdo Macdonald

This anthology collects together work by over fifty writers in the Perth and Kinross area. A number of the items were entries in the Perthshire in Bloom creative writing competition, while some are reprinted from other sources, and some have been written especially for this collection.

To call it an 'almanac' hardly does it justice, as there is much more here than simply 'a register of the days, week, and months of the year, with astronomical events, anniversaries etc.' as the dictionary defines the word. Yet the material is loosely organised around the cycle of a single year, from David Ogston's *Candlemas-E'en* (the night of January 31st) onwards with the occasional diversion into times past and other places.

The reader may like to think of it as a journey around Perth and Kinross, meeting with folk of all ages: some extravert, some humourous, some quietly introspective, some musing on the past – but all of whom have something interesting to say about the place they live in, the work that folk there and the characters who populate it.

I hope you'll enjoy the trip.

RAJ

Contents

Candlemas-E'en

David Ogston

We gaed tae Tullybelton, the quine an me, tae pick snaa-draps for the Table the comin Sunday, the day we mark the purirfyin o Mary an the wee Lord comin tae the temple faan He wis forty days aul. The snaa-drops (som caa them 'Mary's tapers') mak a bleeze o fite finery faan they sit in raas on the lang board, an syne they get hauned oot for bairns tae gie em tae their mithers or their grannies.

"Is this a tradition?" spiers the quine. She's nae long oot o the college, and she his a lot tae forget.

"Oh aye," said I, drivin by Dewars and slowin doon for the new roondaboot, "We did it last year." The quine lauchs. "Seriously," I gaed on, "We dee it faan we can get the flooers. Some years there's nae eneuch. Some winter's laist."

We got tae the place I hid mined on, a place I sklentit a glisk at ae day on a stravaig. Sure eneuch, there wis banks an banks o em, wytin tae be pooed.

"Should we nae mak sure we can tak some?" the quine says. "There's a hoose close by."

So we chap at the door on a young lass comes oot. We tell her oor eerin. She says the laird is a man nae ower fond o folk comin tae reive his grun like we wint tae dee, bit we should caa awa onywye. So noo we're stappin em, haunfu efter haunfu, intae the back o the car, an we get back tae Perth an tie em in posies ready for the morn.

Neist day twa veesitors come tae St. John's. Een o them wears a lang fite goon that haps him fae the thrapple tae the cweets, the tithers buskit nae near hauf sae braw in black, a monk's cassock bi the look o it, an him a monk himsel wie his shaved pow. They glower at the snaa-drops, an the quine in her fite alb. The steens o the kirk ring tae the dirlin measure o 'All the people that on earth do dwell', bit throwe the psalm I hear thochts that flichter throwe their heids, the wirds that tummel fae their steikit moos, for the fite goon an the black cassock are gey loath tae sing.

"My place," says the monk, his een roamin fae crossin tae chapel, "my place was there, when we sang Vespers, and for all the offices, escpecially the great Completonum. They have taken my place and made it theirs now, without so much as a by-you-leave, and where are the tapestries in cloth-of-gold, the sumptuous linen, the vestments for high days and feast-days? I see a man in black and a lass in my place."

And the man in fite said, "They have taken something from Tullybelton, I can sense it, my earth-tuned perception wards me that living power from my old domian abides here in a faint, a fragmentary whisper. Maybe it is the flowers they have ranged upon that table. Ah, ages back, when the fire we tended lit up the sky at Beltane, these here would have trembled before me and come as supplicants, not to this fickle God whom eye cannot see nor hand of flesh reach out and touch, but the ancient power, the energy we tapped into from the heart of this old earth. The great fires have died."

And the monk said, "I feel it too, that cold wind of passionless religion." An the Druid turned an melted oot o sicht ayont a pillar. Bit the monk cam closer, richt up tae the Table, an he raxed his haund oot tae touch the timmer o't.

"There used to be forty altars here," he whispered laich. "Have they taken the Saints away as well? Have they taken everything and discarded it?"

I took peety on him. Faan the prayer cam tae the Kyrie, I said it the wye he kent it "*Kyrie eleison, Christe eleison, Kyrie eleison.*" The congregation wis stammergasted. Bit the Benedictine beamed, and his een shone like stars in a glimmer o recognition.

"Ye see," I sent the thocht tae him, doon seiven hunder eer o history, "The best and bravest flooers nivver fade. They fin new places tae growe in, new wyes tae be themsels."

Efterhin, the quine speired, "Is *that* a tradition, the Kyrie eleison?"

"Oh aye," I said, "We dee it ilka Sunday, only maist Sundays we dee it in English."

The Creatures in the Stone

Patricia Doubell

Bull

Did they bring you from Crete?
Not in the stone, but in the eye of the mind?
Did they store your drinking water in the pithoi?
Your happy smile speaks pleasant memories—
Did you father the Minotaur?

Wolf

They found you here as you were in every place,
Slinking and lean, a scourge of flocks and herds,
Your howl of hunger by night made feet to run,
Reach gate before it closed, and friendly fire.
Your smile proclaims you well fed.

Goose

They saw you then as clear as I do now,
Resting on frosty fields, head on your back,
Snug among down, or skeining north at thaw,
And back again on the run from Arctic winter,
And you were good to ear, so they roasted a few.

Horse

Ridden or riderless, a status symbol,
A proud humility trots out its joy,
No open wound, flank ripped by spear or tusk,
Appears in stone, as it must have been, but you,
Inspired to serve, give out with a glad "Ha ha!"

Sea-Anemone

A muscle holding the rock,
Two tails? Or searching hands? Or kicking legs?
And in between, is that the Pictish smile?
A cornucopia? A happy womb?
Was it for you the Spirit moved on the waters?

Boar

A firece and deadly quarry, prize of the chase,
Kin to a goddess, sacred to priestly swineherds,
A royal head to grace a silver platter.
And see you now, sporting the blue rosette,
Waddling bland and obese – a commercial success.

Deer

Always the hunted monarch – watchful grace,
And sacrifice – a look of Herne the Hunter,
You dominate the tomb of a Cretan king,
Your rising and running was a magic long before
The merry orgasm was tamed by that sweet singing.

Eagle

Grounded and solid,
Dependable as death,
Unclean, protected, uneatable, sacred bird.
What made you defect to the banners of the legions,
The French dictator, and the U.S.A.?

Salmon

You swallowed hazel nuts of wisdom, deep
In the muddy dark of a river of hidden name.
Now in fresh water you feel the need of salt,
The sea wakes cravings for rivers of birth and death,
Where leaps a restless Solomon, glimpsing new worlds.

Serpent

Seraphim, curling around the ancient symbols,
Proclaiming that Genesis has already occurred,
Else you'd have legs – a dinosaur, a dragon—
Wise in the dust, mystic and timeless symbol,
Seraph-in-Cloud.

The Pictish Beast

There's always a maverick,
Settlement in the wrong place,
Evidence missing, brooch in an alien style,
The stones and bones confound the archaeologist,
And so there's you—

A joyous contortionist writhes on a silver brooch,
In stone conforms to no anatomy,
Elephant? Water horse? Snorkel on top of your head?
I conjure you, what manner of beast? – Who are you?
With salt of wit you answer "Do not puzzle me!"

The Burial Mound at Fowlis Wester

George Gunn

It's easy to wait here, the wind blowing through
the branches of the elms stills my heart
I came in uninvited although that was not strictly true
my troubles asked me to come here & be with them

they who built this they knew how to honour
the dead but now in life I circle it
round clockwise a couple of times
once for the rain and twice for those other hands

I would like to read the stones but they won't
show me their language instead I read
the trees & one of them tells me that
in 1896 John Martin carved out his name

I wonder if like me he held his breath
& let the time turn to sunlight
some startled crows get even more startled
as the traffic rolls by but not these thoughts

which cluster in this circle & the rabbits who
burrow here do they understand time
& does it hold them as it does me
a beguiling set of stones travelling to our deepest

distance the gods of their flight are worried
about strange concessions & I am jealous
of them & what they have seen because
I am part of a river here in Strath Earn & I am flowing

from one silence to another & make no mark
I have no stones I just watch the shochads
bringing in Spring I say my farewells
I get my bus & I'm back in the river

The River

(for Aileen)

Louise Moran

Oh! The river,
It brings life
Fertility,
Beauty.
We walk and fish and swim
On sunny days,
It is our friend.

But now the snow is melting
Smoothly seeping,
Drop by drop
And it has rained.
The river now is full,
Brown with mud—
Fast, deep
And silent
As you are now.

The day smiled
Chirping, shining,
Life awaking
After winter sleep.
The river running by your side,
Sunlight glistening,
Stopping
Listening
You hear its call.

"Come, come, I will keep you safe.
My arms will shield you
From the pain.
Come to me,
Dance in the glancing light—
Be one with me.
I will make you free."

You feel your burden
Ease.
The arms enfold you now
And you find peace.

Oh! The river
It brings life,
Fertility—
And death.

Moving to Perth

Joan McGirk

The translucent powdered, light diffusing, U.V. protected,
beige silk chin dropped.
The long lasting, extra moisturised, kiss proof,
scarlet mouth gaped.
A momentary gobsmacked, silver tinged black hole.
A disbelieving "Where?"
"Perth!"
An incredulous "Why?"

Recovery.
The luscious long-lasters curl up. Fixedly.
"I'm sure it's wonderful for children.
It's even got M&S (phew).
It's just not exactly premier league."
Smile. "No, but maybe next season."
Dead blank. Foreign language.
Say something.
"I suppose it's different with babies."

Months struggling to keep afloat in vanishing cream
turn into cold cream years.

Then
A flood of recognition
A deluge of national interest
Hurrah, a human tragedy
Television news,
Renascence!

The anti-aged, liposomed one calls
She's dug out her old school wellies
She's coming – What an adventure!
She came.
She liked it.
The Mauve Ice eyes became speckled with Golden Jade.
A touch of green, carefully applied, is recommended for blemishes.
And it worked beautifully for a while.
But it wasn't tear proof.

I don't know where she is now.
I think she's moved.

Tay Pearl

T.S. Law

Whaa reads as easilie as this is written,
kens nocht is skeelie that's laid past less care.
Yit lay this bye ye till yer guid doon-sittin
can gar it growe groo licht as onie pearl
intae the Tay an bonnie, caller, rare.
Here is yer mairriage wi yersel and hame
aa tho yer benner sheen were bebblin cleir
as grace laid bye ye till it licht the same
lang gaet lays past yer fame.

Falkirk, Grangemouth & Carronshore

Carl MacDougall

Ever since I saw the James Gang rob a train and make off with the loot; ever since I knew they gave their money to the poor, I wanted to be Jesse James. I especially wanted to be Jesse at the end of the film, when he was shot in the back while fixing the clock. In my version, that wouldn't have happened, though I liked the idea of a funeral and wanted to be there to see the crowds disobey the marshall's orders and stand by the roadside as my coffin passed, girls and women weeping.

I even liked his name; and though I didn't have a brother Frank, I appreciated the way he arranged the funeral.

Let me bury my brother, he said to the marshall.

And what if I don't?

Then I'll kill you.

They were sitting in the corner, a mother and daughter whose faces were a shadow of each other's face. The mother had looked that way when she was her daughter's age. Now, she had a certain dignity; in the dark and changing lights of the pub, she looked tired with too much make up. Every now and then she seemed preoccupied, but the daughter was always staring, moving in and out of darkness.

The bank of swirling disco lights crossed them like a cloud. Sometimes they were one colour, then another. I thought she smiled, then she wasn't there. When she appeared again she wasn't smiling.

I went to the bar, wondering how to proceed, when she spoke: Going home?

I was going to get another drink. Want one?

Rum and coke.

And what about your sister?

You mean my mother.

She looks more like your sister.

That's what everyone says. I'll tell her. She'll like that.

What does she drink?

Same as me. Rum and coke.

She moved down the bar like reeds below water, swivelled along on four inch heels, back to her seat where she whispered to her mother who looked across at me and smiled when I put the drink in front of her. Her daughter turned her eyes upwards into my face and smiled.

Here's to you, the mother said, raising her glass. We haven't seen you here before.

I told her I was passing.

You picked the right place, she said and stared across the bar; then didn't say much for the rest of the evening. She let her daughter and I do the talking.

I wasn't used to this kind of conversation, chatting to pass the time, as we waited for something to happen. We couldn't get a last drink and the music had stopped. I thought of offering to buy a carry out. That's it, said the mother. No point in hanging round here.

Would you like me to run you home?

It's all right, she said. We just live along the road.

You could give me a lift, the daughter said, and her mother laughed. Well, it was nice to meet you, she said. I hope we'll see you again some time.

The daughter looked at me. Well, she said. Let's go.

I did not know where I was driving, but kept to a steady 35 miles an hour through rows of grey four-in-a-block council houses with a television aerial on every chimney and a TV dish on the side of the house or in the garden. The sodium orange street lights gave the illusion of moving through fog. Beyond the houses on a country road, I asked if we were heading in the right direction.

Anywhere along here, she said. Well, maybe a bit further.

I reversed into an empty lay-by. The concrete bins were full.

Is this all right? I stopped the engine and doused the lights.

Fine, she said.

And we sat there, staring at the rainy patterns on the windscreen. I turned towards her but she did not move. Outside, the rustle of wind in the trees.

She offered me a cigarette and when I shook my head she lit her own with a gold plated lighter as I pulled at the ashtray. She wound down the window and smoked quickly. I watched the way the treetops waved against the sky as a damp breeze filled the car. She did not let the ash grow on her cigarette, but scraped it off the sides of the ashtray till she threw the filter out the window.

Where are we? I asked.

No idea. When I was fifteen I used to cycle round here all the time. It seems as if it went on forever, splashing through the puddles, coming home with mud on the backs of my socks, sometimes my dress would get caught in the chain and be covered in oil, but that was me at fifteen. Do you want to go back?

I'm not sure I know the way.

Are you cold?

Not really.

She wound up the window and faced the litter, her breath misting the glass as she spoke. What are you doing here?

I was seeing my sister, went for a pint and here we are.

What do you know about this place?

I know where my sister lives.

I bet that's in the snobby bit. New houses. She laughed. I've seen the day I'd've loved to live there.

Fancy a walk?

In the dark?

Why not?

The land rippled off in a series of shadows. Every now and then moonlight hit the roadway, pale and clear. She took off her shoes and walked with her hands behind her back.

Wait here, she said and ran back to the car.

In the middle of the road, the wind in the cornfield and the moon in a puddle, the sounds of night felt entirely alone.

I took off my tights and make up, she said. I combed out my hair and have no idea how far I can walk in the bare feet. It's lovely.

Isn't it wet?

That's the good bit. Like paddling. I thought I'd never do it again, she said. This isn't the same, but it'll do.

What age are you?

Nineteen. Don't tell me. I look older.

Are you working?

There's nothing here. I've done a couple of training schemes.

What sort of schemes?

For things I didn't want to do.

And what do you want to do?

I wanted to be a teacher like Miss MacLean. I thought she was brilliant.

Our breath cut into the air and vanished, as if the night was filled with wires. We stared across the field and watched the way it crumbled into darkness then flared in the moonlight, fringed by a thornbush with a single flower.

And what about college?

What about it?

Have you thought of going?

Thought about it.

But never done it.

No point. I'd have to move.

Is that a bad idea?

I'm getting married.

And somewhere over to the left headlights swept the air as they turned a bend, the engine noise drowned in the night. The sweep of light moved the other way and the car disappeared over a hill, brake lights flaring.

So, you're going to be a housewife?

You have to move if you want to do anything. If you decide to stay, you've to be like them. I was good at school, she said. I wasn't brilliant, but I was bright, so they stopped talking to me, and stopped anyone else from talking to me. They did rotten things. They threw my schoolbag in the river and beat me up going home; they didn't speak, made me sit alone and so on. You've no idea; they kept it up till I was like them.

How did that happen?

Start smoking, skip school, hang around the chip shop, start drinking, get pregnant, you know. You've seen them.

Are you pregnant?

Not yet.

She tilted her head as a cloud crossed the landscape. I wondered about people just like me, people for whom life's a mystery, who never know what to do, who want to hide rather than deal with whatever it is, who feel unique, as if they don't belong, who feel as if they need something extra to be the same as everyone else.

It started raining, the landscape suddenly wet and dark. We were soaked by the time we got to the car. I put on the heater and she shook her hair, turned towards me, but her head swivelled as I moved across and she brought her mouth over to mine.

Of course there was the moon and the rain, the wind and the steady poit of water. The moon grew bright when she was sleeping and the smoky world seemed to waver and slide. As she shivered awake, she smiled at me, embarrassed.

Driving back with the hot air blowing, she crouched in the seat like a child. This'll do, she said.

Will I give you a ring?

I'm not on the phone, she said and ran away.

Three days later, the mother opened the door and smiled. It's for you, she shouted into the house.

I looked at the pub with no windows, the place where we'd met. When I turned she was at the door.

What are you doing here? She looked into the house. For Christsake. I'm getting married.

When?

I don't know. When he gets the licence. Look, you'd better go. He'll go off his head if he sees you here. He knows about the other night. And she shut the door.

I took a road that went somewhere north and stopped by a field, where cows in a corner were waiting for rain.

They made no sound. I heard a stream and the flow of water over stone and thought I'd like to bathe my face. The cows moved aside as I approached, their breath fogging the air like mine. I rested my hands on the heat of their flanks and felt their slow, solid muscles bunched beneath, their sweet eyes staring through me as I found the stream and smelled the snow that had already settled on the hills to the north.

First Born

(for Kathleen J.)

Eileen Duncan

I was young, unknowing then,
My learning all in books.
Then, on the farm
Birth was calves and lambs.
A quick push on to hard ground
The caul cast,
Cold and wet the trembling legs
Guided to milky warmth.

My learning all in books
Nothing prepared me,
Rigid with pain and weeping fear
For this new pulsing life,
Till tiny nails scratched like kittens
On my swollen breast.
Such a poem was this
My sweetest true creation.

Nipples first raised and hardened with love
Now blossomed for their true vocation
To spurt and stream
Till splash and surge near over-whelmed him
Then tiny, toothless mouth
Clamped shut with gums of steel
And held me fast
Hostage forever to fear and fortune.

Now I see an unknown man asleep
Who once lay heart to my heart.
This stranger son
Whose thoughts and fears I cannot know
He binds me still,
Though I am old and knowing now.
My learning all in blood
My life in thrall.

Winter is Ending

Susan Paterson

Winter is ending,
Spring is coming
Plants are unbending,
Snowdrop and primroses blending.

The snow is going,
The sun is showing
The breeze is flowing
The world feels all mine.

Lambs are bleating
Snow is melting
Buds are unfolding
Birds chirping all around.

The mystery of growing
Is quite baffling
How do they know
When it's time to grow?

The winter is ending
Spring is coming
The world is happy
and so am I.

Alison Fearn

I miss winter, I miss winter
all the fun, all the fun
I miss all the snowball fights
and I really miss
the snowmen games

Winter's great fun, winter's great fun
Never ever boring, never ever boring
We ski, we sledge, all day
So I miss winter, I miss winter,
It will come another day.

Who Needs Spring?

Gino Sambucci

Spring is when the baby lambs are born
and make such a noise with their bleating.
Spring is when Scotland is supposed to get good weather
But doesn't.

Spring is when the trees start to blossom
And the dreaded bees come out.
Spring is when winter is over
And there is no more snow fights.

That's why I don't like spring.

Julie Rasmussen

Spring is when all the flowers bloom and all the birds sing. When Perthshire blooms the sun shines and chases the clouds away. Sometimes in Dunkeld I smell the air and taste the blossoms. The birds fly around my school and dive among the purpling heather. Spring is the key to open up new life. I watched the honey bee. What more could I want?

Megan Steward

Perthshire in bloom
Smells like flowers growing in country gardens
Feels like the breeze running over the heather
Looks like the bumble-bee flutter its wings
Sounds like the rustle of leaves of new growth

My pony kicks up her heels now it's spring
The smells, the sounds, the feelings
Give me a golden feeling.

Jim Steward

When the wind flies past it brings the smell of hill and river.
Amulree comes alive after a long winter sleep. The river
flows past my house and the sound of water fills me with joy
for the world. Golden daffodils are growing in my garden.
They make me see happiness in the world.

I touch them. I smell them. I have a good feeling for
Mother nature. The birds are everywhere. I want to sing with
them.

Danny Boatwright

Lambs jumping up and down. The sun shining on a spring day.
Flowers and their sweet smell Birds singing and the river
lapping. This is our lovely Amulree.

I touch the heather I taste the wonderful air. I watch from my
window and see the countryside in bloom. This is Amulree
with its winding glen road and high craggy hills.

This is our lovely Amulree in bloom.

Victoria Margaret Riches

Bonnie Glenquaich – sunshine and a fresh blue sky. Our wee Highland school is surrounded by grazing lands and hills. Lambs are skipping and playing and the house martins have returned to our school eaves. From the school window I gaze on the green hills of Amulree. I imagine a secret garden with flowers of every colour. Here we are surrounded by beauty which can only capture your HEART!

James Mackie

First light sunlight
The morning's fresh pure light
Starting off a brand new day.

Birds are singing
On this new spring morning
Waking the early bird up.

Ready for work
Toast to start the day
In the car and off to work.

Achoo! Achoo!
The hayfever's started—
Months of terror for me!

Edwin Jamieson

Winter dragged on,
But now it has gone
We shall have snow no more

We shall have sun,
lovely hot sun
For three months or more.

Why does it happen each year?
This may sound stupid,
But why did the snow disappear?

River Almond

Rory Hamilton

Running towards the River Tay the Almond waters flow
In spring the water sparkles bright and starts new life to grow
Vegetation bursting greens begins to make life bright,
Each new fern frond unfolds itself and reaches for the light.
Rippling over rounded rocks then glossy smooth in pools,
the fresh spring water, clear and deep, is wonderfully cool.

All around curlews and lapwings fill the air with songs
Little fish dart and flash in their lively throngs.
Many salmon lures still decorate the trees,
Overhead the buzzards mew while soaring on the breeze.
Not for me the fast lane life where things can seem so mean
Down by the Almond waters, life's good and pure and clean.

Buzzard

Thom Nairn

For four hours now
The rabbit has been cooling.
Slowly, surely
As the dawn comes down
To touch and enfold.

Dead, battered and tangled,
The life crushed out in seconds
By the rough spin of a tyre tread.

A field and half a sky away,
A dusty buzzard stirs and balances
Leg to leg and stretches.

Eyes open as clocks
And sparkling, sparking vicious.
Talons are tried, hard and tight
Around tired bark as a brace.

Bristling at a shallow moon,
Wings open like doors.
Movement takes over
And the world rolls on

To Breakfast,
Cool and stringy with a still,
Warm heart to be burrowed and found.

Lambing at Duncrub

Robin Bell

Because the round roofed apse was blue
and starred with wafers of bright gold,
the stained-glass shepherd's crook renewed
the plain walls of his private fold.

From first safekeeping at the font
through doubtless years of being so
beneath the well-starred firmament
the shepherd watched out fathers grow.

This was their order: truth revealed
without the need of asking why.
Glancing from prayer, their eyes could feel
the solid structure of their sky.

The flock has changed. The structure holds,
stripped of its sermons, hymns and pews.
Sheltered from the February cold,
the shepherd puts the past to use.

Straw bales stand stacked against the walls.
The table of the Lord makes way
for narrow rows of wooden stalls
with new born lambs and pale, sweet hay.

When memory is all we trust
to show us where the pulpit stood,
the questions of the Right and Just
bear no more form than burned churchwood.

A lamb dies. He takes another
and clothes it in the dead lamb's skin.
He lays it by its new found mother
to suckle and shelter once again.

Ma Freend Jim

Jean Massie

Wis an orra cheil.
Nickie tams an
torn breeks,
tacketie buits an aa.

Ma freend, Jim—
took tent o
a wee bairn,
wha trailled aboot efter him,
feedin kye an horse,
muckin oot byres.

Ma freend, Jim—
had a guid hert.
Fed her i the bothy
oan cauld beans an rowies.
Took floors tae his mither's grave
fae sumbody else's gairden.

Ma freend, Jim—
wis mensefu,
tho the cast was aa agin it,
thon bible fae
schuil's first day,
is testament tae that.

A Plooman's Lot

Chris Willox

The octogenarian poked the fire and continued to reminisce on his youthful days.

"The feein market was held in the main street on the twa term days, May 28th and Nov. 28th. A single man's employment wis reviewed every six months but a merried man in a cottar hoose wis usually employed for a year. If they "werna bidin" they gaed tae the feein market.

"Fermers an ploomen wandered up an doon Duke Street. A fermer would approach a man an the conversation micht gang something like this, 'Ye're thinkin o lavin Muckledykes?'

" 'Fairly, aye.'

" 'Am needin a man for ma second pair. There's a guid cottar hoose an a the usual.'

" 'A'll think aboot it.'

" 'You dae that,' answered the fermer, 'an a'll awa an hae a wordie at Muckledykes aboot what kind o character he gies you.'

" 'Aye,' said the plooman, 'an a'll hae a news wi your lest plooman.'

" They met again aboot an oor efter.

" 'Weel,' said the fermer, 'Muckledykes says ye're a guid worker an honest – a bit heavy on the drink at the weekend, but naebody can ploo a strechter furrow. So ye'll be workin for me fae Monday mornin!'

" 'Na, na Drumgeldie,' retorted the plooman, 'yer lest plooman tells me ye're a grippy, ill natured auld stott, an a bloody leear intae the bargain, for yer guid cottar hoose has a ruif wi as mony holes int as a tattie riddle. On Monday mornin a'll be plooin straucht furrows in some ither chiel's fields.'

"There wis a recognised hierarchy in every ferm toun. A ferm o aboot 350 acres wad hae, besides the fermer himsel, three pair o horse. The foreman worked the first, an best, pair. Then cam the second and third pair an their ploomen. Each man groomed, fed an muckit oot his ain pair. Forbye, on a ferm this size there would be an orraloon wi a single horse tae dae fetchin an cairryin - athing fae muckin oot byres tae puin neeps. The unmarried men lived in the chaumer abune the stables, often twa tae a bed. Mod cons were scarce. For a W.C. there was the midden and a horse trough for ablutions. Apairt fae beds the chaumer had little furniture, perhaps a chair an mebbe an auld table. Aince a week the kitchie deem wad gie the place a sweep cot. Each man had his ain kist which held his claithes an special possessions – a melodeon, a few horse brasses or a special bit o harness only used at plooin matches.

"It was gey cauld in the chaumer in the winter. The only warmth came from the beasts in the stable below. The men wore woollen semmits an thick, lang, woollen drawers, usually pinkish in colour, wi loops for their galluses on them. On tap o this was worn a dark, heavy, cotton workin sark – neckband only – nae collar. Breeks were 'moleskins', thick corduroy that 'cheeped' as the plooman walked, at least when nearl new. Abune his sark he wore a weskit. In richt cauld weather he micht wear an auld tweed jaicket on tap wi a woollen grauvit crossed ower his chest an tucked alow his oxters. Abune his ankles were strapped his 'Nicky Tams' – broad leather straps wi siller buckles. If gey dirty job was afoot the straps micht be replaced by bits o seckin tied wi binder twine. On his feet he wore muckle tackety boots. On Setterday nichts, arrayed in the splendour o best claithes – a blue serge suit, aye three piece, an boots o bricht broon, locally kent as 'yella beets' – the men would set aff for the toon on their bicycles. The summit o their dreams as far as transport was concerned was to possess a Raleigh 3-speed wi a gear case. Tae save the guid blue breeks they wore orange bicycle clips.

"On ordinary workdays they rose at five thirty tae groom an feed the horses. The men were fed in the ferm kitchen. The kitchie deem would hae the kettle bilin on the swey ower a roarin fire. Each man wad mak his ain brose steerin the bilin watter intae his bowlie o meal wi the wrang end o a fork. Wi his brose there was a bowlie o creamy milk. The horses were yokit atween six an six thirty. The foreman took the first rig an set the pace. The men knipit on till eleven. By this time the horses needed feedin an a rest. The men filed intae the kitchen for their denner, the foreman aye first, followed by the second and third horsemen. the orraloon wis aye at the coo's tail. The first bowlie o broth wis aye for the foreman. The ither men were served in order o importance. Nae wunner the recruitin sergeants aye hung aboot the feein markets. The country loons had the idea o rank ingrained fae their earliest days. The workin day feenished aboot six. When the beasts had been attended to the men gaed into the kitchen for their supper. Later on they micht foregather in the chaumer wi melodeon, trump an mebbe a fiddle. They would while awa the nicht tellin stories an singin sangs. They sat on their kists – hence 'bothy kisters' as the sangs were caad.

"The merried men lived in the ferm's cottar hooses. There wis aye a bit gairden whaur the tenant could grow kale, leeks an rhubarb an mebbe a buss or twa o reid or black currans or grossets. Maist o the cottars kept a puckle hens. They were supplied wi milk, meal and tatties fae the ferm. As sune as a cottar's bairn was a auld enough to lave the schule his father would find him a fee on a ferm roon aboot. Lassies would be sent oot tae serve as kitchie deems or dairymaids. Often eneuch if the ferm was sma she would work in baith kitchen and byre. The country folk were brocht up tae work lang an hard."

Going the Messages

J.S. Law

This morning – surely as everybody knows it
was crystal-clear as it was keenly cold,
the near side of a frosty sort of feeling,
the wind a bittockie the south of north,
and I padding-the-hoof, traiking through town,
going the messages as cannily
as easie-oasie not too far too much.
Not many old men go the messages:
if I did not, I'd exercise elsewhere,
and could not write like this of what I see.

In Auchterarder High Street, then, this morning,
a fine old womanbodie passed me by:
she was as dacentlyke as nicely-manned,
and when I tipped my bonnet-skip at her,
saluting kindly femininity
as always, she responded gently as
amiability her half-a-smile
as totally into her sort of charm
that was like winsomeness of the expression
surely was hers in youngly lively youth.

Back home for bone-fed broth as cauf-lug-thick
as holds the vegetables densely packed,
accomodating two Kerr's Pinks potatoes
per plate makes them changeful as subtle as
the cunning in a metamorphosis;
but wait, the broth is also changed like that!
To say such a thing is so, is to make it such.
If you can make kail like that, then you will know
it can be made no other way the better,
and like this poem, minds a pleasantness.

Calipso

Grant Cameron

Do bhòichead fhuasglaidh
chan fhaigh me greim oirr'
mun cuairt gun tèid mi
gun amharc as m'dhèidh
ach thig thu daonnan
an àm ainneart ìnntinn
is mi nam ònrachd—
cha ghoirt leam duine mar thu.

'S tu rèidh ri Dia
thug e treis dh'a chrùn dhuit
a chum feum do dhain-fhèis',
do dhannsa soirbh le tìm.

Ach lorg uaigneas mi, le òige air ghoid
mac-talla thusa mun mo chuairt,
Bu tu an t'oisean na mo chearcall
uair bha m'chearcall fhathast gun chuing.

Your cathartic beauty—
out of reach.
So round I go trying—
not to look back.
But you always pass
as my mind gets violent
when I am on my own—
no one hurts quite like you.

On good terms with God,
he lent you his crown
for your searching carnival
and easy dance with dance.

Solitude found me, with youth stolen,
as you echoed around.
You were the corner of my circle
when my circle was unbound.

Birth

Patricia Ace

The child dropped like a plum from a tree, was caught on a
towel by the skilled hands of the midwife. It seemed strange
that babies really did need catching at delivery but this one
came hurtling out, a purplish-grey rugby ball, attached to an
umbilicus of mother-of-pearl. The umbilical cord shimmered,
its twisted skeins glistened in a pale rainbow of surprising
colours – sea green, sky blue, pink-tinged, it spiralled and
coiled, a miraculous lifeline which had anchored the new life
inside for the best part of a year. The child was no longer
suspended in the eerie, uneasy silence between life and
death. She had cried as a head emerged into the bright
sunlight of the late morning and was bleating still in a tiny
shocked alarm. The mother lay motionless, reeling, like a
massive ancient tree, spectacularly felled.

Parallel Lines

Bob Hughes

With a grunt and a swipe of her mouth with the back of one hand the girl opposite comes awake just as the train clanks into Glasgow's Central station: she's been out since Motherwell.

One across: our eyes meet, briefly, then mine drop again to the *Scotsman* crossword passing her embarrassed smile en-route, embarrassed myself. The answer still eludes me and the thread is lost as other signs and faces appear outside the window.

A near clash of heads as we rise to grapple coats and bags from the rack and there's another exchange of smiles as we're thrown together by the stopping train. Then, caught up in the bustle of alighting passengers, we arrive together on the glistening platform with other strangers: fellow travellers no more.

And yet, tuning in my walkman: shouldering my rucksack; I catch a last sight of her as she mounts the escalator and begins rising before she is cut off by the platform indicator; her long legs, like the grin of the Cheshire cat, last to disappear.

And then, over the pop song I haven't identified yet, I hear a louder noise; a shushing noise. That background noise you hear in every railway station: that pre-diesel sound you used to hear from escaping steam and that's now made by air brakes. It's the sound you get when you open and close your palms over your ears: or when you've just dived into deep water and come up for air, or when you wake up from a dream into a room that's suddenly no longer familiar.

The main concourse is crowded with queuers and movers and a kind of miasma. People of all ages, shapes, sizes, colours and – mercifully – whole glide across the floor. And I drift through them: moving forwards in space; an atom avoiding collision. Just me and my walkman and my noise: and my memory; that most selfish possession.

Before walkmen, when I couldn't have afforded one, and when I didn't really feel the need for that isolating luxury anyway, I worked on the railway: the Permanent way: the P-way, as we called it. And it seemed like it then: permanent; steady, a job for life. At twenty five, I'd pee away the bulk of my wages in the pubs of Leeds and work all the hours I could get so that I could do it all over again. I was fit, and it was freedom now and fuck the future.

Then came the accident.

That's what they called it: an accident. It was in the *Yorkshire Post*: a few, terse lines: hard lines; bare facts:

On the main line between . . . the body of a woman . . . in the early hours of . . .

Just a paragraph then. And, next day, a statement from her husband, a Bradford policeman, equally terse; jejune:

In the past few weeks . . . under a strain . . . .

Just the facts. They're part of my memory now. A small part. Like the scribbled note on the back of a holiday snap:

Yorkshire. Summer. 1976

Yorkshire. Summer. 1976. 6 am. The sun's already high: the sky a flawless blue: the birds are singing and we're all swearing and waiting on the platform of Burton Salmon station to board a stone train. Twenty wagons filled to the brim with grey chippings, an engine and a guard's van: all that's needed now are the men to supply the muscle power to turn rusty wheels that will open doors to release the ballast, and one wanker in a shirt and tie (the inspector) to tell them when to do it.

There's ten of us to do the donkey work. That means four wagons to each pair – two men, one wheel apiece. It means climbing on and off the wagons. It also means near-suffocation from clouds of thick granite dust. Nobody is happy about it as the inspector waves us aboard and climbs up behind the engine.

A sweaty two hours and five wagons later we stop: suddenly. The driver's applied the brakes and we've all been jerked back against the guardrails. We're clinging on and cursing. Heads appear as we lean out and look towards the inspector who's hanging out in space himself trying to see beyond the engine that's stopped on a curve. Then we're all jumping down and crunching our way to the front through clouds of stone dust, swearing and asking each other what's happened.

What has happened, according to a bloke who appears from the other direction is that: "Some poor fucker's been skittled."

What happens then is that the inspector goes forward: the older members of the gang head for the back of the train and the guard's van, muttering about "a brew:" three of us go on, and reality gets derailed.

There's a group of orange-waistcoated figures a hundred yards ahead and just standing.

To the left, breast high in yellow barley, two uniformed men are making as fast an approach as they can, while behind them a silent ambulance emits a blue light in feeble, rotating flashes. We're in single file as we beat the ambulancemen to the scene and there she is: there it is.

Lifeless and, for all we can see, bloodless, a pair of legs without a trunk: butting against the rail: splayed outwards towards the high banking: one toe jutting through the foot of a pair of tights which are otherwise intact: they are; it is; *she* is . . .

Tension, or the relief of having confronted the unknown? One of the men says: "I'll need to get the missus a pair like that," and there's laughter; but not from me.

Maybe I'm in shock. All sound, save for a shushing like a wind through the barley field, ceases. I feel as if I'm rising up, lifted by the wind until I'm floating above the track and above: everything. But then there's a scrabble of loosening stone and raised voices as two men clamber up the slope.

And then there's a steady, somehow comforting, rhythm of our crunching boots as we make our way back to the guard's van and the brew.

Two days – one of compulsory "rest" – later and I'm in our caravan making tea when the rest of the gang arrive. They're talking loudly and there's a stranger with them, a man who walks the track looking for jobs for us to do. A garrulous bastard, toothless and tactless and tasteless: rebarbative.

Between mouthfuls of sandwich and swigs of tea he tells us all about the dead woman. About how she'd travelled all the way from Bradford and flung herself from the door of an express out of York: and about how you could still see where it happened on account of there being no rain. He's banging on about what dopey bastards the railway police are then he starts laughing and spitting crumbs at us and fishing for something inside his shirt.

It's a box, long, narrow: plain, grey cardboard. Still laughing like a drain, he slides the thing apart in two sections and produces it's contents with a flourish; and it's a pink, new-looking vibrator.

Then he's waving this fucking thing like a conductor with a baton and he says: "At least she died happy."

Everybody laughs: me too. But then it happens again: the shushing and the rising sensation. Only this time it's different. The sound is coming from me.

I can still hear the laughter but it's kind of far away. And what I'm hearing now is the sound of air brakes being released and the clanking of couplings. And I'm moving forward now, picking up speed.

I'm moving forward now. I'm going somewhere and behind me is the arched entrance to the Central station. And behind that is the buffers, and the track that's connecting everywhere to everywhere else; and everything *with* everything else. And in my breast pocket, crumpled and holed, is my return ticket.

Osprey Watch, Loch of the Lowes

Honor Inglis

The ringed master stands poised and proud
Atop a green canopy. He, his future guards.
They tremble in rough bare-wood nesting shroud.
We, extant, expectant, home in on their back yard.

Elsewhere, she, like slow-winged devil,
Makes circles over water, and conjures
Fishes from their deep, secret revels.
Suddenly . . . she drops.

Shattering water crystal as sequinned fragments fly,
Her spine-clad talons grasp firm
The gasping, motleyed, shining prize,
While We and He and They, await her return . . .

And the thunder drums roll
And survival holds its breath . . .

Surrendering

Margaret Gillies Brown

The bike was ower big for me
An' the fairm road
I learnt tae ride on, rouch,
Dubby at times.
Whiles I gave up
But aye cam back tae it.
After I couped,
Scartin' ma knees on the stanes.
I'd been telt hoo tae ride it,
Kent a' the theory.
Noo and then, Faither or Mither
Wid hing on till the seat,
Let go wi' oot warnin',
I'd wobble and crash
Till ae evening'
Wi' the yorlin singin'
And the sunlicht weepy wi' shooers,
For no parteeclar reason,
In a split second
I for the w'y of it and nivver forgot—
Findin' my balance they cried it—
Och! – the joy o' that moment!

Hoo can ye explain it
Tae ony ither?
This mystification
Has tae be foond oot for yer sel'—
The discovery—
Then gie'n in tae the wull o' the bike
Syne warkin wi it:
"It's easy," I said,
"When ye ken hoo."

A lang while efter
I made another surrender
Tae a g'y muckle wull
That, too, in a split second!

1971-thing follows another

Wendy Birse

I remember Jim
He came from Teesside.
Teas I'd share with him
Through forbidden hours
In college sleeping quarters.

Sleeping. Quarters of each hour marked
By the chimes of the clock in the steeple on the corner.
I wondered why the time chimed
All through the night.

All through. The knight departed bearing tarnished armour.
Only the trail of his weary steed remained.
One plus one make three. Let's count the aftermaths.

After maths, biology and then the bloody physics.

For six months no love, no lust,
No carnal knowledge
No fun, no games, no pleasure.

Nope. Leisure must take another form.

I remembered Jim.
He came from Teesside.
Tease? I'd rib him till with rage
His face would flush a deepening mauve
That seemed, for all the world,
Beetroot to me.

The May Queen

Mary Sutherland

Pastel-pink petals
Floating softly
Down from a blossom tree
Landing as snowflakes do
Carpeting grass,
Pavement and roadside
Being sent down as confetti
For a May bride.

I look to this tree as the 'May Queen'.
She, being dressed in a gown
Heavy-laden with fink florettes,
Her branches waving gracefully
Against a blue heaven
In the brightest of Spring sunshine.

Pansies, in their colourful dress
Circling the bow of the 'May Queen'
Their faces upturned beaming with joy
Taking part in the celebration
Of new life—
—Another year.

An End to Innocence

Eileen Duncan

I always remember his little feet. They must have been about a size five, narrow and dainty like a woman's. He generally wore very highly polished black shoes, or, in the summer, little brown plimsolls.

I don't know what age he would have been – late sixties I suppose – though he always seemed ancient to us children. Small, nebby features, watery, grey eyes and sparse grey hair, usually covered by a flat cap, or a panama in very warm weather. A thin tortoise neck poked out of a striped flannel collarless shirt, over which he wore a baggy grey cardigan and baggy serge trousers. I don't recall ever seeing him in a suit, although he sometimes wore a linen jacket in the height of summer, and always a brown overall jacket in his workshop.

There was a dry, fusty, slightly sour odour about him, but it was not unpleasant and was easily lost in the general smell of tobacco smoke, coal dust, old newspapers and woodshavings which permeated his house and workshop.

Everything about him was precise. A cigarette hung constantly from his narrow lips, smoked precisely to half an inch from the end. No filter tips in those days. These were collected in an old tobacco tin and, when it was full, whichever child was visiting at the time was allowed to snip the paper off the butts with little sharp scissors, shred the remaining tobacco into another tin and make new cigarettes with a little machine which to us was the height of technology. In spite of this he lived to a ripe old age, although in retrospect this may have been only into his seventies.

He was precise too in measuring kindling wood to exactly nine inches, just right for fitting into the little grate. Logs were sawn to just this dimension, coal was split along the grain with a little hammer and old ashes were riddled, anything over an inch and half being kept to add to the fire after kindling. He had a particular method of twisting up old newspapers and laying the kindlings on in grid fashion to allow air to percolate which I use to this day.

We ranged the countryside far and wide with him, collecting burdens of broom for kindling, and sticks for the fire. This got him and me into tremendous trouble one day when we released a rabbit from a gin trap, unaware that the gamekeeper was doing his rounds just a few hundred yards away. We scurried off with his shouts ringing in our ears and, as my father worked on the same estate, I lived in terror for several days fearing that the keeper would complain to him and I would be in trouble.

We used to help him saw the sticks too with a Bushman saw, which was kept well polished and efficiently sharp, as were all his tools. In fact his workshop was immaculate. Boxes of nails and screws were arranged in order of size on the shelves and axes, saws, chisels and planes hung neatly on the walls.

This was a far cry from the state of the house, though I suppose in his own way he considered it quite orderly. The house consisted of two rooms and an attic, a real but and ben. I was never 'ben the hoose' where I think he kept his clothes, suitcases and bicycle. The main room was both living room and bedroom with a grate for heating and cooking. A single table stood in the window with an enamel basin on it, where he shaved and prepared food, with two enamel pails underneath, one for clean water from the spigot outside, and the other for slops.

There was a large bed behind the door, the bottom of which was totally covered by neat bundles of newspapers and magazines. At right angles to the end of the bed was another small table, neatly spread with newspaper, the salt, pepper, butter and marmalade jar ranged with neat precision at one end, against the wall of newspapers. There were four small chairs tucked under the table and a horsehair armchair sat at one side of the fire opposite the pails of coals, graded in size, and kindlings, on the other side.

There were four children in the village and we all visited him regularly. We filled coal pails, prepared his tobacco, peeled potatoes, carried home sticks, and took his flagon with ours when we went on our daily visit to the nearby farm for milk. For this we would each get a 12 sided brass threepenny piece and a Highland Cow slab of toffee every week.

But a greater attraction were the nightly games of cards. We learned whist (if he could get three of us squeezed into the room) otherwise two-handed rummy, Beggar-my-neighbour and my favourite, Speed, which had wonderful paintings of race-horses, racing cars, planes and steam engines on the cards. Even better than that were the magazines, comics and papers. He got them all, *Rover*, *Hotspur*, *Wizard*, *Wide World* and *Geographic* and we got to read them all in turn, better than nuggets of gold to children in a rural village, five miles from the nearest newsagent.

When I went to secondary school, homework took up more and more time and I was able to buy my own *Schoolgirl* and *Jackie*. Like the other children I still helped the old man occasionally with his chores and still enjoyed the odd game of rummy or whist, but childhood was drawing to a close. One evening a blue-veined hand hovered indecisively over the cards then moved towards me. With eyes cast down he whispered, "Can I touch you – there?" A robust, country-raised child, I brushed him aside and snorted dismissively. The game continued – but for the last time.

The Village Schoolmaster

Margaret Gillies Brown

He is like a father to them,
A rather boyish one
Who hasn't quite grown up himself,
Seeing the world from their own point of view
As well as his own.
They are his till their twelfth Summer
To mould just how he wishes,
He knows their homes, their histories,
Their origins,
Sees what makes some right
And others wrong,
And like a good parent would
Takes equal interest in them all.
The aim is happiness.
Oh yes he gives them the rudimentary
Rules of education,
The three Rs
But there is so much more he tries to tell them,
How the world is,
The excitement of sport,
The glory of winning,
Magnanimity in losing.
With Pied Piper persuasion
He takes them for several days
Away from green, hilled, flowered
Treed, cropped country side,
Leads to London
Where with Dick Whittington delight
They see through clear young country eyes,
Palace and Parliament,
Cathedral and Tower
And endless streets teeming with foreign tongues.
Opens up whole new worlds for them,
Whole new realms of though
For some distant grown-up dream time.

Nae Fare fir the Schael Bus Hame tae Hunter Crescent, 1957

Yvonne Pirie

We're jinglin
—be the sweetie shoap—
oor fares, tuckt in wer poackets.
Stoap fir a bit;
jist tae see whits whit . . .
AW!!! moothwaterin granny sookers.

We're dribblin noo . . .
Mmmm!!! we cannae? . . .
we do; twa pokes o dolly mixtures;
sticky moo'ed an belly fu: SPEW!!!
It's a lang hoof hame tae Hunters.

We've sneaky sneakied oan the bus.
We're cute! tae Bella's temper;
clips the bell and raises hell,
fairly gangs hur dinger.

Creepie creepie it's derk in here,
we're belly creepin fae the hud, doon stair.
Look . . . shoosh . . . deck aboot . . .
git ready tae dive we'll syn be there.

Stoap! stoap! ahink wer shoapt;
is yon yellie skellie mouthin?.
She is! . . . up – jump the bus—
burl the pole – we're skitin.

We're fleeing . . . she yells,
'Ye've no peyed a'll tell'.
'BELLA!, they twa are scivin'.

AW BELLA YER BELL . . .
AN YOU GAE TAE . . . Well!,
it's nae damn fair . . .
is clypin.

The School Cleaner

Grant Cameron

She stooped,
her back a ruler that wouldn't break,
to emulate the implement she pushed.
Her haircut a short statement of efficiency,
eyes fidgeting warily behind
her spectacles' steel cage,
years tirelessly crushing
any figment of youth.

The years rolled round each day,
her song a whistle,
content in her cleansing brethrern.
Her boss trusted her,
as a workhorse.
She resigned every day,
and everyday, returned.

Not able to grasp reflected light,
she feels the sky laugh as
she works towards her
nine carat carriage clock.

Her childrens' eyes grateful,
as she delivers the tea,
smiling.

Strathardle

Rhona Johnstone

Massed cumulus blown by a strong May wind
Sweep the vault of the Spring-blue sky
Chase their shadows across the hills
As sunlight comes and goes.

The rising slopes, once heather moors
Now marked in regimented squares
Of tax-deductible conifer plots
All by vanquish the native oaks.

Green fields along the valley floor
Hold new-born lambs and black-face ewes;
White blossoms scatter the sparse hedgerows
And highlight the peat-dark river flow.

Twenty Visions

Angus Brown

1.   THE DESERT

The red discs rise over flatness. As the light spreads on the dark surface, pockmarks come into focus on the ground. A kind of hulk like rock, hollow in places under the surface, the dark marks the entries to holes. A silence in the air. A bareness over which life must crawl. A burnt out ember.

2.   WATER

There is no water. Nothing to drink. We leave the holes and emerge into the grasping heat. The necessity for survival is going to lead us to violent acts today. The ground over which we feud is well known. We had it before them. Then they had it. Now we are thirsty and we want it. The dusty weapons are primed. There will be casualties. Them and us. Them or us.

3.   THE MEN

Some people get wise. Some substances make you wise. Some proteins tickle the neurotransmitters and jog up the grey matter. We want to be clever, cleverness breeds survival. We don't want to return to the dust, the glowing bowl of no hope. As our ancestors pulled themselves from the seas, we will push ourselves into fresh pastures of the mind. We can colonise the soul. In a world with no cars, telepathy is far more use than oil.

4.   THE FISH

These fish, resting from the heat in a cool pool, are haemaphrodites. Two sexed, non-reproducing. I examine them, running my hand over the smooth scales. The last of the family line. My food for today. They swim silently around the pool, trapped by my hand and by evolution. But new phases must mean new solutions, and like the dinosaurs I suppose we, or whoever else, will remember fish in some way.

5.   THE CULT

The procession of people pushes on through the sand and rock. I watch as the leader raises his head and chants mournfully "Ceau, Ceau." The others join in, dismally in the dust. The line stops as we come to a large hole in the rock. Below it I can see embedded a large statue of a man's head. From some lost world. Why are they remembering him? Somebody told me that he didn't really die (when was this, 30 years ago, I don't know) and that he is living still in the rock. The same old myths.

6.   LIMBS

Before the War I had limbs. Real ones, flesh and blood. And I suppose I'm lucky that I was grafted before the circuit boxes ran out and the anaesthetic pumps went dry in the hospital. Semi-solid, semi-flexi, semi-human I suppose, they live on me and in me, a kind of challenge to Mother Nature lives in them, as they circulate with blood, sense my pain or sense the wetness of rain. If there ever is any rain.

7.   SATELLITE

My satellite is still out there somewhere. When I was a kid my father bought and sold them. This one belonged to a rich man who used it to spy on his wife. It was programmed to track her DNA chain. Satellites had got beyond the necessity of fixed orbits and used to hover in the sky for months before a battery change, so it could see all her lying and cheating and screwing around. Except she didn't, certainly in the short time before her implants burnt out and she died in hospital. Since then it tracked anyone with a similar DNA, wherever it could, confusedly spinning around the world, staying with someone, then realising the match wasn't quite right. It could never find its match again.

8.   WORKING THE LAND

Some things grow. I pull a carrot out of a space in the rock and look over to the field. A labour gang weaves across the middle distance, extracting rock from rock in an attempt to make a plantable plot. It has to be done, every day, then fiercely defended. And I'll defend my carrot if I have to. I came by them and I'm sticking by them, the little bit of security I've got, trying to give them water occasionally and clear out the biggest of the rocks. Out of little things . . . grow disasters.

9.   HOME

I was dreaming of home. Whatever that is. Before the heat shock fried my memory I think I had a home. I dimly remember light, artificial light, and shadow. Is that what made it a home? I think again, my mind struggling with inner colours and patterns jostling for my attention like spectators at a fistfight. I try to see it through the bits of electronic data which lodged in my cells during the fallout. I'm like a wallpaper library, a what, what did that mean?

10.   COMMANDMENTS

The commanders told me to do it. At least I think they did. The neurocommand entered by head as the plane was tilting backwards, the result of my fear interfering with the auto thought pilot. Involuntarily, or nearly so, I turned the craft round in my head and came over the centre. I think I destroyed my town, at least I unloaded the plane on it. What happened next? I can't remember.

11.   REALITY LOOP

Outside the settlement we see, at periodic intervals, a pseudo-neo-quasi mirage: a vision of things I remember, things the others remember too. We stare at it together, the repeating light and sound patterns. Some say the rock is magnetic, that its fields picked up old signals or data streams from long-defunct computers. Others say the visions are our collective unconscious speaking to us, as everyone sees these repeating visions in a slightly different way. Occasionally someone, upset or excited, jumps into the swirling patterns. They black out and wake the next morning with a heavy head, hungover from last night's reality.

12.   TWO SUNS

I did see two suns one day, or maybe there always were two, one behind the other. I know it was "proved" decades or centuries ago that we had one sun here, so maybe it split in two.

13.   JIGSAW

Every time I try to reconstruct the past I get more confused. Does it really matter what we did, or the events which led us here. Will it make me feel more secure to know where or how I came here? We do our own form of fossil hunting from time to time, digging in the rock, searching from clues. But when I recognise something, a shoe, a comb, a circuit board, it just feels out of place and I throw it away. The past disappoints me.

14.   MY CAR

I dreamt last night I was in my car. A long time ago. I remember the smell of oil and plastic. I woke up on a road with lots of other, fast cars. But I was going the wrong way. The sinking feeling, the mouth dry. I tried to explain it to the others, some of them flashed recognition, others thought I was mad, deranged.

15.   THE CULTURE

Is no more. I think it was alive, but perhaps there is a dead culture too.

16.   GHOSTS

I think the past really is haunting us. The echoes of people, pulses of energy, where are they all now? I can feel them pressing down on me. An old religion, in America, I think it was, used to think it was important to track down everyone who ever lived, to save their souls, perform a ritual. They said they had information on 80% of all the men and women who ever lived. Right from Adam. Where are they now?

17.   TIME MACHINE

There were rumours of a time machine in Centre 4, long before we saw reality playback or any of this really happened. But people were scared to use it. I saw a man prematurely aged, a lifetime in 10 minutes, irreversible at the time. But at what time?

18.   WALKING

I walk for hours, my muscle implants queasing and seizing up beneath me. And sometimes I skate on the sand, like a disabled surfer, tottering against the wind on a piece of wood. Is the earth flat? Well I've never seen the edge, and it goes on and on. Or maybe time is in reverse, dragging up old concept and plugging them into my brain? Is it in the air, in the sand, the sand going up the hourglass?

19.   99 PIECES OF STONE

I counted them out. 99 pieces of stone. This must be significant. Am I forming a new ritual? Can I persuade the others that it is important? Is this how cultures start? I rub them against each other. Rounded by the years, then cracked by the force. Little tombstones from our past.

20.   PARALLELS

I am convinced there is a parallel universe where this didn't happen, where I'm somewhere else, someone else. Sometimes I can see it in my mind's eye. We used to have equipment to track it. Some people tried to split it. Maybe that's what caused the War. The two suns. We don't know what else to call it except a War.

The Fall

Linda Cracknell

Jim was spread-eagled over the bonnet of the car with the open map. He pinned the edges down hard with his palms. Marjorie held her face up to the early morning sun and waited, her small rucksack already on her back. She gazed at the mountains and hummed. Something light and tuneless. Humming was good for that – filling the spaces, taking your mind of other things. She was only vaguely aware of doing it. It was her family who'd forced her to realise, after all three grown-up children had trailed her around the house making dying bee noises. 'The Humbug' they called her.

'See, it'll be much quicker this way,' Jim said. Marjorie didn't bother responding. Likely as not he wasn't really talking to her; briefing himself for the expedition.

'Don't you want to see where we're going?' He cranked his neck round to see her.

'OK, love.' And she put a hand on one of his shoulders and leant over too, towards the map. 'Show me what I'm in for then.' Maps were not Marjorie's forte. There were green bits for trees, blue bits for lochs; she understood that. But all those lines and squiggles. Well.

'See, we'd have to go all the way around there.' He drew an arc with his finger along a dotted line.

A path, then. 'Yes?'

'When we can just go straight up here.' His finger stabbed a short distance through a cluster of irregular concentric circles. He looked up at her, smiling triumphant.

'And what are those amoeba things?'

'Amoebas?'

'Those squiggly circle things.' She pointed at the concentric circles.

'Marjorie.' He put one hand up to the back of her neck and swivelled her gaze in the direction of his pointing finger. 'See those high pointy things? You've come across one or two in your time?' She nodded. 'Well on the map they turn into contours and look like 'squiggly circle things'.' He peered into her face to make sure she was following. ''Hills'. They're sometimes known has 'hills'.'

'Ah', she said. 'Thanks, Jim. It's ringing a bell now.'

He cuffed the back of her head. A sprinkle of rain drops tapped on to the map from an apparently clear sky.

'Better not get the map wet', she said. And he folded it back into its plastic wallet.

'Are you sure about this route?' Marjorie said to Jim's back a little later. He was already laying the trail towards the sheer face of the hill. The terrier, Bobby, clung to his heels, nose down, tail up. Marjorie had stopped to stuff a jumper into her rucksack. At first she thought he hadn't heard, but after a few more strides, he stopped and turned back to her. She thought she saw something dart behind his eyes, like a goldfish in a dirty tank.

'It's just that it looks steep. Too steep,' she said. He turned away from her again to look at the hill. Jim and Bobby stood next to each other. Marjorie was amused by their similarities; they seemed to imitate each other. Short legs planted slightly apart; noses upwards sniffing the challenge. A solid pair. But Jim didn't pant. Of course not.

'It'll be fine. It's much quicker this way. I showed you – remember?'

She picked up her rucksack, mentally re-packing the small parcel she always carried on hill-walking trips. The Jim-is-always-right parcel. It was compact and durable. Like the first aid kit that they carried in a tupperware box containing essential treatments for cuts, strains and insect bites and which they re-stocked religiously from the bathroom cupboard. The Jim-is-always-right parcel allowed them both to feel confident. After all, it was so much easier to let Jim take this role; to trust him. True enough, in the early years of their marriage she had fought it a bit. And it hadn't been just about walking. There was the choice of schools for the children, the best pension scheme to buy into, even what sort of dog to have (Marjorie always wanted a collie). But the painful negotiations died down as they settled into their married life. A collie really was too big in a suburban house, she accepted that now.

Marjorie relaxed, the parcel safely back in her rucksack.

'It always looks steeper than it really is, remember?' he called over his shoulder as they set off again. He was right. Going up *and* down. Like when they'd stood on the Aonach Eagach ridge in Glencoe, their senses tumbled in deep-sea mist. A chink in the cloud had framed the silver line of the river and tourist cars in the glen below, and he's said, 'We can go down here', and pointed at a slope of impossibly sheer scree. She shrugged and followed after a few protestations, and they scrambled down, breaking into smiles as they joined the sunshine and day-trippers in the glen.

She was almost reckless in her trust. She had to admit, Jim extended her, forced her into situations she wouldn't have put herself in. Friends were amazed by her escapades.

At their joint retirement party a few weeks earlier, Marjorie had stood, embraced by a circle of her teacher friends, tearing at wrapping paper on a small gift.

'I'll be able to find my way to the shops now, anyway', she laughed. 'Look Jim, I'll be able to find my way to the shops.' She beckoned him over from the bar and took his sandwich in exchange for the compass. He turned it over.

'It's a good one, that. A very good one.' They swapped back again.

'Thanks, girls', she hugged them one at a time. 'Maybe I should learn to use it now I've got all this time on my hands. What do you reckon, Jim. Will you get bored with being my guiding light?'

'Never, my darling. Not till I drop dead with that heart attack on the hill.' He retreated towards the bar with his sandwich.

'I suppose I ought to know which direction to carry you in,' she called after him. She turned back to her friends, 'Though I have a feeling a ghostly voice will shout directions through the clouds.' A smirk passed silently around the circle of faces.

She followed Jim and Bobby on gently rising ground towards the hulk of the hill. Bedclothes of cloud unravelled from a peak, allowing it to stretch up into the bright morning. She sucked in a lungful of air and stretched her arms over her head. She was like Julie Andrews, tripping weightlessly through mountain meadows studded with wild flowers. She had to recognise her limitations though. She might be a little over-stretched by trying to sing and look beautiful as well.

There was joy in following, she decided. Not taking the responsibility meant she didn't have to think. She just luxuriated in the sensations. She mentally caressed the flowers, naming the ones she knew – tormentil, heath bedstraw – and trying to avoid walking on the orchids. Patches of black moss were silken and moleskin under her fingers. Reed pricked her bare calves. Her steps flicked frogs out of the squelch. The rocks were decorated with lichens – antique white and green. And some had tendrils that reached out into the air, like corals escaped from the *Underwater World of Jacques Cousteau*. She stretched her arms in front of her, swum a few breast strokes through the air. Why not? No-one was there to see. Certainly not Jim, way up ahead with no idea of the fun she was having.

It was getting steeper, and she felt the warm grate of rock on her hands as she pulled herself up. The wind increased as they got higher, lifting the hair away from her face. Her lungs started to hurt, and Julie Andrews faded to black and white. Marjorie stopped to draw breath. Jim was up ahead, standing on a ledge. He was pushed vertical by a rock in front of his chest. His arms were spread open to hold himself to it. His head twitched to left and right, looking for the next part of his route. They were scrambling now, not walking.

Marjorie followed Jim and Bobby into a gully to the right where they continued upwards, sheltered on both sides by moss and rock. Ferns sprouted from a gurgle and spout of water, unseen under the rocks in the deepest part of the gully. Her boots slipped on the wet surface. Despite the shelter, she understood why Jim moved back to the left, onto the drier, but more exposed rocks. She didn't look down, followed Bobby along a wide ledge. Jim was above them, but neither she nor Bobby could see how to follow him. She stopped, faced the rock, leant into it.

Jim looked down and said something that the wind lifted away from her and then, 'You stay there. I'll go and look around the corner. Find the best way.' Grey-bottomed clouds lumbered between Jim's head and the sun, flattening and blackening the peaks and corries around them. The sparkle disappeared from the straight white lines of waterfalls. The rock started to cool under her hands. She didn't feel like moving anyway.

Jim levered himself upwards until he knelt at the next level. Then he stood up and disappeared from view. Bobby trotted to and fro next to Marjorie, looking upwards for a way to follow, rocking back onto his haunches every now and again to look higher, front paws lifting off the ground.

'Stay here, Bobby', Marjorie said. Her voice was like a wisp of something tossed in the wind. The dog ignored her. He hurtled up at the ledge where he'd seen Jim disappear. His front paws caught the lip of the rock, and she heard his extended claws scrabble against it, saw the urge of his head and neck upwards, before he peeled backwards, swivelling into a roll of fur that carried him down. Past Marjorie. Down.

She let out a low wail. Bobby. Indestructible Bobby. Her eyes followed him downwards and one of her knees started to beat a rhythm against the rock in front of her. Several feet below, Bobby's paws found purchase on another ledge. He scrambled upright. Shook himself. Under his fringe, he rolled his eyes up towards Marjorie without moving his head. One of his 'did-she-notice?' gestures. He was embarrassed. That was all.

'Are you OK Bobby?', she shouted over the wind, leaning down to see him. The her senses lurched and swayed. As he bounded upwards by another route, she re-focused. Off Bobby, onto what was beyond him. She saw a sheep. Far below. Directly below. Like the speck she suddenly felt herself, pinned against a rock face. She'd climbed all that way. So far up. And she could fall all that way. Rolling and bouncing like Bobby. Except she was heavier, would have more momentum.

She reached deeper above the rock with her hands, gripped the rough heather stems. As if they would save her. The thing was to stay still. Jim would come back with a solution. He'd find an easy way, just out of sight; a staircase, even an escalator. Wouldn't he? She waited. Clung to the rock. Stared into its lined face. Heard the insane whine of her own humming. And below her, above her, inside her, time contracted and expanded. A tide went way, way out. And she thought about Jim moving away from her around the corner. Had his shoulders looked less robust than in the old days? Were there other hints she should have been taking?

A boot scuffed into sight above her. Coming down. And then Bobby's whiskery face appeared crouched between paws, one of them bloody. They both joined her on her ledge. She continued to cling. Jim's sweat-smell, the heat he seemed to project, enveloped the three of them like a familiar mist. She stopped shivering. Waited to know what would happen next.

'It's too chossy,' Jim said. 'Too dangerous when it's this steep. We'll have to go down.'

'Down?' Marjorie stared at him. Down. All that way back to the tiny sheep. Across the mass of contours he'd shown her on the map. It was horrible going down on steep ground, feeling backwards for footholds you couldn't see.

'Sorry love.' He seemed to avoid her eyes. 'We'll take it slowly. I'll lead you.' She continued to stare at him till his eyes were forced to meet hers. It reminded her of Bobby's look earlier. Yes, she thought. I did notice. She grew braver. Turned on the ledge so that she faced Jim rather than the rock. Felt the vastness below her on one side. She wasn't clinging any more.

And then it happened. The fall came as she knew it would. She saw the compact parcel she had carried all those years fall out of her rucksack. Tumble like the dog. But this time it crashed on downwards, bouncing off rocks, displacing lumps of bog, scattering sheep in its radius. The contents were displayed across the hillside, messy and embarrassing, like a rubbish bag pulled apart on the street for neighbours to see. It took several minutes for everything to settle. For her to see the hillside clearly again. To feel a thrill at the devastation.

She let him lead her down. Slow and meticulous. Accepted his instructions.

'A bit further to your left, love,'

'A small stretch more.'

She heard his questions, 'Are you OK?' and the reassurances, 'You're doing fine. We're nearly there'. And she didn't question; knew that they were safe.

And when they got to the bottom and were back on the firm path that led to the car, she walked in front. And her rucksack felt light on her back.

Kepa Rasmussen

Alive and refreshed the mountains and fields
flood over with colour and beauty.
Alive and rippling the streams and the river Braan
flood over the swaying weeds.
Alive and growing an animal world
Flourishes and is content.

Birds sway gracefully in the breeze
and on the ridge the eagle studies the land—
the true ruler of the Amulree skies.

Heather and bracken dance like waves
on a sea of green.

Hilary Drysdale

As I watch the River Tay I feel excited,
With butterflies in my stomach.
The water chases logs down and under bridges.
It is almost as if the river is screaming
to stop the speed of it racing away.

There is a sense of danger but yet
the rails hold me back from falling
into the excitement.
If you look closely you can see
The foam bubbling like witches' potions.

Summer

Amanda Noble

The sun dancing in the sky, watching the people below
Children playing in the park, a red and blue football flies through the sky.
The leaves rustling in the soft evening breeze.
Grass dancing to the song of the ice cream van.
Children run to where the white van waits, pulling parents along,
Stand in an eager line, for the ice creams to come.

    The sun shines through the bright green leaves of an oak tree,
    Making patterns on the ground.
    A red and yellow kite is launched into the clear blue sky.
    A child starts running, trying to catch the mischievous kite,
    Tossing, dancing, with a wicked smile on its face.

The sun beats down on the contented picnickers lying in the sun.
The children in the paddling pool lightheartedly throw water
Over sleeping fathers, still smiling when they're told to get out.
Regretful now, throwing water over dad wasn't such a good idea.
The angel fountain bursts to life, spouting water from its mouth.

    The sun shimmers on the water's surface,
    Reflecting all the tall pine trees that stand nearby,
    That send dark shadows over all the joyous people.
    Flowers bright and colourful line the beds,
    Daisies scattered all around the grass,
    As bumble bees fly by while working
    And birds call to each other in the even sky.

Dreamin

Irene Gunnion

Time tae dream – by ma river
Flowing serene – an sae calm
Enjoyin a moment o stillness
Lord – sae lucky A am

It's a heavenly simmer
Birdies dartin aboot
The water maks its ripple
Playin awa's – yon Mr Troot

Everything sae perfit
A'm in anither time
An A'm no goin hame
Fur – this meenit – is mine

No a soon – aroond me
A'm fair smilin – tae masel
Hoo a wish – ye could be wi me
Fur – ma words – they canna tell

Jist whit this feels – tae savour
River – trees – an peace o mind
Treasure rich – ma freend – like this
A'll go a lang way – tae find

The View Frae the Knock on a Simmer's Day

Francis Armit

Man it's gran' jist tae stan' on tap o' the Knock
and be maister o' a' ye survey.
What mair can beguile than a view that has style
and gies pleasure as pairt o' yer day.

Ye can look Ayst and Wast and then become lost
in the beauty that lies a' aroond.
God be thankit nae less for the heavenly dress
o' the countryside richly festooned.

Ther's maist a' thing there, and naught can compare
wi' its hills, and its rills, and its 'ley.
For Strathearn is Queen if ye jist yeese yer een
and pause tae tak in what ye see.

On tap o' the Knock ye'll enthuse when ye talk
as ye gaze ower the Strath leisurely,
Splendid scenes tae applaud, Creiff's entitled tae laud
the Cnoc View tae the highest degree.

Here's tae The Wyfie

(for Sheila and Ken at Coille Bhrochain on 3 June 1976)

T.S. Law

"Here's tae the wyfie that made brose for Robert Bruce,"
said I, in the green o Coille Bhrochain, staunin
fornent whit's left o the guid auld bodie's hoose,
toastin six hunder an seeventie year growne thrawn
an vyve as the aitmeal and usquabae o ma dram.
Whaa neebors freedom bydes as leeberatit
as the skowthe o a sang, and in sang here it 's I 'm
yin wi the-thither nynetie-aicht, an wi
thon wyfie I toast the day.

Note: It is said that Robert Bruce, in flicht fae the English efter the Battle o Methven on the 19th o June in 1306, was gien brose bi the wyfie whaa bidd at that timm in the bit hoose that stuid in the wuid that efterwarts was caad *Coille Bhrochain*.

Tam's Excuse

Janet McKenzie

Your Honour, here's the explanation
o this ridiculous situation;
the factors that cam intae play
an brocht me before you the day.

Ever since I was a wean,
I couldna thole a craitur's pain
I'd bandage up a thorn-cut paw
or splint the wing o some auld craw,
an that's why, whiles, I'm tae be found
daunderin the woods around,
tendin ony beast in pain
an – och, I maybe should explain
the shotgun? It's become a habit
in case I spy a myxy rabbit . . .

Weel, June the first? I took a turn
alang the bank o Lunan Burn
an doon intae Meikleour Estate—
a shortcut! It was wearin late.
Then, aa at once I heard a shot!
A theivin poacher was ma thought!
An this puir bird crashed at ma feet
in such a state – wad make you greet.
I gently picked it up, but saw
that naethin could be done ataa.

The keeper caught me wi the bird.
The cuif – he'd no believe a word!
But that, Your Honour, is the reason
I had the pheasant oot o season.

Mary Murphy

Patricia Ace

The first week of Mary Murphy's marriage, she carried her pendulous frame around with an unbecoming, smug jauntiness. Her arrival into what she considered full-blown adult life did not pass quietly in Mary's soul. On the contrary, she heard birds singing in at her bedroom window, experienced revelations of shattering importance whilst waking up. Every waking minute felt load and jangling, contagious, discordant, like some echoing Turkish melody. It was the newness, the strangeness which shocked her to the core in this way; a new name, a new identity, her rebirth was complete. And out of the dull hush and pastel shades of her parents' living room, Mrs Mary Murphy emerged, shining and bloody as a new born babe, wailing for all the world to hear, into the tender bruise-purple hills of Perthshire.

Sic Transit Gloria

John Herdman

"Right, Carstairs! This is your baptism of fire!"

Two guides and a piper, who had been lounging round in the vicinity of an open window in an upper-floor room of Balsillie Castle, appreciating the balmy breeze of a beautiful June afternoon and contemplating the distant splendour of Beinn Mhuic Ghorm, drew themselves up at the approach of Jake Duff, the Chief Guide, and endeavoured to appear ready for duty. Or rather two of them did, namely Carstairs and the Australian piper, Keir McFadyen, perhaps the tallest and thinnest man ever to wear a kilt. Heinz-Dietrich Schlossmüller, the Bavarian guide who conducted the German-language parties, never looked as if he were either on or off duty, he merely emanated an aura of being wonderfully and permanently at peace with the world.

"Amanda's been took ill," announced Jake with evident satisfaction, eyeing Carstairs shrewdly. His crinkly red hair and stocky physique gave him something of the appearance of a truculent Highland bull. "There's six coach parties expected this afternoon. That means you'll have to conduct a tour, Carstairs. Maybe even two."

Carstairs groaned inwardly. He had managed to get through the first month of his season at the castle without having to conduct a coach party, and he had been in high hopes that he was going to get away with it altogether. There were two classes of guide employed at Balsillie Castle, those who gave guided tours and those who merely patrolled the corridors and chambers to answer questions and keep a weather eye open for thieves. Carstairs was of the latter variety, but all had to be prepared to turn a hand to anything in case of emergency. This, it seemed, was an emergency.

"Do not worry," said Heinz-Dietrich comfortingly, "all will go well." He was a wonderfully reassuring person to have at one's side, with his kilt which drooped at the rear and his ecological, environment-friendly black beard. Not one of your anaemic, grudging, carefully-trimmed beards this, but a magnificent bushy affair with all sorts of tufts and excrescences, a holistic, gentle and caring beard which emphatically said Yes to life. At quiet times Heinz-Dietrich would sit in the Tower Room with his hands extended palm-upwards on his thighs, in an attitude of determined yet gentle receptivity. It was understood that at such moments he was meditating, and perhaps even at one with the Universe. At the very least he was centred in the deepest and most real core of his being, encountering himself as a fully authentic human person, and so on . . . there is no need to elaborate.

Jake Duff faced Carstairs in an attitude of smug triumph. "So what are you going to tell them about this room, Carstairs? I've took you through this routine a few times now. Let's have a dress rehearsal."

"It was in 1756," Carstairs began, drawing a deep breath and launching into his memorised spiel, "that the Fifth Duke of Badenoch commissioned Messrs MacTaggart, the well-known cabinet makers in Inverness . . . "

"Na, na," Jake Duff held up his hand, "hold it there. Make things easy for yourself, Hugh. See when I get tae this room, I just extend my arm in the direction of that lovely piece and I says, 'Ladies and gennlemen, would ye's look at the craftsmanship that's went intae that.' Try saying that."

"Ladies and gentlemen, would you look at the craftsmanship that's went into that." Carstairs was deadpan, expressionless.

"Say it with conviction, for God's sake!"

The piper guffawed, and Duff swung around on him with fury.

"You – what are you standin' there for, snickering? There's a busload of bloody Yanks oot there awaiting your services! Skirl o' the bloody pipes – wantit now.' Get oot there!"

"Ciao," said the happy-go-lucky Australian, and loped off, turning to give Carstairs a huge wink as he went. His ginger hair and moustache testified to his Scottish extraction, but he was not allowed to speak to the tourists so that he should not betray his national origin and thus be the cause of profound disillusionment.

"Do you think I could say 'gone' rather than 'went'?" suggested Carstairs innocently. "I always find it hard to utter grammatical solecisms with conviction."

Duff gazed at him with baffled, uncomprehending rage. "Say anything you bloody well like, but sound sincere!" he shouted. "And there's another thing. When you're sitting on the grass at lunch hour eating your sandwiches, keep your knees down. I saw how you were sitting today – any ladies passing could have seen everything you've got under your kilt."

"I believe I am not paid during lunch hour," observed Carstairs with some loftiness.

Duff reluctantly conceded the implied point. "I'm only trying to spare your blushes, Hugh," he said.

"It would take more than that to make me blush, Jake." That was so far from being the truth, as a matter of fact, that Carstairs was blushing fierily at that very moment. The thought that Amanda might have had the opportunity to inspect everything he had under his kilt had just struck him, carrying in its train a riot of conflicting emotions.

Duff turned away from him in disgust.

"You're on duty too, Heinz-Dietrich. There's a German party expected. They'll both be here in five minutes. You'll go first, Carstairs. Right – on your way." He strode off.

"Where our master leads, there we must follow," said Heinz-Dietrich equably.

When Carstairs reached the Entrance Hall his party of Americans was already beginning to assemble. They were radiating a sense of complacent expectancy. Panic clutched at his heart.

The Controller, Marcia Brocklehurst, a magnificent statuesque blonde of about forty, approached him with a beam of encouragement on her broad features. Her head was, if anything, just a shade too large for her body.

"You can do it, Hugh, you know you can. Sock it to 'em, baby!" Her Midlands accent contrasted most fearfully with her tartan-bedraped person, yet for once he would willingly have prolonged the encounter. But in an instant Marcia was gone, and Carstairs was alone, utterly alone, with forty elderly and middle-aged Americans pitilessly hungry for history, culture, information and kilts. He cleared his throat, stammered out a few introductory remarks, and then – seizing desperately at a firm, unyielding fact – struck out boldly and with every appearance of confidence.

"To the right of the entrance, ladies and gentlemen, you can see a portrait of the thirteenth Duke of Badenoch by the distinguished Spanish waiter, Sancho Panza."

He knew instantly, from the horrified expression of one woman, that something was wrong – had he mistaken the name of the painter? It was certainly something very like Sancho Panza; but no, right enough Sancho Panza was someone else – who the devil *was* Sancho Panza? His brain felt like cotton wool . . . But never mind, the gaping disbelief on the face of that one woman, that look that dared to confront the awful possibility that this strange guide might be sending them all up, was not mirrored on any other, all the rest of them seemed divinely contented . . . He must just press on.

Something, as fortune would have it, had moved them to sympathy, those forty travel-hardened Americans. They were aware, perhaps, of his fetching awkwardness without for a moment suspecting the anarchic impulses that underlay it, and a warm glow of sympathy was kindled in their collective bosom. Something of this must have communicated itself, subliminally, to Carstairs. The influences which determine our moods and their changes are sometimes so subtle, so insubstantial, so fleeting and evanescent that we are unaware of their moving hand upon us, yet they have the power, like faith, to move mountains. So it must have been with Carstairs, for once he got the Americans out of the Entrance Hall and down the first corridor, under the bright and steady gaze of long-ago murdered birds of prey, his nerves began to come under control and the leaden phrases from the guide-book to fall lightly and almost trippingly from his tongue – so, at least, it seemed to him. His self-esteem recovered a little he became all at once conscious of his authority, of his position of command.

After the Gun Room they ascended the Staircase of Trophies; the Mauve Drawing Room succeeded to the Pink Dressing Room, and the Glenpartan Ante-Chamber to the Great Dining Room, and all was going well – Carstairs was aware of no further *faux pas*. He might have delivered this oration a hundred times; the Americans were clearly interested and even impressed, questions were asked which were really quite intelligent; a certain sentiment of warmth entered his relations with the party, a warmth, even a respect, that was perhaps mutual – they were, in fact, eating out of the palm of his hand. Carstairs experienced suddenly an unwonted surge of psychic power, and with it a delirious sense of inner freedom. He could, he realised, do with this party whatever he wanted, precisely whatever he wanted – anything at all. The whole universe of possibility laid itself open before him: just how would he use this freedom?

"Excuse me, sir, can you tell me the difference between a Dook and a Marquis?" The questioner pronounced the latter word 'Marquee'.

"Indeed I can. It is impossible to hold a wedding reception in a Duke."

There was a brief silence.

"Hey, is that right?"

"What's he say?" came a puzzled whisper.

"I dunno . . . seems kinda wacky to me." Shoulders were shrugged and they moved on. Shortly they came to the portrait of the cross-eyed man. Carstairs knew exactly what was coming. The party hesitated, muttering in wonder, collectively astonished.

"Hey, do you suppose he *really* looked like that?"

"Let me put it like this, sir," Carstairs responded with patient seriousness, "would you like to be portrayed that way if you *weren't* cross-eyed?"

That question proved too profound for the Americans: they were deeply and audibly disturbed. The party progressed for some time without further incident, the prevailing tone now markedly subdued. They had completed the top floor and were proceeding down again when Marcia Brocklehurst appeared round a corner in all her splendour, but looking just a shade concerned. She approached Carstairs, laid a hand on his arm and whispered confidingly in his ear.

"Hurry it up a little, Hugh, there's a ducky. The next party's arrived a touch early and they're, you know, a bit *restive.*"

Carstairs nodded impressively – he was utterly in control. "Will be done, Marcia. Don't worry about a thing." Marcia beamed back her confidence in him; but no sooner had she disappeared than Jake Duff stormed into view, his breath almost steaming.

"Get a move on, Carstairs, for God's sake. There's another party down there champing at the bloody bit, the Germans are behind you – what are you playing at, man?" His stage whisper, delivered a few inches from Carstairs face, must have been fully audible even to the most inattentive, the most hearing-impaired member of the party. "Amanda would have had them at the walrus tusks by this time! Get moving!"

At that, something inside Carstairs just seemed, as they say, to snap. And, as we all know, when something just seems to snap there is nothing, really nothing at all to be done about it – one is, it appears, no longer a free agent A moment heavy with fate had arrived. Perhaps, indeed, it had been a long time preparing, somewhere deep in the subterranean reaches of Carstairs' soul. At any rate, on hearing those words of Jake Duff he knew that he was leaving the castle, and the job, there and then, right at that moment; he was in fact already on the way and powerless to stop himself. But he was leaving at his own pace, and his manner of going would be his own.

Carstairs continued to walk through the rooms, slowly, with the Americans behind him, but he no longer spoke. He described nothing and he ignored all further questions. At first there was only a kind of audible puzzlement, then a few whispers and jokes and a little nervous laughter, and finally a heavy, embarrassed silence settled upon the abandoned group. When they had passed through three entirely mute chambers a voice said, *sotto voce,* "Do you suppose this guy gets paid for this?"

Carstairs swung round on his heel. "Extraordinarily little, madam, I can assure you."

That said, he abruptly left the official route and cut off down a spiral staircase leading to the first floor. It was not his intention that the Americans should follow him, but when they did he made no move to deter them. In a window ledge there stood precariously balanced a bronze bust of the present Duke of Badenoch. On his lonely rounds Carstairs was accustomed always to pause in front of the bust in order to tweak its long, drooping nose, and in full sight of the leading Americans he did so now.

"Holy snakes" someone exclaimed; but they kept following him, as if under an enchantment. Having reached the first floor, they were progressing along the narrowest and most over-furnished corridor in the Castle, when they came face to face with the Germans under Heinz-Dietrich Schlossmüller – for Carstairs and his Americans were now moving in the wrong direction.

Heinz-Dietrich at once endeavoured to halt his party and line them up so that the Americans might pass, but the Germans were having none of it. They knew their rights, and they knew, too, that they were *in* the right; so they shoved and elbowed their way forward with stolid, stony-faced pertinacity. Very quickly a leader arose from among their ranks, who started shouting commands in German; Heinz-Dietrich was at once rendered superfluous, and coming to terms with the fact instantly, and with commendable realism, he fell to calming and shepherding as best he could the now-panicking Americans.

The chaos was indescribable. American ladies were uttering little yelps, not yet quite screams, their menfolk were protesting loudly, and the Germans ploughed on regardless, stepping ruthlessly on all their toes . . . A priceless statuette of Sporting and Sleeping Putti – delightful, plump little cherubs with delicately formed wings – crashed to the ground from the cabinet on which it was displayed, smashed to smithereens and was trampled underfoot. Carstairs, meanwhile, was on ahead, cutting a relentless swathe through the last of the advancing Teutons. And suddenly it was all over.

Battered, dishevelled, shaken to the marrow of their being but grateful to have survived, the hapless party at last arrived at the first-floor landing of the Great Staircase and saw their leader, Carstairs, descending the last flight with slow and stately mien. Meekly they followed him – what else could they do? Heinz-Dietrich, completely rejected and now quite forgotten by his own charges, could not leave the sufferers in their hour of need; and gathering them together like chickens under his wing, with many a soothing word and gesture he escorted them back to the Entrance Hall. Under the vigilant eye of the thirteenth Duke, as portrayed to such life-like effect by Sancho Panza, the brilliant Spanish waiter, they passed through the Great floor; and blinking a little in the bright afternoon sunshine, followed the princely Carstairs down the steps. Briefly he turned and inspected his troops, a hint of pride in his splendid eye.

"Where do you suppose he's taking us?" whispered a nervous old lady.

Keir McFadyen was seated lazily on the balustrade, a genial, happy-go-lucky grin on his freckled features.

"Strike up, piper.'" commanded Carstairs; and nothing loth, the tall Australian shouldered his pipes and with a terribly protracted groaning, squealing and retching launched into 'Hugh Carstairs' Farewell to Balsillie Castle', a jig which he had composed two or three weeks previously in anticipation of just such an eventuality. Carstairs set off, the towering piper just behind him on his left, and the Americans followed, instantly in raptures. All their troubles forgotten, with wonderful and joyful ebullience they marched off across the gravel in the direction of the drive. In the rear trotted benignly Heinz-Dietrich Schlossmüller, his beard mutely offering sanctuary to thirty-two endangered species of stick-insect, his kilt sagging touchingly behind.

"Well, whaddaya know!"

"How *about* that!"

"Hey, swing those kilts."

"Wow!"

Their coach-driver, who was standing by the door ready to welcome the adventurers aboard, gazed in astonishment as they swept past him without so much as a glance and set off down the drive. Back at the Great Door of the Castle Marcia Brocklehurst could be seen staring wistfully at the backs of the rapidly disappearing column, her great mouth with its strong, even teeth parted in wonderment. Jake Duff pawed at the gravel with his hoof and ran forward a few paces then stopped, baffled; over the colourful little procession Beinn Mhuic Ghorm brooded inscrutably. Carstairs strode on, the pipes skirled, and the brave-hearted little party followed exultantly, seeking the sunset, headed for the Mexican border.

Perthshire

Joy Hendry

There will be no escape
and no restructuring of local government
can blot out the contours of this,
most diverse of counties.
I pine for your solace,
being too far to the south.
I need to know, and see
that everywhere I look
will be a real hill,
hillsides, mountains, mountain ranges,
raging waterfalls, sudden lochs, bleak plains
then fertile fields, as luscious as any anywhere
and the peaceful cattle munching their own.

It is not so, in the barren south.

I drink you, and drink you,
long for you at dawning,
crave for you when white clouds chase
a high sun over the zenith
and in the lengthening shadows
The breadth of your horizons
take on the hue of mystical evenings
that smell like incense.

There, where I belong
I am a stranger
Here, where I am a stranger
I almost belong.

John F. Petrie

Two people side by side,
Each knowing other through and through;
There is nothing to hide,
Nothing to hide from you.

The room is still; dusk thickens,
Curtains flash in summer wind:
My body stirs, quickens,
In tune with my giving mind.

There is no joy for me as here,
Nor ever been for half my days:
Soul-stiffness – blank, austere—
Melts and floats away.

Wrapped in warm velvet
Of skin-touching, love-giving you;
Stretching yet – and yet,
More we need to do.

Words float from mouth to ear
So close, they barely stir
The warm silence enough
For listening mind to hear.

Sleep comes blessedly slow;
I wonder there is time enough to rest;
Yet you and I melt, flow, relax
And curl softly together.

You are present joyful pain,
A hope of ever-giving love;
Life is unlikely to gain
Any sense, reality, without you.

Ossian's Grave, Glenalmond

After Burns, after Wordsworth

Robert Alan Jamieson

Panting hard, we struggled through the scree
and walked along the ridge towards the cairn.
The Sma Glen scarp across from us so near,
the crisp blue sky devoid of signs of rain.
The Celtic hero Ossian's buried here—
or so our book-fed fancy would believe,
if only for this day, this climb, so that
the stone we touch is more than merely real—
like Berkeley's tree, an attitude of mind.

Below we saw Clach Ossian by the stream,
the boulder General Wade had his men shift
when Roman straightness was offended by
its bulky stone-age presence in that glen—
where underneath the warrior-poet's bones
appeared burnt-brown in stone walls deep confined.
What was it that we walkers hoped to find?
Some relic of an older, purer time,
before the bard Macpherson struck his pose?
Or just to lay a stone atop the cairn,
to walk the way that those Breadalbane men
had walked near on three centuries ago
behind a piper, sympathising with
those few who saw a Redcoat present push
the past aside with levers and massed strength,
to wake the sacred ancient from his sleep?

And how were they to know this warrior,
his spirit so displaced, would stalk the world,
from Lexington to Waterloo would storm
and not be pacified till Buonaparte,
in St. Helena, cried, "C'est moi! C'est moi!
My head is filled with Ossian's sweeping mists.
'Twas I who made him fashion – it was I!"
An arrogance that only emperors
can utter to the satisfaction of
the noble ghost that haunts and taunts us all.
No, none of that dead and rotting history.
No idealistic revolutionary talk.
Romanticism that day was manifest
Only in the quivering form which hid,
the leveret cowering underneath the cairn.

I gently slipped my hand between the stones
and felt the tiny heart beneath its bones.
I drew the creature wriggling to the light
and held it as a father might a child—
a frightened child who wakes up in the night
and seeks for comfort in its parents' bed.
I stroked it gently on its twitching head,
this life that coursed around the warrior's grave,
and passed it to my friend who, laughing, said
"Oisien, the little fawn, is now a hare."
To find the living where we'd sought the dead
was worth far more than all the books we'd read,
and as we watched its bobbing tail run off,
it seemed that moment's capture was enough.

Ruchill Linn

Robin Bell

I heard a curlew in the almost dark
of midnight June. I heard it wake
among the wheat and free itself from fear
with one clear call.
    The waterfall
was to itself a waterfall,
a moving in water, a white arc
of foam. It did not seek to slake
the trees nor thirst of you not here.

Heavy green branches overhung the pool.
The water formed itself on stone and formed the stone.
Its swirling rings
              succour the movement of bright wings
and hidden roots and mindless bones.
Ruchill Linn. The world relaxes its hermetic rules

and lets us be tonight. Lie on the ground
and listen to the curlews' calls
         and waterfalls
and the innocent sounds the world makes going round.

From A Glenlyon Childhood:
Rounders and Raspberries

Carol Burgess

The last day of summer term was wonderful. For the few weeks which preceded it we practised and rehearsed for our summer concert. This annual event was attended by proud and doting parents who came to see their offspring sing and dance, and perform a simple one-act play. Afterwards a veritable feast was laid out in the dining-room, and we mingled with our peers and their families, munching tiny iced biscuits and slurping watery orange squash, leaving a trail of sausage-roll crumbs in our wake as we showed off our paintings and story-books, wall friezes and project tables. All of us quick to point out the particular touches of our own ingenuity. On this day we were attired in our Sunday best, party frocks in various hues of stiff taffeta, with huge satin bows tied in a flourish at the back, pig-tails neatly ribboned. Boys with slicked down hair and ties with elastic bands slung round pristine collars. Apart from going to Church on Sunday, it would be the last day for seven weeks that we would wear anything other than T-shirts and shorts.

Those seven weeks were measured only by the calendar, feeling to us like a life-time of freedom while they lasted. Somehow it was always sunny; long hot days that started being fun from the moment we tumbled eager and dishevelled out of bed in the morning, and only finished when our eyes could no longer stave off the Sandman and the sky transformed from clear cloudless blue to pink and red shot through with the gold of the setting sun.

Within days of the end of term we were brown as berries, sunburned legs and arms adorned with cuts and grazes and bruises gathered in our daily adventures.

We lived about four miles from the hamlet where most of our schoolfriends stayed, and deep in the heart of a highland glen. Our mother didn't drive, and our father was a gardener on a private estate and summer was his busiest time of the year so he worked from dawn to dusk in the big walled garden just yards from our little white cottage with its hen-house nearby, and surrounded by pink and white lilac trees which filled the air with the scent of summer. We were almost cut off from our school-time companions, so the four of us roamed wild and free from the end of June until well into August.

From somewhere my father acquired a large black ladies bicycle, ancient and rusty but in perfect working order, and this became mine by default of being the oldest and largest. Even so, I was far too small to sit on the sharp saddle and pedal at the same time, and so learning to ride the monster was a difficult and painful process, but eventually I mastered it. I discovered that if after mounting, I pedalled like fury for a while I could then leap up into the saddle and coast for a bit with legs swinging wildly, ready to jump down onto the pedals again when my speed dropped. Needless to say, this object had no gears, and so I could only sit on the flat or going downhill. Being an avid reader of schoolgirl stories in which all the little Geraldine and Erica's had their own ponies, I decided to christen my iron horse "Eastern Star".

My brother and arch enemy Charles fared worse than I in the two-wheeled world. His bike had been handed down from our older brother Tom, and although it was a much more reasonable size, it had one rather obvious defect. There was no chain!

We would get up in the morning and pack our brown leather school satchels with what we considered the absolute essentials for a hard day's cycling; marmalade sandwiches and a screw-top bottle filled with water. Slinging these on our backs we mounted our trusty steeds and took off down the little road from our house towards the main road, me alternately pedalling and leaping, he beleaguered by the lack of traction hurtling along behind, toes skinning the ground as he rode hobby-horse fashion, half running, half coasting. Both of us were glad when on a piece of road with a long downward slope!

Eventually we would arrive at whichever destination was that day's stopping place and, after parking up our unruly mounts, would proceed to devour our travellers' fare as if we hadn't eaten for hours.

The garden which Dad worked in was far too large and produced much too much produce for the needs of the tea-planter and his wife who owned the estate, particularly since they weren't permanent residents. The excess was a very saleable commodity, especially the summer fruits. Countless punnets of gooseberries, strawberries and raspberries emerged from the walled enclosure for daily delivery to those who had answered the advert in the paper. When we were at a loose end, or when a particularly large or urgent order had come in, we would happily help with the fruit picking. Each of us had our favourite berry. Strawberries were back-breaking to harvest, but Peter adored the taste, and would always volunteer for them. Charles liked to gather the black-currants as instead of individuals the currants were taken from the bush in clusters. I liked the raspberries best, both for the taste and for the easy way they slid off their stalks like pulling gloves off tiny hands. Marion, who was really too young to effectively glean any soft fruit, would gladly run the risk of being sharply stabbed a thousand times to get in amongst the gooseberry bushes, picking more of the big fat hairy yellow-green berries to eat than to pack. Our parents were well aware of our ulterior motives for helping, and would strike up sing-songs as we worked on the theory that we couldn't sing and eat at the same time.

In the evenings, after tea-time and listening to the news on the radio, and when it had become a little cooler, the daily bounty would be loaded in baskets into the back of the Land-Rover and we four would set of with Dad to deliver them. It was one of the best times of the day. We sat in the back beside the evidence of our hard work as we bowled along the narrow and twisting glen, heavy with greenery of every description, and fragrant with the scent of grasses and pine. With each stop to drop off a delivery we would be treated to sweets and pennies from the recipients, to compliment us on the quality of the goods and on our efforts in procuring them. Sometimes on the return journey, if the day had been particularly long and arduous, my father would stop at the hotel in the village, disappearing into the bar to emerge with bottles of Coca-Cola and packets of crisps. We would sit on the tail-board, swinging our legs and enjoying our treat as he went back inside to have a well earned bottle of beer.

On one of his solo-delivery trips he had attended an auction which was taking place, and on his return we watched mystified, as he unloaded a great bundle of khaki-coloured material, and several long poles. As we lay in bed that night we could hear howls of laughter mixed with sharp retorts as our mother and father engaged in some external night-time activity. Ordered to remain in bed, and not to look out the windows, we finally fell into a frustrated sleep, anxious to discover the cause of their mirth.

Next morning we did not wait for breakfast, but piled outside to see what had been happening the night before. There, in the field outside the front of our house, stood a great old army Bell tent, which we were told could sleep sixteen men. It quickly became our gang hut. Two old mattresses were dragged from the loft to line the ground within, and in the heat of the day we would retire there to lounge and plan the rest of our activities. It gave off a peculiar smell, musty but dry, which seemed to mingle with the diffused light which permeated the thick canvas walls.

Now our games of Cowboys and Indians had a new dimension, although we all wanted to be the Indians. We would launch Apache-style raids on the garden in the evening. Single file we would creep silently from the tent to the woodpile beside the garage, climbing from the logs onto the roof. From there we had access to the garden wall, and would crawl along this until we came to the fruit trees which were trained along the inside at the southern end. One by one we lowered ourselves onto the branches of the honey-pear tree, and would clamber down it to the ground. For these raiding parties my sister and myself would wear dirndl skirts, brightly patterned pocketed affairs, with elasticated waists. Holding them aloft we allowed our brothers to raid the fruit trees for pears and plums, and bundle them into laps. The return journey was certainly more difficult for us girls, as we now had to traverse the various stages while clasping to ourselves full bundles of stolen booty, pretending they were our papooses! Upon descent the fearless tribe scuttled into the wigwam to feast upon our spoils of war.

Our little stone-built two-storied hen house was home to a strange mixture of fowl. There were gloriously strutting black and emerald cocks, fat and fussy Rhode Island reds, big pale yellow hens with vivid red bonnets, little shiny black bantams, a couple of weird looking Guinea fowl, and five Aylesbury ducks. All wandered at will, there being no chicken-wired restrictions. We gave our favourites names, such as Dinah, a really plucky little bantam hen, who got caught in a fox-trap which had been set by our gamekeeper, and consequently only had one scrawny leg to hop about on as she swung and dipped amongst her sisters. The ducks were a recent addition to the flock, as my mother had a great fondness for duck eggs. My father dug a small pond for them, which they largely ignored, preferring instead to waddle in the always open front door and up the lobby, to stand looking quizzically into the kitchen as we ate. We loved those ducks; like little dogs they followed us around, excited by our every activity, far more curious and outgoing than the hens, and better natured than the cocks and guinea-fowl.

Always in the summer there were various wasps nests lurking around our play areas, bothering us not a bit except when we were sticky with juice and they wanted to play on our faces. We kept hives of bees, and viewed both insects simply as little pests, of no particular danger. The ducks saw them differently however, and rudely attacked one nest which had been built in an old rabbit burrow near our tent. Snapping their bills and quacking in delight they rummaged and flapped until the wasps had had enough and swarmed at them, stinging them countless times until all our poor feathered followers lay dying and dead from the venom.

We were heart-broken, and my brothers swore vengeance. Armed with long sticks to poke into the nest and smash it to pieces, they sallied forth.

Each of us had at some time been stung by an irate little striped body, but this time, enraged by the behaviour of the Aylesburys, the wasps were determined to retaliate with every last droplet of poison. Gathering themselves into a single deadly entity they hurled at the boys. Peter saw the danger first, and broke into a run, little legs pumping him away from the protagonists. Charles was not so lucky, and in the melee he fell and was defenceless as they buzzed and crawled over him, infuriated and careless of their own death which followed the sting. By the time my parents were alerted by our terrified screaming, he was semi-conscious, and his skin was already beginning to rise in a mass of hives, his body swelling with the toxin, and his throat constricting to choking point. Dad never broke his run, through the hellish swarm he darted, sweeping the little form into his arms, batting off the stray insects which still clung to it as he tore towards the Land-Rover, depositing my brother on the passenger seat and leapt into the driver's seat himself, throwing the thing into gear and shooting off in a screech of tyres.

We waited by the phone until the call came; they had safely arrived at the cottage-hospital, and my brother had been given a massive injection of anti-histamine just in time to save his life. This hitherto unsuspected allergy of his radically changed our attitude to these creatures, which were subsequently regarded with fear and loathing. When they returned home, my brother was put to bed, smothered in calamine lotion, and father set off again grim faced, with a bundle of old rags and a can of petrol to burn out the murderous invaders.

On Sundays we had a family day. After church and Sunday School, we would either set out together in the Land-Rover, or the little Morris 1000 which we later bought, to visit, or we would play host to family and friends who wanted a day in the country.

Often visitors would arrive by the car-full, unheralded, and unprepared for. My mother's lovely lackadaisical nature was always completely unfazed by this interruption of our quiet day, and she would send some of us to the henhouse to gather fresh brown eggs, and the rest of us to the garden to pick lettuces and tomatoes. My father would be despatched to the greenhouse to get the trestles out and set up hasty tables covered by bedsheets, while she retired to the kitchen to make up platefuls of egg salad and whip up a batch of griddle scones and pancakes. We would eat al fresco in the fading sunlight, chattering and laughing with cousins while hens and dogs pecked and snuffled round our feet.

When we were the visitors, returning late at night in the darkness after a day of eating strange cakes and biscuits which came from cellophane packets, and shop-bought jams and jellies, we would sometimes be too tired from the day's exertions to stand. Our grey-haired sinewy father in his Sunday jacket and sports trousers, and plump dark-headed mother wearing a bright floral print, would lift us one by one from the back of whichever vehicle we were in, and carry us to our beds, pausing only to remove our shoes and socks, and drag a wet wash-cloth across our sleepy faces before tucking us up for the night.

My mother was never house-proud, and during the summer she would often suddenly dump some household task to join us outside in the field for a game of rounders. Great hilarity ensued as her round, apron-clad body tried to match our speed and agility in running from base to base.

All too soon the dark would begin to creep earlier into our tent, and the last of the raspberries had been picked. We would set out on the once a day mail-bus which ran between our nearest small town and the top of the glen, to be measured and fitted for our new school clothes. All of us had sprouted like carrots during the forty nine days of freedom.

On the night before our return to schooling, we would be submerged, two at a time, into a steaming bathtub to be vigorously scrubbed and soaped, and then our father would get out his home hairdressing kit to trim us all into respectability.

Awakening reluctantly the next morning we trooped into the kitchen for our tea and porridge. There, in front of the Rayburn stove, were four pairs of shiny new black lacing up Clarks shoes, ranged in size. As we waited at the end of our road for the school-car, clean and tidy for the first time in two months, we knew the summer was over for us.

What we dreaded most was the essay we would have to write, entitled "What I Did In The Holidays". While our classmates described trips to Torquay, and the delights of sea-side bed and breakfasts, we who never went away until autumn and the end of the fruit and vegetables, were stumped.

We never did anything during the holidays.

Strawberry Field

Margaret Gillies Brown

They cover the dark green field
In many-coloured patches,
The pickers,
Kneeling on earth, straw, leaves,
Held in an envelope of air
Smelling of fresh-cut strawberries.

Away from the supermarket, road rush,
Quick-green-man they pick with ink blue fingers
Into yellow buckets
Sometimes thrusting the pitted half-juice fruit
Through parched lips.
At lunch time they find coolness
In the shadow of a tree,
Open sticky flasks
Eat 'pieces' made with early morning haste.

They laugh, talk, work.
It's hot, sun-splitting afternoon – they tire.
A Mother clouts her daughter,
"Get off your lazy arse
Get doon that dreel and pick!"
Two bored, baked laddies flare
Fling berry bombs
And sudden war breaks out.

A bell – a slow voice shouting berry-up!
Pickers drift to the weighing-in
Arms long to earthy leaves:
They argue, banter.
Hot money falls into stained and sticky hands;
Red buses rev and wait.

In the sun
A low swallow swerves,
Catches what nourishment it can.

Re-carnation and Rasps

Janet McKenzie

Dear Marjorie Proops,

I'm writing to you on a dead serious subject, because Dayveen – my best pal – says you don't only deal with girls having toatie wee tits and worrying if they'll ever get a boyfriend, not that that's a worry of mine, I've always been well-developed for my age! Anyway, what I want is some advice about the theory of Recarnation. Do you believe in it? I never did – although Dayveen does – until I went up to Blairgowrie for the berry picking this summer and had a strange encounter up a dreel.

There I was, picking rasps into punnets for the quality freezing, when I heard this voice down the next dreel. I never bothered, because it was the first dry day for ages and I wanted to make some real money, but then it came from right opposite me, through the leaves. It was dead weird.

> Wee modes't crimson-tinted fruit
> Ye'll maybe think I'm juist a brute
> As wi ma clumsy hand I put
> Ye in ma punnet,
> Or even worse, beneath ma foot
> I let ye plummet!

Well, I was that astonished I bent down to keek through the bushes, and couped all my lovely berries over the ground!

I said something I don't think you'd be allowed to print in your column and the next minute this weirdo appeared at the end of my dreel. A right poser, I thought, with a high-necked shirt and neckerchief and dead tight trousers.

Well, he actually turned out to be dead decent and helped me to pick up some of the okay ones and gave me some of his own to make up. He'd lovely eyes – all soft and brown – and old-fashioned hair with side-burns.

Mind you, if my pals had been there, I'd never have taken him on, but they'd all skinned off back to Glasgow because of the rain and to tell you the truth I was feeling browned off, so when he sat beside me at piece time I said I'd meet him later.

Well, we went to Micawbers. I can pass for eighteen when I've got my make-up on. He didn't look so odd there cos it's always full of posers anyway. He never asked me what I was drinking. He brought over two glasses of red wine and moaned that they didn't have his usual – clarty, or something! Sounds dead disgusting!

He said his name was Robert and when he heard mine was Jayne he started calling me Bonny Jeannie! I soon put a stop to that! He said he was on his way to Edinburgh to read poetry. At the festival, I suppose. You get all sorts of arty-farty things going on there, though I don't think there's much money in it.

I must say, for a person who wrote poetry he seemed very ignorant to me! He never even knew about Micawbers or David Copperfield who wrote it! I'm doing them for O-Grade.

Afterwards we went for a walk up the side of the River Ericht. My, could he talk! Sometimes quite posh, and sometimes – well, I could hardly understand. Dead Scottish.

Then he tried to get all romantic, but he just hadn't a clue how to chat up a woman! Absolutely useless. Said be wanted to take me to the corn rigs and barley rigs. There's only the berry dreels around here, I says, and they're no good, what with the berry-bug! He whispered in my ear, "My love is like a red red rose". I told him not to be so pass-remarkable. Wine always gives me a flaming red face. I should've stuck to vodka.

After this, he talked lots more, about everybody being brothers and sisters and caring for all the wee animals and even plants having feelings too, but I was busy gazing into his fab eyes. He really was pure dead handsome, but now I wish I'd listened better.

This is the dead embarrassing bit, Marge. I know now he didn't mean what I thought he meant, but when I heard him saying "And I will come again my love" I was affronted. "You're not on!" I says. "Not likely. What kind of scrubber do you think I am? And who do you think you are, anyway? Get lost, you big chancer!"

Well, he took me at my word. He just kind of disappeared into the shadows. I looked for him at the berries next day, but I never saw him again.

I told Dayveen all about it. She's into burning joss-sticks in her bedroom and that kind of thing and she says "coming again" means recarnation, when you re-enter this world as another person or a caterpillar or even a cabbage.

So Marge, do you believe in recarnation? I now realise that he was the great and only love of my life and that I will be a tragic person from now on, unless I can be recarnated too. I hope you can advise me how this is done. I enclose a stamped envelope for your reply.

Hoping to hear from you soon,
Jayne

P.S. Marge – I've got it! Writing this made me think back over all the things he said and did, and I see now he was giving me lots of clues, like when he wrote the initials R.B. on the table in Micawbers in spilled wine, and when he told me lots of women had found him very sweet but other people had said he was rude. Get it? A sweet taste, but a rude sound, starting with RB! It has to be RASPBERRY!!!!!

P.P.S. Marge, does this mean he was once a raspberry, or that he has still has to be recarnated into one? Please hurry and let me know how this recarnation works.

One thing's sure. I can never ever go back to the berries, even if I make good money there!

P.P.S.S. Oh My God! I can smell it! Oh no. what'll I do?

Mum's making raspberry jam . . .

First published in Z_2O magazine.

Nine Lyrics From Strathmore

George Gunn

1

The brave white dogrose & the red
wild garlic, foxglove, the living dead
who walk but cannot see
this family of green beauty

2

& now the moon ducks behind the clouds
& rainbows hang onto the day
who could not love these sweet placings
oh, you Sidlaw Hills, you sing of love & that we may

3

The brave white dogrose & the Red
wild garlic, foxglove, the Strath's bed
is made, oh river, your silver word, your language bled
now the blind man leads the led

4

The wild peas form a green cream starred
hedge in front of my eyes
behind purple lupins the broad throat
of Strathmore sings the ancient heart of Angus

5

Here is the yellow flower of the whin
see it, that perfect colour
how it reminds me of you
how the shoals of memory swim to you

6

Who are you, sad listener, hearing these
sad verses from the glad smile
of Strathmore, all you can know
is that love lies beyond these hills, these verses

7

Tell me your story, Strathmore, oh yellow heaven
is this the truth? the orange
flame which is your tongue
you are broad and shifting, this is the geology of courage

8

You are swimming through the heart
of Scotland, Strathmore
you cannot govern us, you cannot
imprison us, your quilted shoulders heave

9

The tears of morning tell us that
we must swim & when you grin
our river boils, & it cannot be
oh, heaven, let the earth in

Gladys

Nanette Fleming

Blairgowrie has in the past had its share of characters, but Gladys Stewart – known only as Gladys to all and sundry – was very much a present day one.

Born in London of Scottish parents, she came back North with them at a very early age. From the very start of her life, Gladys had her cross to bear. She was born blind in one eye, and when her parents and younger brother and sister left Scotland to seek a better life in Canada, she was only four years old, and the victim of an illness called St Vitus Dance. An extremely caring great-aunt and uncle, with no children of their own, brought her up.

By all accounts, Gladys was a bright child at school, in spite of her infirmities, and she was well read, as well as being an accomplished pianist. As she grew older and her handicaps became worse, she was more and more alone, and she turned to cats for company. She must have, in her time, fed every cat in Blairgowrie and Rattray, and many of them stayed amongst the rhubarb in the large garden of her home. And, as the situation got out of hand every now and then, the RSPCA came and collected the animals. This annoyed Gladys intensely, and she regaled everyone she met with the tale.

Her appearance, because of her illness, was odd. About five feet tall, her head continually twitching, partly because she couldn't see properly. Her dress sometimes bordered on the bizarre, although latterly her home help saw to it that she was turned out reasonably well, often in a warm coat and hat rescued from the Church jumble sale. She was never without her handbag, her stick, and the inevitable polythene carrier bag.

As a result of her blindness, which was affecting her other eye, Gladys often walked in the middle of the road. Trying to avoid her was like taking an advanced driving test. If the sound of the engine went to the right, so did Gladys. It was a constant source of amazement that she was never run down, and even in the dark she seemed to lead a charmed life as she went about delivering her religious tracts. She was a regular visitor to the Manse, where she exchanged her tract for the Minister's wife's pancakes.

A great Churchgoer, Gladys never missed a service, but if she did have a Sunday off, nearly always when the clocks changed, the congregation was greatly concerned about her. She invariably arrived late, either during the first hymn, or in the middle of the prayer, the 'Gladys-proof' door, especially installed to close quietly, banging shut behind her, Sunday after Sunday.

She attended every social occasion in the Church, from the Woman's Guild to the Boys Brigade Parents' Night, always arriving late, usually brandishing a pint of milk, the top of which was tied with a rag, her handbag, plastic carrier bag and stick. In season she always brought a bunch of flowers wrapped up in a newspaper. Gladys never arrived anywhere empty-handed.

In her almost illegible handwriting, she carried on a number of correspondences, and Howard Lockhart was the recipient of many a birthday request from her on his Sunday morning programme. When she died, he mentioned her passing. She would have loved that.

Gladys died in 1983, in an ambulance, on the way to hospital after a burning accident at home. Her brother, his wife and family, and her sister, came from Canada for the funeral, instead of the seventy fifth birthday celebrations they had intended to hold later in the year for her.

That day in January, with a foot of snow on the ground, and a blizzard raging, Blairgowrie said goodbye to Gladys Stewart. The large Church was full, the congregation made up of all walks of life, from every denomination. The Catholic Priest sitting alongside the Presbyterian and Episcopal Clergy. The hymns were her own choice, with the good-going gospel tunes she loved, and although saddened by the circumstance of her death, one could not mourn her passing. There was no doubt in Gladys' mind that she was going to meet her Maker.

In her own way she had made her mark in the town, and in her own way she was leaving it, praising God. And when the Gladys-proof door sometimes bangs shut during the first hymn on a Sunday morning, one can't help but look up, expecting the rustle of a polythene bag, and the thud of a stick.

The Pity of It

Helen Waugh

Now I must take my turn at dying.
I am of the genus solanaceae,
the last of my species.
I came here silently, by stealth
at the end of sixteenth century.
There was neither government nor patron
to urge my acceptance.
I won the confidence of the people,
fitting readily into the economic structure
of lives already torn apart by civil unrest.

For centuries,
I was the perfect instrument of the masses
I contributed to this, my adopted country,
the sole diet of many. Man and beast
survived on the nutrition I supplied,
though mixed with salt and milk to taste,
alone, I was a complete provider.

You, my master, created a dependency,
an economy around me, and both you and I
developed a time-honoured association
with this once fertile earth.
I blossomed in this fair land,
delighted in your cool moist atmosphere
and rich deep, friable soil.
Prayers and rituals accompanied
both my planting and my harvest.
I could be relied upon to be pregnant
with the promise of plenty.

This trinity worked well – I, the father,
earth the mother, you the tiller,
each respectively giving and taking.
Then you became careless, you would not
cultivate between planting, became forgetful
of denshiring – therefore, no nourishing.

We made so it insignificant a demand upon you,
your enery and skills, and yet you neglected us.
Throwing us into the soil, you left us
to the mercy of the elements.

We gave you many warnings, but you,
you never heeded them. The earth was too tired,
it tried to nurse us – but it turned sour
could not cope with the diseased spores
that fell from me. Now my once proud head
is bowed in sorrow – no more bold displays.
Then I had been resplendent in my dark green leaves
and yellow male bloom – strong and fertile,
yielding abundantly.

You with your lazy beds and lazy ways
you divided me, halving the goodness
I could pass on. I was made to lie with myself,
my brothers with sisters, till because
of your demands we became fused and crippled.
Our young were miniature and watery specimens
steeped in a black evil-smelling slime.
You weakened my strain, we became exhausted.
All that is left now are fields of corruption
like some peculiar botanical form of incest
and I behold with sorrow the waste
of putrefying vegetation.

Now both of us have suffered. At least
for my kind all was over in a few days.
You and your poor nation have many trials
to endure. Your famine will be severe,
continuous, and heavy of heart, afraid,
you will scatter your seeds to the corners
of the earth. Take heed, master, do not
neglect your strain as you did ours,
or they too will grow genetically impure
defective, doomed and diseased.

I served you well – and who knows
who was the exploiter, the exploited.
And does it matter? It is for others to decide.
I leave you to your sorrow, my pitiful cottier,
you will never see our likes again,
your once lusty Irish apple.

Grip

Thom Nairn

The berry bushes in their full, lush red,
Sparse black branches for narrow limbs,
"For the birds", well that's what they said.
Light caught in pinpricks, white ace glancing
In straight cool lines, for the birds, we all need fed;
The tractor ruts and mud,
Horseshoes imagining magnets,
Bums and ditches, hares, a tyre twist
Wide as a wrist, the rough, deep tread,
A crumbling hut and cuts in the rising banks;
Beyond, over barbed fences,
A cool glaze of clean grass,
Blue stubble in the morning haze.
At the road's end the pylons mesh.
Concrete aitches, grey terminals,
High wired hummings, homing in, cutting out,
This is the heart of the web,
Raw meat in a string bag, a sac,
Scrotal stretching, pulsing, clustering,
Broadening the net,
Each straining weal rich in blood,
Arteries pulse on veins to break out
Slashing the deep dark before dawn,
Everything needs fed.
Muscle, ligament, soil and cell,
Lush blood, full milk breasts,
A strength resonating and rumbling
In the doored steel box,
For the man, "The Electric Man",
Well that's what they said.
Knuckle cluster, all full-span,
Power in the long, slick strands,
Always bigger things to take in the grip.

Berry Money

Airlie Fleming

For the last few summers, in a gallant attempt to earn some money, I have tried my luck at berry picking. Unfortunately, it was a skill which I could never quite master, picking one bucket in proportion to everyone else's three. I gave in gracefully, and, instead, landed a job paying out money to pickers as they weighed in. I had figured this to be a more relaxed method of bringing in money, but this theory was soon to be shattered. And so was I. This is an account of a typical day at the berries, seen from the 'other side'.

9.00 a.m. I arrive. The first and worst task of the day is to somehow climb on to the back of the high truck where the scales and money are. Not known for my agility, I wait until no-one is watching before making several feeble attempts to jump up.

9.05 I make it on to the truck at the 10th attempt, and congratulate myself on managing to avoid the eyes of the pickers. But to my horror, I turn to see a group of children applaud my efforts and a farm worker yell, "Well done hen!", followed by a loud cackle.

9.45 The first weigh-in. I start to hand out the money. "That's £2.40, thank-you." – "Is that ALL?" A picker insists on getting a re-weigh, and goes on to examine the scales thoroughly. Beaten, but still not entirely satisfied, he wanders off, muttering under his breath.

A teenager gets his money and asks where the nearest shop is. He's eaten his dinner already. On finding we are miles away from civilisation, he wanders off, dejected. Another satisfied customer.

10.15 A sudden downpour. The rain comes down in sheets. The pickers stand under a tree in a vain attempt to get some shelter. They look on at me with envy, as I sit happily on my dry truck. Unable to ignore their stares for long, an immense sense of guilt creeps over Sue, and I offer some pickers my umbrella.

10.20 The ice-cream van arrives.

10.30 The rain clears, and the pickers return to work.

11.00 A number of mothers emerge from their dreels, and there's a mass nappy-changing session, over a piece or two.

12.30 After a steady stream of weigh-ins, there's a lean period. All is quiet. I decide to have my lunch.

12.31 As if by magic, hundreds of pickers appear from nowhere, and stand in a never-ending queue, impatient to weigh-in and have their lunch. Chaos ensues.

2.00 p.m. I finish my lunch.

The sun is now shining, but as I'm not in the direct sun-light and not moving about, (*I daren't leave the truck in fear of never getting back on again*), I feel quite cold. I sit on an up-turned bucket wearing a large, heavy winter coat which resembles a sleeping-bag, and is fastened up to the neck. Meanwhile, the pickers roam about in shirt sleeves.

2.15 The children start to feel sorry for me and offer me hot cups of coffee from their Mums' flasks, and a scarf borrowed from a scarecrow in the next field.

2.20 I begin to feel a little stupid, and as I an getting a little warmer, I venture to actually take off my jacket. A picker comments, "You've stripped off I see."

3.00 The children start to get very bored and one asks if she can climb up and sit on the truck. Thinking she'll never manage, I say "If you like." She is up beside me in 3 seconds flat.

3.05 Unfortunately, when one wants up, they all want up and before I know it, I'm by screaming children. I decide the situation is out of hand, and it's time to exercise my authority. "Could you er . . . get down now um . . . now . . . please?" To my surprise, no-one takes a blind bit of notice. Suddenly a farm worker appears and yells "Get offa there NOW!"

3.06 There isn't a child in sight.

3.15 I give a child ten pence for his small punnet of berries – his day's work.

3.16 Confronted by an irate mother "You gave ma wee Jimmy a foreign coin! Tryin' tae do ma wee kids oot o' their money!! It's disgusting!" I apologise profusely and change the coin, deciding that the 10p was more trouble than it was worth.

3.16½ The scandal of the foreign coin ripples through the berry field, up and down the dreels. Every picker who weighs in now studies their money with great care and suspicion. I decide I am never going to live this down.

3.45 The last weigh in. We all heave a sigh of relief. The scales and money are cleared away, and the pickers return to their buses, ready to move.

3.46 A man with 3 large bucketfuls of berries is found down a dreel, still picking furiously, completely oblivious to the fact that everyone else is finished, and the field virtually deserted. Out come the scales and the money, and the pickers wait in their buses, more desperate than ever to get home.

4.00 Home

4.15 Sleep.

MacCaig Country

Angus Watson

A sea-loch with a wind-swept craggy face,
A twinkle in its eye,
A glint to show it doesn't suffer fools,
Has couplets strung austerely round its bays.

Beaches form in crooks of epigrams.
Multiple Highland rogues, the Bens
Take on as many shapes
As there are syntheses of opposites.

The sun lies ahead
But may not be strictly true.
The rains blow paradoxically,
Measured in easy squalls
Or polished floods.

And in the corries poets sit,
Legs crossed above the knee,
Ashtray and dram to hand,
Disputing in never-closing howffs
They've carved with words,
Out of the living rock.

Lucifer

Angus Watson

I was a dream, ripe to fall
Into the mind of Man.
A journeyman keen to be out and about
Enjoying a fine sense of doing useful things.

So when I flew down,
Secure in my own disrepute
I set to.
Transforming the Glory of God
Into a carbuncly little believing.
Issuing each man
With his own little devil to hang at his back.

The Curlews Crying

Kenneth C. Steven

Down at the river and always far away
I hear them, high voices crying
The sky is over that way blue and pale as opals.
Until it is dark I hear them mourning
Like lovers leaving for another land,
Circling over the summer river pools
The sea in their wings now, in their voices,
As they rise, relentless, still cry and cry
Till the first white stars have flowed like pearls
Through the water of the skies.

from The Lady of Kynachan

James Irvine Robertson

As Lochiel's runner trotted over the pass and along Strathtay, the news he carried spread ripples of disturbance through the townships.

He paused briefly at the alehouse in Weem and took on board a few mouthfuls of oatmeal and some whisky before continuing on his way. The soldiers lounging against the parapet of the bridge had challenged him but then waved him past on hearing that he was on Lochiel's business. Had they suspected the nature of that business, the messenger would have been detained. Their loyalty was to King George, whose interests would not be served should his enemies be roused before the forces of the state had time to nip a putative rebellion in the bud.

Cameron had told the news to James Menzies, the innkeeper, who left his wife in charge of the establishment and hurried through the gateway leading to the wooded policies of Castle Menzies. Before the castle, the formal knot garden wilted in the sunshine, and the innkeeper was grateful to escape the heat when he plunged into the cool darkness of the castle itself.

The hall porter, dozing in his chair, opened a bleary eye at the sound of James Menzies's feet on the stone flags.

'Is the laird about?' demanded the innkeeper.

The porter jerked his thumb. 'He's outside somewhere but he'll be back for dinner.'

The smell of roasting meat drifted tantalisingly down a stone passage.

'I must see him. I have news.'

'Well, you'll have to find him yourself.' The porter paused. 'What news?'

But he was talking to himself, as the innkeeper had already left. The porter thought for a moment, then closed his eyes again. If the news was worth hearing, he would hear it soon enough.

At the back of the castle, a scullion was tipping waste onto the midden, disturbing a swarm of flies. In response to the innkeeper's query, he waved his hand towards the hill. James Menzies hurried up the path to the walled garden, which lay on the slope facing south and was as big as many of the estate's farms.

Gardeners, busy tending fruit trees or weeding amongst the ranks of vegetable and bushes, straightened their backs to watch the innkeeper climb towards the terrace, where the laird seemed to be sleeping peacefully in a hammock, his wife and daughter chatting quietly beside him as they sewed. The terrace was higher than the castle roof, and the view encompassed the strath, stretching as far as the peak of Ben Lawers, fifteen miles away, where patches of snow still skulked in the corries. Across Sir Robert's unbuttoned waistcoat lay an open book.

'Laird!' called the innkeeper as he approached.

Jerked from his slumbers, Sir Robert grabbed for his book and looked wildly about him. His eyes settled on the messenger.

'Oh, hallo, James,' he said. 'It's a bit hot to be running around. Will you have some lemonade?'

The innkeeper was tempted. Sir Robert was the only man for a dozen miles with an underground ice-house capable of preserving its harvest from the winter loch through the hottest summer. And the cost of a single lemon would pay the wages of one of the gardeners for three days. Struggling to regain his breath, James Menzies shook his head.

'A runner from Lochiel has just been through, Sir Robert. He carries word that Prince Charles is in Scotland and is raising the flag of rebellion.'

Sir Robert sat up. The book finally left his chest and knocked over a beaker of lemonade on the table alongside him. Swaying, the hammock nearly tipped its occupant to the ground.

'What? What?'

'Rebellion, Sir Robert. The Highlands are rising.'

'At last!' exclaimed his wife. Lady Mary, born Lady Mary Stuart, was the daughter of the Earl of Bute and a descendant of Robert II, founder of the deposed royal of house.

Sir Robert waved his wife to silence. 'Where is this runner? Where is the prince?'

'The runner's run on, as runners do, Sir Robert. He gave no further information than what I have told you.'

'It'll be no more than another rumour,' said Sir Robert. 'It's too late in the year to begin a campaign. Besides, the French have no troops to spare.'

'Don't be such a killjoy, Robert,' said his wife.

'Killjoy, my dear? There is no joy in rebellion. Brother pitted against brother. The country laid waste by warring troops. Decent men dying in ditches or decorating gibbets. Joy comes from peace and stability.'

'How can you say that, Father?' demanded his daughter. 'Scotland is oppressed by the German usurper.'

Sir Robert glared at the girl, his eyes popping. 'What nonsense has your mother been feeding you? Look around you, child? Are we oppressed? Can you feel the tyrant's boot upon your neck?' He turned his attention to the innkeeper. 'What do you say, James? Are you oppressed?'

'Should we not be doing something, Laird?'

'And think what would happen if the bloody man really has come to Scotland.'

'Robert! Your language!'

'I'm sorry, my dear. But the first thing that always happens when there's trouble is the invasion of our home by soldiers.'

'If they're the soldiers of King James, they will be welcome,' said Lady Mary.

'Not by me,' said Sir Robert grimly. 'My father and my grandfather supported the Protestant settlement. I've no time for some flashy young papist on a fool's errand from Italy. James, go to the bridge. Alert the sergeant to what you've heard. It's the Watch's job to sniff out tales of rebellion.'

'So you won't be calling out the clan for the prince, Sir Robert?' spoke up one of the gardeners, a dozen of whom had sidled over to be within earshot.

'Absolutely not! If there's any troop-raising to be done, it'll be for the government.'

'But Robert—' began Lady Mary.

'But me no buts, my dear. It is my duty and my desire to keep my people from becoming embroiled in a madcap escapade.'

The innkeeper was now answering questions from the huddle of garden workers. Sir Robert shot him a malevolent look.

'To the bridge, James Menzies, this instant. The rest of you, back to work.'

'Robert—' began Lady Mary again, a dangerous glint in her eye.

'Peter!' interrupted her husband.

One of the gardeners looked back.

'Find the factor,' Sir Robert said. 'Tell him I'd be obliged if he'd meet me in the castle as soon as convenient.'

'Shian?'

'Of course Shian, you blockhead!'

'Mind yourself, Laird.' said Peter. 'You don't want to be have a seizure.' The gardener was concerned, never having seen his sunny-natured chief so angry.

'Do not be insolent, man.'

'Och, it's not that I'm being insolent, Sir Robert,' said the gardener. 'It's that Shian is in Rannoch, as you well know, and not expected back for a while.'

'Well, send a messenger to hurry him here.'

'As you wish, but I doubt he'll be back any sooner.'

Lady Mary's warning look instantly silenced her daughter's giggle as, with an air of injured innocence, Peter clumped down the steps towards the castle. The Laird of Weem cleared his throat noisily and picked up his book, but the calm of his summer afternoon had been irrevocably shattered.

Misty Amulree

Jim Steward

The cold wind covers my body like a sheet of silk.
The frost covers the ground like a rug of white cotton.
The mist hides the Amulree hills like clouds hiding the sun.
The colour of the heather pierces through the mist.
Like the sun bursting through clouds.

The Haunting Beauty of Loch Leven Castle

Katie H. Maitland

The wind was cold.
The sky was grey.
The waves lashed our little boat.
Our thoughts went back six hundred years,
As we neared the castle, afloat.

The tower loomed up.
The walls stood firm.
The gun loops rimmed the stone.
Well-made to keep the enemy out,
Or yet the prisoner, alone.

Thicks walls enclose
Dark rooms of stone,
Cold stairs meander high.
We think of Mary imprisoned there,
Alone and left to die.

The Days of Early Winter

Danny Boatwright

The mist is shutting out the sun,
The clouds swirl like cotton wool,
The frost sparkles like tiny stars
and puddles lie like layers of silk.
Trees stand coated with white soft mist,
and in the breeze frost falls
from the telegraph wires
like sugar through a sieve.

Ghislaine Egan

In late autumn the streets are covered in a deep crisp golden brown carpet. The High Street is busy as early Christmas shoppers look for gifts. The River Tay flows swiftly along beside the twinkling fairy lights. The cold harsh wind blows as the children fly their kites. The jacuzzi pool is filled as cold swimmers relax and warm up.

Kinnoull Hill is brown with leaves as cold hillwalkers trudge up. The City Hall is full of buzz and excitement as concerts take place. The bright lights of Christmas decorations shine in the dark evenings. The Inch is quiet as people stroll along, walking their dogs. The Ice Rink is full of people practising their skating in case the pond freezes over. The plants wither and the waterfall in the Norie Miller stops. The thought of Christmas forms in everybody's mind as the bare trees sway slowly in the bitter wind.

Paul Clarke

Perthshire wearing its coat of many colours
Gold, red and brown.
Crunch go the fallen leaves,
All across the town.
The man of the world has shed his coat
And he lays it on the ground.
Now the old lady with her icy fingers comes
And the snow lays itself silently without a sound.
The cold mean lady of winter
Hangs on with all her might.
But all of us are lucky
Spring is in sight.

The Long Wait

Elma Wood

"Weel, I'd best be off. There's a long way to go and don't want to be late back."

Rose, Iris and Ivy were so excited. For ages they'd pleaded in vain for a pony. Their farmer father had finally relented. It was war-time and there was no petrol to spare for luxuries like fetching pets. Dad had a long walk over the hill to the moor where the Shetland ponies were kept. He had to take a right of way round the Haugh, a flat field near the water liable to flooding. It was more than just a right of way, it was an old coffin road that had to be kept tidy six feet wide. Before the days of cars, when country folk couldn't afford a horse-drawn hearse, coffins were carried to the kirkyard. It was still the church road, and although a few folk had cars, it was considered proper to walk to the kirk, and on the way home all the news of the week would soon be exchanged. After he'd rounded the Haugh, he had to cross the wide burn by a shooglie wooden bridge and climb all the way following the farmtracks till he reached the moor. It would probably take him more than an hour to get there and getting back would depend on the willingness of the pony. But the lasses were jumping up and down with excitement and Mum was sorely tried. At last she gave them all tasks to pass the time.

"Rose," who was twelve, "Will you set to and clean out the wee hen hoose? Iris, you take Ivy with you and find out where the hens have been laying today. Take care not to break any. The van man will want as many as I can give him when he comes tonight."

Rose, who normally couldn't stand the smell of the hen houses, and always had a grumble at this job, set off quite happily this time. There was fresh hay to be carefully placed in the nesting boxes, the dropping board beneath the perches to be cleaned and the perches to be scraped as well, if they needed it. Only then could the floor be cleaned and the fresh chaff scattered over it. Rosie had never got through this horrible job so quickly before.

Meantime, Iris and Ivy were looking in all the usual places for the hens' eggs. The nesting boxes in the hen houses were always neatly prepared for the hens to lay in them, but mostly the doors were never shut in time. So they found whatever place suited them: some had got into the habit of roosting on the branches of the trees that sheltered the farm buildings from the worst of the winter gales; some nested in the cart shed, some in the barn among the hay, some under hedges, and some would even fly up into the stacks in the stackyard and burrow in to lay their egg. This meant climbing up to reach it. Sometimes the nest would even be found near the top of the strae soo, a huge stack built from big bunches of thrashed straw used for bedding the beasts, and they'd have to use a ladder to reach them.

Mum thought she was doing them a favour, because as a young girl she had loved looking for eggs. For her it had been fun and not a chore. But today, with all the excitement, they too set about it willingly and the eggs were searched out in extra quick time. She couldn't believe that they were all back so soon. And again it was "Mummy, when will Daddy be back, he's taking an awful long time."

"For Goodness sake, is there no peace with you? I've got my work to be getting on with. Your daddy will be ages yet. Why don't you run over to the neighbours? Mrs McTavish might like to help you choose a name for your pony. It might cheer her up."

Mrs McTavish had come to this country from Europe long before the war, and had married a Scotsman. She was very unhappy most of the time because she didn't know what was happening to her family in her old home. Communication was impossible due to all the fighting. She was delighted when they turned up at her door and invited them in to the kitchen. They explained why they were there and she asked them about the pony. She suggested 'Mooi', a word meaning beautiful, since all they'd been able to tell her was that the pony was a girl and that she was dapple grey.

They went happily home with the idea, only to find that Daddy still wasn't home. They were beginning to get really impatient by this time.

"Can we go across the Haugh to the burn and wait for him there?' they asked.

"All right, on you go, but take good care of Ivy."

They shot across the Haugh and soon were at the burn.

"What do we do now?' they asked each other. They looked at the bridge nervously, remembering how shooglie it was. But they also remembered how in the summer they'd stood on it, watching the wee trooties swimming. In a while they picked up courage and went on to it very carefully. It had been much easier when Dad was with them, to make them feel safe. They looked in the water but it was very dull and grey, so they couldn't see any fish. But they got a surprise to find that after a while of looking into the burn, it seemed as though the shooglie bridge was floating down the burn! This amused them till they began to feel cold. Then they began to wonder if this might turn out to be another disappointment.

"Do you remember the time we asked Daddy to bring us a pony home from the market and he brought a baby goat?" Rose asked.

"It was good fun but it wasn't a pony," Ivy answered.

Iris wondered, "Do you think it could happen again? Daddy always says that pets have to be fed."'

Wearily they crossed back over the Haugh, hands in pockets and feet dragging despondently in their wellies. But a surprise was waiting for them. Dad had taken a different way home and there she was, the pony! Excitement wasn't nearly enough to describe how they felt. They danced round and round the "beautiful" pony. They had had no idea what dapple grey meant, as they'd never seen a horse of that colour before, but she was well and truly named. And there was another surprise. Because very soon she was going to have her own first baby. Of course, this meant she'd have to be very gently treated in the meantime. They were a wee bittie disappointed that they wouldn't be able to play with her much in the weeks to come, but they did understand.

Their mother had a bit of a phobia about closed doors and, during the daytime at least, all the three doors into the house were kept wide open. As a result they got a big shock one morning as their mother was getting them ready for school. Mooi walked right into the kitchen and helped herself to an apple out of the bowl on the dresser then walked right out again! They wondered at this strange happening, but didn't have long to wait for the reason. Next day she produced a foal even more beautiful than herself. It was black with a perfect saddle marked in pure white. Mooi was so proud of this first foal and they all thought she'd been very clever. They named the foal 'Dinkie'.

Mooi had many foals over many years, but none was ever so beautifully marked as this, her first one.

Horses

Patricia Ace

As she approached the gypsy horses, her full white skirt billowed out in the wind like a flag of surrender. The Spanish tan stood square and brutish like a runner on the starting blocks. Solid and athletic, she saw the power in its shoulders, the thick muscular flesh which could spring into motion at any moment. He came to greet her, in search of food; she ran a hand down his thick, matted mane. Like witches hair it was black and copper-red with odd white streaks. It was beautiful, the wild hair of a Goth girl in her late teens or early twenties. She stroked his velveteen nose, tickled his sensitive curling lip. He threw back his head in violent disapproval. She traced a finger along the intricate pattern of wet curls on his back; to her it was irresistible, like a man's short hair after rain.

Charlie Graham's Last Dram

Sheila Douglas

The early morning mist hung over Strathearn as Charlie Graham, King of the Lochgelly tinkers, six foot three and built like a barn door, stood in a clump of young birch trees at the side of the field where the grey stallion was shaking the dew from his mane and tail in a graceful canter. He watched it for quite a while, his eyes taking delight in the fine proportions and movements of the animal. Then he put two fingers in his mouth and whistled a long low call. The horse stopped and listened. He whistled again and the horse came slowly towards him. Charlie stroked its nose and fed it a sugar lump, then slipped a halter over its head. The horse whinnied and stepped back. Charlie gave it rein, making soothing noises, speaking gently, and presently it moved back towards him. He stood for some time, caressing its nose and its flanks before leading it away through the trees to where his horse was tethered. He attached a leading rein to the stallion's halter, then mounted his horse and took it down into the shallow waters of the burn that wound through the wood, following the burn's course, until it passed the dyke enclosing the field and he reached the little humped back bridge. Up onto the bridge he guided his horse and the stallion followed, then he set off at a good pace towards Fife, before the sun was up.

Halfway up Glentarkie, he found a band of his people encamped in a hollow, among them his brother Sandy, who greeted him delightedly as he dismounted.

"Oh weel dune, man! Ye got the stallion! That's bluidy great!"

"Tak chairge o him," ordered Charlie. "Keep him hidden, mind. Ye ken whit ye've tae dae."

Sandy nodded. The gelding tools were ready in his tent, and the dyes for changing the colour of his coat. He and Charlie were practised hands at this game. There'd be a great hue and cry raised to find the stallion, and they would be prime suspects, but all anyone would find in their possession would be a brown gelding. The landowner they'd stolen it from, Archie Smeaton, was the only one in the neighbourhood who would never let tinkers camp on his land or lodge in his barn.

"My, he's braw!" said Sandy admiringly, stroking the satiny haunches of the stallion. Other brothers and cousins gathered round to view the handsome beast.

"I'll awa tae Perth noo. I've business tae attend tae afore the mercat gets owre thrang." Charlie remounted his horse and galloped off, leaving the grey stallion to its fate. He had plans for the noble animal, which made him chuckle quietly to himself as he crossed the Baiglie Straight towards the Brig of Earn.

Before he got to Perth, carts and wagons, herds of cattle and people on foot were all coming in for the Midsummer market by every road into the town. Charlie's first port of call was John McQueen's shop in the Shoegait to deliver a consignment of horn spoons.

"Weel, Chairlie," John McQueen greeted him, "here ye are on the dot as usual. I'm gled tae see ye, man."

Charlie laid the bundle of spoons on the counter, "There ye are, John. Six dozen as ordered."

John McQueen counted out the price of the spoons. "I wish aa my suppliers were as dependable as ye are, Chairlie."

Charlie pocketed the money. 'Ye can coont on me, John. If I gie ma word, I keep it."

"Aye," nodded John, "I've aye fund that tae be true."

Charlie smiled to himself as he left the shop. The delivery of the spoons gave him a legitimate reason for being in the town on a market day, or any day for that matter. Others of his kin would be in among the market crowd, also selling spoons, willow baskets, tin flagons and bowls. Their womenfolk would be telling fortunes, begging and selling ribbons and laces to the country wives. At some juncture, one or other of them would create a diversion of some kind.

But before he gave the signal for that, Charlie had another matter to attend to. As the bell of St, John's Kirk struck nine, he rode round to the entrance of the old jail, dismounted and waited. After a few minutes, the heavy studded door swung open, and a woman in a ragged cloak stepped out. She was tall and very good looking and ran over to Charlie, who embraced her warmly.

"Oh Da!" she cried, "God bless ye for comin!"

"Hoo are ye, Meg lass?" he asked, looking her over affectionately. "Ye're gey pale o the cheek."

"Nae wunner. Shut awa in yen place, wi nae air, nae sun, an naethin fit tae eat."

"Tak tent, noo, lass. Keep oot o their clutches. Ye're owre wild, ye ken. It's nae worth it, tae gie up yer freedom for the daft things ye dae. Mind yer grandfaither? He got up tae plenty o nonsense, but he never gied them the chance tae prove onythin. They used tae hae him up in the coort, but they'd aye tae let him gang. If ye askit him whit he was up for, he'd say, 'Och, just the auld thing, but nae proof.' Noo, ye've got brains, lass, the same as me. Use them!"

Meg hugged her father, "Aye, Da, I ken ye're richt. But I canna help it. When ye see aa thae lang-faced sheep o tounsfolk, an thae fat-bellied, mealy-moothed maggots on the Cooncil, I just has tae annoy them! As for that dreepin-nebbit Bailie Caw, may the Deil choke him for giein me sixty days for fechtin in Lucky McKendrick's. It wis thon cantankerous hoor o a fishwife that got ma dander up."

"Jist forget aboot it," Charlie advised her. "Come on noo, we'll awa roon tae the Ship Inn and hae a guid tichtener and a dram afore we dae onythin else."

The prospect of a decent meal and a drink put Meg in a better frame of mind. Charlie tethered his horse on the outskirts of the town and they made their way to the inn, where they were soon enjoying mutton broth and salty bannocks.

"Weel Da," she said, when a mutchkin of porter was slippin over her throat, "whit's the ploy the day?"

Charlie winked solemnly. "Noo Meg, ye should ken better than tae speir. The Grahams come tae the Midsummer Mercat in Perth wi jist the ae thing in mind: oor lawfu business." The two tried to keep their faces straight, but soon they were laughing as if what Charlie had said had been the greatest of jokes.

Just then, a short, thick-set man came into the crowded taproom and pushed his way over to where Charlie and Meg were sitting.

"Eck!" said Charlie, recognising one of his cousins. "Whit's the news, man?"

"There's a battle brewin in the High Street," replied Eck in cant, "atween the ferm lads and the weaver lads. They're shoutin the odds at the moment, but they'll be comin tae blows afore lang."

Charlie got to his feet right away, paid his bill and he and Meg followed Eck out into the Skinnergait. A great rabble of noise was coming from the direction of the main street, and cries of "Horsemen aa!" vying with yells of "Up the weavers!"

"Ca canny, noo," warned Charlie. "Wait tae we see whit's happenin." He went ahead and took a look out into the High Street. By virtue of his height, he had a better view than most and saw the weavers were outnumbered by the farm lads.

"The lads is aa doon in the Shoegait," said Eck when he returned. "They sent me tae fin ye an get yer orders. Maist o the trouble's up near the Watergait, so we could jouk through the Meal Vennel and jine up wi the ithers."

"We'll dae that," said Charlie. They slipped out into the High Street and fought their way against the tide of folk, who were all making for the source of the hullabaloo to see the fun. At last, they got to the Meal Vennel and made their way through to the Shoegait, where a large numbers of Grahams were hanging about in twos and threes among the crowd there.

"Pass the word roon," Charlie told Eck in cant. "We side wi the weavers." Eck scurried off to do his bidding.

Meg tugged at her father's sleeve. "Da, whit aboot the morts?" The women always backed up their menfolk.

"Grib the lour chates an the haben," Charlie told her, meaning "Take the valuables and the food."

She ducked away through the jostling throng, whispering in the ear of all the sisters, aunts and cousins she could locate. Very casually, all the Grahams began to move through the Meal Vennel towards the High Street. As they worked their way through the stalls and the sideshows, the noise of the disturbance grew louder. The two sides armed with sticks and staves were battering at each other and the cries of the wounded could be heard in concert with the yells and shrieks of the spectators. When he saw the farm lads were driving the weavers slowly down the High Street, Charlie seized a length of wood from a man selling fencing posts and charged forward, followed by his band, shouting, "Up the weavers!"

The weavers were surprised, but delighted to be given such support and renewed their efforts. Stalls were overturned and stallholders and spectators fled in terror, as all hell broke loose. Hens, ducks and geese escaped and scattered squawking and quacking in among people's feet. Neeps and tatties rolled everywhere, butters and cheeses rolled on the cobbles, peep shows were knocked over and towers of gingerbread collapsed. Children were crying, dogs barking, windows were smashed and the whole market was reduced to a shambles. The farm lads were slowly but surely pushed back down the High Street towards the river. At the height of the uproar, the sound of kettle drums was heard and down George Street came the sound of marching feet. It was the Perth Volunteers resplendent in their scarlet and blue and their white feathers, called out to quell the riot, with their muskets at the ready.

All those who were able tried to run away, but were hampered by the crowd closing in on them again, in the hope of seeing them all marched off to the jail.

"Bing avree!" called Charlie, and all the Grahams who had been battling valiantly for the honour of the weavers, melted away like snow off a dyke.

Charlie made for where his horse was tethered and as he jumped on it back, Meg appeared at his stirrup and he hoisted her up behind him, before galloping off towards Craigend.

They were the first to reach the camp in Glentarkie, but one by one, the rest arrived on horses and ponies, some with carts, in great spirits after the day's diversion. The womenfolk put down their bundles on the ground and the men gathered round to inspect their booty. Live poultry, loaves of bread, vegetables, measures of meal, as well as wallets, watches, brooches and rings, lengths of cloth and leather boots were produced from bags and pockets and the folds of plaids.

"No a bad day's work," commented Charlie.

The next time Charlie was in Perth, along with Sandy and Eck to deliver orders for horn spoons, baskets and tinware, it was also a market day. They were refreshing themselves in the George Inn, when who should appear but the farmer, Archie Smeaton, whose white stallion had been spirited away. He was with his friend Duncan McCandlish, another farmer, and his face turned purple with rage when he saw Charlie sitting there.

"Villains like yon shouldnae be allowed in places amang decent fowk," he muttered to Duncan.

Charlie continued to enjoy his dram, scarcely glancing in the direction of the angry farmer.

"Whaur's my stallion?" called out Smeaton across the room. Still Charlie paid no attention. Archie moved closer and repeated the question, adding, "I ken fine you had a hand in takin it awa, so dinnae deny it." He thumped the table Charlie was sitting at. Charlie turned with great dignity and asked, "Dae ye hae some business wi me, Mr Smeaton?"

"Aye!" raged Smeaton. "My stallion! It's disappeared from ane o my parks on Midsummer mornin. Dinnae tell me ye ken naethin aboot it."

Charlie looked reproachfully at him. "Noo, noo, Mr. Smeaton. Dinnae be owre hasty wi yer accusations. I'm sorry tae hear ye've lost yer stallion. He was a braw beast. Aabody in Strathearn kens that. Hoo could I tak him ? I'm nae a magician."

"I'm no sae shair o that," growled Smeaton. "Let me warn ye. Ye'll nae get awa wi it!"

Charlie spread his hands and shrugged his shoulders. "Ye're on the wrang track, Mr. Smeaton."

"I'll get the proof, dinnae fash," promised Smeaton grimly. "I'll hunt it doon an I'll get it."

"Mr Smeaton," said Charlie with great authority, "ye are welcome tae visit ma camp at Lochgelly and any ither o ma camps in Fife and Kinross. Ye'll no find your stallion in ony o them. I'll tak ye roon them aa masel."

"Na, na," replied Smeaton, "I ken ye fine, Graham. Ye'll switch the beast fae here tae there and I'll never see it. Dae ye tak me for a bairn?"

Charlie put on an air of injured innocence. "Ach, Mr Smeaton, I cannae win, can I? I'll tell ye whit I'll dae. I'll tell ye whaur aa the camps are, an ye can jist turn up unannounced at ony o them. Is that fair, or no?"

Smeaton looked doubtfully at Charlie. "Hoo will I ken ye'll tell me aboot aa o them?"

"Jist ask aa the Fife folk. They aa ken."

"They're aa feart o ye. They'll tell me onythin you want them tae. I wouldnae trust ye as far as I could throw ye."

"Weel, Mr Smeaton, if that's hoo ye feel, I cannae help ye."

Duncan McCandlish tugged at his friend's sleeve. "Come awa, Erchie," he said, "he's jist makin a fule o ye."

"Aye, maybe he is," Smeaton retorted, "but I'll get him yet. He'll mak guid the hairm he's dune me, I sweer tae God he will."

"If ye're luikin for a guid horse, Mr. Smeaton, ye need only come tae me," said Charlie. "I cannae bring ye back yer stallion, but maybe I can sell ye another animal jist as guid."

"Awa ye go! I wadna buy a dug aff ye, let alone a horse."

"Weel, please yersel."

Smeaton walked away in disgust, followed by his friend, and Charlie and his brother and cousin continued with their meal. The two farmers sat at the opposite end of the room and called for broth and bannocks and large drams, but all the time they were eating and drinking Archie Smeaton continued to grumble and complain about his stolen stallion.

They were joined by a third man dressed like a farmer who came into the taproom in a very agitated state.

"Oh me!" he exclaimed as he sank down on the bench beside Archie, mopping his brow. "This is nae ma lucky day!"

"Whit's adae, Tam?" asked Archie, while Duncan commented, "Ye look fair forfochen."

"Nae wunner!" gasped Tam, "I've been robbit. I sellt aa ma stirks fur a guid price the day, but some bugger's awa wi ma wallet."

"Naw!" The two friends were shocked, as they could well imagine how they'd feel in the same plight.

"Wis there muckle in't?" asked Duncan.

Tam nodded miserably. "Forty pun," he said in a voice little above a whisper. "Oh, whit am I gaun tae dae?"

"Did aabody hear that?" Archie shouted, so that everyone in the inn could hear him. "Tam Guthrie's had his siller taen!"

Sympathisers quickly gathered round and commiserated with Tam. "We'll hae tae dae something," said Archie. His eye fell on the Grahams. "Maybe we'll no hae faur tae luik!"

Charlie Graham met his gaze calmly and laughed. "I dinnae ken why ye're luikin at me, Mr Smeaton. It's naethin tae dae wi me."

"Dae ye expect us tae believe that?" sneered Smeaton. "Forty pun gaes a-missin and there's Grahams in the toun. Of course, it's jist a coincidence!"

Some o the bystanders laughed, but Tam himself protested. "Noo, noo, Erchie, ye cannae jist pit the blame on them. I've never been onywhaur near them the day."

"Wis ye at the cattle sale?" demanded Archie fiercely of Charlie.

"No me. Nor Sandy, nor Eck neither. We've been up and doun deliverin orders. Ye can ask ony a oor customers. John McQueen, and Jeanie Wilson, and auld Mattie Gibson and Robert Bain."

"Aye, ye've been aa roon the toun, in aa the vennels and closes, aa thrang wi fowk," said Archie. "They were maybe richt ahint ye, Tam, an ye never saw them."

"I dinnae think sae," replied Tam, who often lodged Charlie's folk in his barn.

"Ye ken me, Mr Guthrie," Charlie said, "I widnae rob ye." He produced a leather bag, from which he took a handful of sovereigns and threw them on the table. "There's my share, noo, gentlemen. If ye aa pit doon the same, we can help Mr. Guthrie oot o his difficulty."

This did not in the least appeal to Archie, or Duncan, or any of the other farmers present, who were all noted for their reluctance to part with money.

"Aye, it's easy for some fowk!" commented Archie bitterly. "We cannae aa jist shell oot siller like the fairies. For some o us it's hard tae come by."

While they were all conferring about the best thing to do, without adding anything to Charlie's contribution, another man came in, with the look of the Grahams about him.

"Andra!" Charlie greeted him. "Ye're the very man!"

"Whit's adae, Chairlie?" asked the newcomer.

"Ye're jist in time tae help Mr Guthrie, here. Ye ken Mr Guthrie?"

"Aye, indeed. Hoo are ye, Mr. Guthrie?"

"He's nae verra weel, the day, Andra. Some thievin bugger has taen his wallet."

Andra looked very concerned. "Is that richt? Noo, that's a damned shame!"

"I wis thinkin, Andra," said Charlie, "that as Mr. Guthrie has aye been guid tae wir fowk, we should maybe dae whit we can tae help him, seein his ain kind are owre ticht tae pit their hauns in their pooches."

"Aye, Chairlie. I think that's fairly richt."

Andra took a leather pocket book out of his coat and laid it on the table before the astonished farmer. Almost before he recognised it as his own, and opened it to find his money intact, the Grahams were out the door of the inn, like vanishing ghosts.

There was uproar in the taproom and Archie was all for going after the Grahams, but Duncan McCandlish restrained him. "Ye'd never catch them, Erchie."

"They're damned villains, the lot o them," cried Archie in a fury. "An that Charlie Graham's the worst o aa. He took ma stallion, I'm shair o it. Hoo he did it, I'll never ken, but I've nae doot at aa that it wis him and nae ither!"

"Come on noo, Erchie," pleaded Tam Guthrie. "Dinna be sae ready tae think ill a him. He kent his freen had taen ma siller and he got it back for me. He canna be aa bad."

"If ye want tae associate wi the likes o him and hae aa his rabble cadgin aff ye and bringin their weemin an their dugs intae yer steadin, weel, that's yer choice. It's nae mine." Archie rose and buckled on his plaid. "He liftit ma bonnie stallion, an I'll no rest till I've brocht him tae justice."

He strode out of the inn with a curt farewell to his friend Duncan and made for where his gig was waiting to take him home.

When Charlie and his friends got back to their camp at Lochgelly, he and Sandy took a walk down a lane to a paddock where a brown horse was cropping the grass. They went in and looked the horse over.

"Ye've done a guid job, Sandy," said Charlie. "Archie Smeaton wouldnae recognise his stallion noo."

"Weel, it wouldnae be muckle use tae him for coverin his mares," grinned Sandy. "Whit are ye gaun tae dae wi him noo?"

"Get a guid price for him," said Charlie. "He's worth plenty."

"There's St. John's Day mercat comin up in Perth," suggested Sandy.

"Aye, we'll tak him there."

A tall figure came into the paddock and hailed them. It was Walter MacFarlane, the farmer who owned the land.

"I was hopin I'd see you boys," he said to them. "Ye've been awa for a wee while."

"Aye, Mr MacFarlane," said Charlie. "We've had business tae attend tae. Is there onythin we can dae for ye?"

"Aye, there is. It's aboot this beast here, He's a braw beast. Is he fur sale?"

"He micht be. Wad ye be interested, Mr MacFarlane?"

"Nae me. But I hae a freen that micht be."

"We were speakin aboot takin him tae the mercat at Perth neist Friday."

"Weel, weel, that wad be jist the thing. Ma freen'll be there. I'll tell him tae luik oot fur ye."

"Thank ye, Mr MacFarlane."

The farmer gave them a wave and strode off. Charlie grinned at each other.

"I wunner wha his freen is," said Sandy.

"Disnae maitter," replied Charlie. "There's only ae person I'll sell the gelding tae."

"And wha's that?"

"Archie Smeaton. Wha else?"

"Archie Smeaton!" Sandy was flabbergasted. Charlie played some queer tricks, but this was the queerest yet. "He'll no buy a gelding. It's a stallion he wants!"

"Aye, maybe. But when he's at a horse sale, he aye ettles tae ootbid ilka ither body, and aa the mair gin he thinks the ither body's really efter the beast."

"Ah ken that fine," agreed Sandy. "If MacFarlane's freen's there, it could pit the price richt awa up."

"I believe ye could be richt, Sandy," said Charlie, straight faced. He patted the gelding's hind quarters approvingly, then he and Sandy left the paddock, thinking on the fun they would have at the St. John's Day market.

The horses to be sold at St. John's Day market were moved up to the Brig o Earn the night before. The Grahams had a camping place near the village, long recognised by custom. Charlie himself, Sandy and Eck and three other cousins had charge of the horses and saw them settled for the night, watched over by some of the younger lads, before betaking themselves to the Cyprus Inn for refreshment. The landlord there, Willie Brodie, knew them well and while he was wary of them, he had always found them good customers. His regulars also knew the Grahams and while many of them feared them, and some positively resented them, Willie Brodie had convinced them it was wiser to be on friendly terms with the tinkers than incur their ill-will.

Charlie and his friends were not long installed in the taproom, than a group of well-dressed gentlemen, including a minister, arrived.

"Mr Graham!" exclaimed Willie Brodie, which made Charlie turn his head. "I'm pleased tae see ye, sir." Evidently, it was the minister he was addressing. "Come ben and welcome."

"Good evening, Mr. Brodie," replied the minister, who appeared to be somewhat inebriated already. "I've had a maist agreeable day in the toun and I've brocht some freens wi me tae, tae sample yer best maut."

The party settled themselves round a table. Charlie rose and went over to them. "Excuse me, gentlemen," he said pleasantly, "did I hear the landlord caa ane o ye by the name o Graham?"

"Aye, sir," beamed the minister, who was a jovial, florid-faced man, "Andrew Graham o Arngask Kirk." He held out a hand to Charlie.

"Chairlie Graham o Lochgelly," replied Charlie, shaking the minister's hand, chuckling inwardly as he saw the minister's friends turn pale and tense.

"Will you and your freens jine us in a dram?" asked the minister, and to his friends horror, he motioned to all of Charlie's group to come and sit with him. Willie Brodie served them all with whisky, and the minister's expansive mood increased with every sip. Soon, he had an arm round Charlie's shoulder and the two of them were singing verse after verse of "The Gallant Grahams". The minister's friends were growing more and more worried.

"Let me tell you something," said the minister confidentially to Charlie. "I hae heard the maist affa tales o you fowk, as the worst rogues unhung in the Kingdom o Fife."

The Grahams looked at him fixedly, without a word and the three gentlemen shivered in their shoes.

"But whit I'm gaun tae say tae ye is," and the minister began to assume his pulpit manner, "we are aa God's bairns. Let the man wha wad see a mote in his neipour's ee, tak tent tae the beam in his ain. Judge na that ye arenae judgit."

At this point, the minister slumped over the table and began to snore.

"We'll hae tae get him hame," said one of his friends. They gathered round and hoisted him to his feet, but Charlie Graham barred the door.

"Na, na," he said quietly. "Nae sae fest. Tak yer time, boys. I think ye should bide a wee while langer. Let's hae anither dram afore ye tak yer gait."

They all sat down again, the minister out for the count and his friends fearing the worst was to happen. Willie Brodie and his regulars were also watching the scene with some apprehension, but Charlie sat down and ordered up drams in the most amicable way.

"Come on noo, cheer up!" he laughed at the three nervous looking cronies of the unconscious minister, as Willie Brodie served once more. They raised their glasses in their trembling hands and thanked him. "Dinna fash," Charlie told them, "We'll tak care o his reverence. Meanwhile, let's hae a tune. Is that Jamie Broon in the corner there?"

An old man in the corner tucked his fiddle under his chin and started to play 'Tullochgorum' and Charlie stamped his feet, while Sandy and Eck got up and danced round the room. They were light on their feet and soon everyone was applauding them. The minister snored on and his three friends began to look a little less terrified, Just then, another two Grahams came into the inn. "Geordie! Rab!" Charlie greeted them. "Whit's the news fae Glentarkie then?"

"Barry, barry," they told him in cant, "we've gribbed a puckle lour fae the hantle on the drom." They'd been busy on the Baiglie Straight, relieving passers-by of their money.

"Ye've had a good day then," said Charlie. "Ye can hae yer supper noo."

They sat down at another table and Charlie turned to the minister's friends. "Ye can tak his reverence hame noo." Two of them hoisted the minister up again and helped him towards the door. The third one addressed Charlie.

"Mr Graham," he began. "I think I ken whit ye've done for us, an I thank ye."

Charlie bowed and said nothing, as the man turned to go, and after he had gone, he chuckled quietly, then laughed aloud. The rest of the company joined in, although some of them weren't very sure what they were laughing at.

Next day, Charlie and his friends took their horses to the market in Perth. It was a bright golden September day and business was brisk at the fair. About the middle of the day, Archie Smeaton arrived at the South Inch, where the horse dealing was going on. Charlie wasn't surprised to see him, of course, but could hardly believe his luck when Smeaton immediately fastened his interest on the brown gelding.

"Is this beast for sale?" he asked.

Charlie stared at him. "Aye. Whit fur wad I bring him tae the mercat if he wisnae?"

Smeaton didn't reply, but inspected the horse carefully all over, looking in its mouth, examining its feet, running his hands over its hindquarters, stroking its fetlocks, eyeing it from every angle.

"Aye," he said at last, "a fine beast. I'll offer ye a hunner guineas for him!"

"Mr Smeaton!" cried Charlie in mock surprise. "I thocht it wis a stallion ye were lookin fur!"

"I am, Chairlie, I am," Smeaton assured him. "But I'd like this gelding."

"I'm sorry, Mr Smeaton," replied Charlie, "but I've been asked tae reserve this horse fur somebody else."

"Oh? Wha wad that be?"

"I'm nae at liberty tae say," said Charlie mysteriously.

"Is he comin the day?"

"Aye, I wis teilt he wis."

"Wha teilt ye?"

"Mr MacFarlane o the Mains o Clachmuir at Lochgelly."

Smeaton laughed heartily. "Weel Chairlie, is that no a coincidence? Wattie MacFarlane's a guid freen o mine. It wis me he wis speakin fur!"

Charlie didn't altogether find this too pleasing, but he could hardly grumble. He hadn't envisaged the sale to Smeaton being such an easy matter, and if the price was not as high as it might have been with competing bids to push it up then it didn't matter too much. He was about to strike a bargain with Smeaton when another man appeared.

"Whit are ye askin for the gelding?" he wanted to know.

"Weel, this gentleman has jist offered me a hunner guineas," replied Charlie politely. Smeaton began to scowl.

"Mak it a hunner and fifty."

Smeaton's brow grew black as thunder. "The horse wis reserved for me!" he reminded Charlie.

"Na, na, Mr. Smeaton. I didna ken it was you that MacFarlane wis speakin for."

"Dinna split hairs, Graham!" snapped Smeaton.

"Your offer's a hunner and fifty guineas?" Charlie asked the newcomer. "Weel, that's better than yours, Smeaton."

"Twa hunner!" snarled Smeaton.

"An fifty," added the stranger calmly.

A small crowd had gathered round to listen to the bidding.

"Twa hunner and sixty," was Smeaton's reply.

"Three hunner!" The stranger never raised his voice, which annoyed Smeaton all the more.

"An fifty." Smeaton was almost choking with frustration. The stranger waved his hand and walked away without a word.

"Three hunner and fifty guineas, Mr. Smeaton," said Charlie, "afore aa these witnesses?"

The price was extremely high, but there was nothing Smeaton could do. "Ye're a rogue, Graham. Ye set that up. That wis yin o your cronies pushing up the bidding."

"I've never seen the man in ma life!" protested Charlie.

Smeaton had no choice but to pay up, which he did with a bad grace, and took the gelding away with him. Charlie counted the shining guineas lovingly, his heart jubilant at having sold back to Smeaton the horse he had stolen from him and 'doctored'. He'd really got away with it, and for a high price! That would make a good story for the campfire among the Grahams, for years to come.

The rest of the day passed uneventfully and when the last of the horses was sold, and one or two new ones bought, the Grahams gathered together and prepared to leave the market. Judge Charlie's displeasure when he went to where his horse was tethered to find Smeaton and two officers of the law waiting for him.

"Charles Graham?" one of the officers demanded.

"Aye."

"I have to apprehend you for the theft of a stallion on the morning of 21st June, this year of grace, from the land of Mr Archibald Smeaton of Wester Geantrees."

"On whit evidence?"

"This is the animal in question here, is it no?" the officer asked Smeaton.

"Aye." Smeaton agreed.

"But that's a broon gelding," pointed out Charlie.

"Maybe it is *noo*," snapped Smeaton, "but when you took it, it wis a grey stallion!"

"Hoo dae ye mak that oot?"

Smeaton could not contain himself, although the officers would rather he had kept the information till later. "My stallion had a mark on it, jist a wee scar, that naebody kent o bar me. This geldin has the same mark. Wattie MacFarlane'll bear witness tae't."

Charlie cursed inwardly. Smeaton's smug face was almost more than he could bear. The officers put him in irons and took him away to the jail, while the rest of the Grahams hot-footed it back to Fife with the terrible news.

The day Charlie was to be hanged, you couldn't move in the High Street of Perth, or in any of the other streets and vennels for that matter. When they brought Charlie to the gallows in a cart guarded by four military men such a cheer went up that you would have thought he was some kind of national hero, instead of a criminal being put to death by law. All the principal members of his family were there, dressed in their best, with a piper playing a lament and the womenfolk wailing and tearing their hair. The crowd's emotions were swelled by the steadfast appearance of Charlie himself, who looked taller and broader and more handsome than ever. Archie Smeaton was there too, of course, looking respectable and self-satisfied. It was more than Charlie's daughter could stand.

"Smeaton!" she screeched. "Ye've ruined a better man than you'll ever be! May a curse licht on ye for a fat-bellied insult tae God's creation. May yer lum never reek, may yer horse aye gang lame, may yer drams burn yer hairt oot, may . . . " She was dragged away still screaming curses,

Charlie stood beneath the gallows impassively, as if he hadn't heard Meg's tirade. He looked round the crowd and recognised a face here and there: John McQueen, to whom he'd sold his horn spoons; Tam Guthrie, whose money he'd returned and in whose barn he'd often sheltered; Walter MacFarlane, who'd allowed him the use of his paddock; Jean Wilson and Mattie Gibson, whom he'd supplied with baskets and tinware and who were now red-eyed with weeping. He acknowledged each one of them with a dignified wave of his hand.

The minister from Arngask stood beside him, having requested the right to offer Charlie the comforts of religion. He wasn't quite sober, having fortified himself with a large dram before coming out to perform his duty.

"Dae ye acknowledge Jesus Christ as your Saviour and Lord?" he asked.

"Nae bluidy fear," replied Charlie sotto voce, getting a whiff of alcohol from his breath. "Hae ye a dram on ye, man?"

"Kneel doon," ordered the minister, turning his back on the crowd. Charlie knelt before him and was offered a communion cup, which he drained, as the minister intoned, "Drink ye this in remembrance of me!"

As the strong spirit warmed his thrapple, then reached down to his solar plexus, Charlie felt the rage inside him melt away. Had he known it, this was less due to the dram itself than to the sleeping draught some hand – perhaps the minister's – had slipped into the cup. Town gossip had it afterwards that it had been done on the magistrate's orders. Whether to induce a merciful oblivion, or whether, as was more likely, to prevent an escape attempt, was hard to tell. For whatever reason and by whatever hand it was administered, Charlie Graham's last dram enabled him to end his turbulent life in peace.

The Smell o Hey

Jean Massie

The smell of hey wad dae it—
no the caller smell o new cut stuff,
but the foosty smell o auld stoorie stuff
pit bi i bricht simmer days
that the baists maun hae mait through the winter—
mind me o cairyin the lantern
for ma faither, ower the close
intae the stable;
muckle shaddies o the Clydesdales
clinkin an clankin i the staas.

The canty soond o cud chawin
set us oan the richt airt
for the byre.
Cats gaithered fae aa thae
hidy-holes that cats coorie intae.
Cam for their pairt o the frothy warm milk,
strecht fae the kye.

The sky wis aye clear,
the stars wir aye bricht,
the muin wis aye fu,
as we gaed back intae
the warm safe kitchen.

Hard Times Ahead

Louise Moran

Fingers of frost chase shadows over ochreous stubble fields
Jabbing icy needle tips, spreading warning – summer's gone.
Time to gather
Time to store
Hard times are knocking on the door.

Summer's brilliance mellows rich to golden autumn splendour
And trees put on their gayest dresses, dancing harvest home.
Time to gather
Time to store
Hard times are knocking on the door.

Wanton feasts of Hallowmas, rites of passage in the night
Witches, broomsticks, trick or treat, toffee apples – sharp and sweet.
Time to gather
Time to store
Hard times are knocking on the door.

Rusty bracken crackles, spreading far o'er tawny hillsides,
Woodlands bursting rich with nuts and mushrooms, haws and rosehips.
Time to gather
Time to store
Hard times are knocking on the door.

Autumn Feelings

Chelsie Gibson

Rain,
Black clouds,
Fallen leaves and pale moon.

The hurried flight of birds,
The arrival of lonely autumn,
The time for us to part.

Much has been said, yet
we have not come to the end
of our feeling.

I leave you this poem; read it
where the silence of the world possesses you
or when you're feeling fretted with disquiet.

Long must be this parting,
and remember,
my thoughts have always been of you.

Eric's Million

Dolores Garden

'I've never been to India, but I reckon I know what it smells like. I think you've got it".

Eric dropped beside me on the threadbare settee. His pale face, serious for once, his eyes magnified by thick glasses searched for any sign of a micky-take.

'I don't know, I think it still lacks a certain *je-ne-sais-quois*'.

'Essence of Ganges, perhaps?'

'More 'Bengal Balti''

'Look, make me another cup of coffee, roll on the cookies and let me think about it for a minute'.

Eric went off to put the kettle on and I moved the pile of the *Eric's House and Pet Sitting Service* leaflets on to the floor and put my feet up. I reflected not only on the question of the current concoction, but on how this whole funny business began.

Last summer, I'd accompanied Eric to the local Tech where a chap he knew was letting him have some bird tables going cheap! I was standing in this joinery workshop, lads working on benches all around and suddenly I was 20 years and 200 miles back in time. My dad's workshop in Glenloe; sturdy timber planks, heaps of sawdust, curls of wood shavings. Shafts of dusty sunlight, sounds of sawing and planing. But mostly, and I closed my eyes to savour it – the smell: woody, tangy, musty, mellow, hints of oil and resin. It was almost a surprise to open my eyes and not see Dad standing there in his multi-pocketed overalls and cloth cap, pencil behind one ear, cigarette behind the other (I used to wonder if he ever mistook these). Eric burst my thought bubble, 'Hello! Anybody in? Where have you been?'

'Heaven and back', I answered dreamily.

'Without the use of illegal substances? Tell me more!'

I tried to describe the effect of a collection of evocative smells, 'When I closed my eyes – it was just like being there'.

'You mean it brought back the memory?'

'No, well yes, I suppose, but it was more real than a memory, more real than a photo. I don't know, but it wasn't what I saw or what I heard so much as what I could smell'.

A dangerous light gleamed in Eric's eyes. I could almost hear the cogs whirring in his head.

'What?' I asked, 'what are you scheming up now?'

'Dave, my little blubberchops', he pinched my cheek, 'I have just had a peach of an idea. How about this – bottled smells?' Looking eagerly to me for a response, the best I could manage was a rather weak 'Yeh, great'.

'This calls for a celebration cum planning meeting. Got any money – to hang with Janet's green salads – treat yourself to a McDonalds.'

Over my illicit Big Mac and Large Fries, Eric enlarged on his latest money-making venture.

'Just like aroma-therapy except made to order – like, say you come to me and say, 'I remember my dad's carpentry workshop' and I'd say, 'close your eyes, imagine it, and describe the smell to me. You'd say 'musky, tangy, blah, blah, blah.''

'Got you so far', I chipped in, a tad cynical.

'Right, so, O-level Chemistry to the fore, a few lotions and potions, shaken not stirred and Bob's your Auntie Jean – Eau de Carpentry Workshop. You come back to me, uncork the magic potion, fall at my feet in eternal gratitude. Off you go, instant nostalgia in your pocket, off I go £20 in mine'.

'Well, that's got novelty value, all right, you with 20 quid in your pocket'.

'Mate, you will be sneering on the other side of your milkshake when I make my first million'.

Eric had been chasing his first million since we left school and true to form, he went after this one like a greyhound on steroids. Over the course of the next few weeks, he had bought a whole chemist shop of aromatherapy oils, essential oils and distillations of many and dubious origins. I was even called in as a technical consultant being described as proboscisly enhanced! I left my jar of coffee and a packet of muffins on the chipped Formica table. 'Some folk actually have coffee and biscuits in when they invite a friend round to make use of their sensual organs'.

'Sorry, mate, skint. Spent all my dole on this lot'. He waved his arm expansively with almost a 'Ta-Ra'!'

The single unshaded bulb in the centre of the room cast a 40 watt gloom on a variety of small bottles in wonderful colours piled beside the sink. On a shelf above, neatly on parade, were 10 octagonal dark blue bottles with cork stoppers, each one neatly gold-labelled in Eric's surprisingly fine handwriting. I rose to inspect these at close quarters, but Eric intercepted, placing his wiry frame in front of me, arms outstretched.

'No, no, my friend,' he said pushing me back onto the short spindly stool. 'That is not how we play this game'. He quickly turned each of the blue bottles to hide the labels, and took one in his hand.

'Can't I have my coffee before you set me to work', I pleaded.

'And spoil all your delicate senses, I don't think so! We don't see Milly Winey-person swig a mug of Nescaff before sloshing the old chardonnay round her gums, now do we?'

With something of a nervous flourish, he pulled the cork from the bottle in his hand, waved it back and forward under my nose several times and demanded, 'Well?'

'OK', I said 'give me time, let me hold the bottle – don't worry, I won't look, I just need to inhale it in slowly'.

I held the cool, edged glass in my hand, no hint in the colour. I closed my eyes and swirled the liquid gently under my nostrils. Alcohol . . . beer . . . onions!

'Brannigans', I shouted.

Eric literally jumped for joy. 'Yes, yes, bloody Brannigans, bloody brilliant! Well done, mate!'.

With smug grace, I agreed 'Anybody who's been in that pub lately could have guessed that one – it's spot on. How'd you do it?'

Hopping from foot to foot, Eric picked up several bottles from beside the sink and plonked each one in front of me 'O'Mally's Stout, Seamus' Old Irish Whiskey, Mary's onion bridies, and eau de fagash! Plus a few secret ingredients which shall remain harmless'.

'Fantastic!', I was impressed, 'Mary's onion bridies in a bottle – that could be a big seller on its own'.

I spent the rest of the evening guessing (with 90% accuracy) the inspiration behind the other 9 bottles. They ranged from the local leisure pool (chlorine and chips – there's a café at the door) to Sylvia's Hair and Beauty Salon (shampoo and acetone).

I was more than a little surprised at Eric's successful marketing of these very specialised Aroma-Memory products. He started with Mike Malloy, landlord of Brannigans and with his well-honed skills, soon persuaded Mike that this was just the gift to send of to his many relations in Limerick, Newcastle and Chicago!

Encouraged by this early success Eric's confidence grew. Soon he was able to introduce the customised commissions. These proved to be varied, interesting and very lucrative. Often a great deal of research was involved; a certain member of the local gentry (clients anonomity preserved) paid handsomely to recapture the aroma of her long-lost kitchen garden in summer (many herbs, soft fruits and flowers).

'Hey, now I know you've hit the big time, chocolate digestives!'

Eric laughed, 'It's been great since before Christmas – that Festive pong is still selling well – expensive to make, but it was well worth it. This one's a bit tricky though – he held a bottle under my nose. I pushed it away quickly – 'What is that?'

'You tell me!'

'I dunno – it really stinks – what about sweaty socks?'

'Close – wet dog! No kidding – this old bloke rang me up, said the thing he missed most about his dear departed Mufti was her smell drying off in front of the fire on a rainy day!'

'Sad' I said 'in all senses'. 'Now what's this new departure you've brought me here for?'

Eric suddenly became serious. He didn't quite look round the room, but his tone was lowered as he spoke. 'This could be big – this could be really, really big. How's this for an idea – Smellevision!'

His manner checked my instinct to laugh. 'Tell me more'.

'This is how it works – new programme launch, drama set in Indian restaurant. Big publicity campaign. Free gift in all the TV mags and papers. A foil wrapped tissue. When the programme begins, you place the tissue on top of the TV. Heat from the telly sends out 'Scents of India'. The whole programme comes alive with sight, sound and smell! Isn't that just brilliant!'

This was the bottle I now held in my hands. With eyes closed, I took a deep sniff. I could have been sitting in Omar's Tandoori waiting for my pakora. 'This must've been an easy one' I shouted.

Eric handed me a mug and agreed 'Yeh, it was pretty straightforward, but I've taken a lot of time and trouble on this one. I've even brought out a patent – this thing could be worth a fortune. The chap from Channel 7 mentioned Warner Bros!'

'Are they going to manufacture these tissues?'

'Yes, these TV people give my recipe to these 'make your washing smell like a summer meadow' guys, and they make these moist things. The original idea was the bottled stuff, but I thought – one little slip on the telly, Kaboom, and that's another great idea up the Khyber!'

I was reluctant to introduce a note of pessism at this stage, but I was worried that this time Eric might be putting all his hopes and dreams into this one crazy idea.

'Suppose it doesn't take off?'

Eric tipped himself back on his chair, took a long swig of his coffee and nibbled the top of his double choc-chip cookie. Then, with the merest twitch of a ginger eyebrow said 'There's always the revolving bird-tables!'

The Pity of It

Helen Waugh

Now I must take my turn at dying.
I am of the genus solanaceae,
the last of my species.
I came here silently, by stealth
at the end of the sixteenth century.
There was neither government nor patron
to urge my acceptance.
I won the confidence of the people,
fitting readily into the economic structure
of lives already torn apart by civil unrest.

For centuries,
I was the perfect instrument of the masses,
I contributed to this, my adopted country,
the sole diet of many. Man and beast
survived on the nutrition I supplied,
though mixed with salt and milk to taste,
alone, I was a complete provider.

You, my master, created a dependency,
an economy around me, and both you and I
developed a time-honoured association
with the once fertile earth.
I blossomed in this fair land,
delighted in your cool moist atmosphere
and rich deep, friable soil.
Prayers and rituals accompanied
both my planting and my harvest.
I could be relied upon to be pregnant
with the promise of plenty.

This trinity worked well – I, the father,
earth the mother, you the tiller,
each respectively giving and taking.
Then you became careless, you would not
cultivate between planting, became forgetful
of denshiring – therefore, no nourishing.

We made so insignificant a demand upon you,
your energy and skills, and yet you neglected us.
Throwing us into the soil, you left us
to the mercy of the elements.

We gave you many warnings, but you,
you never heeded them. The earth was too tired,
it tried to nurse us – but it turned sour,
could not cope with the diseased spores
that fell from me. No my once proud head
is bowed in sorrow – no more bold displays.
Then I had been resplendent in my dark green leaves
and yellow male bloom – strong and fertile,
yielding abundantly.

You with your lazy beds and lazy ways,
you divided me, halving the goodness
I could pass on. I was made to lie with myself,
my brothers with sisters, till because
of your demands we became fused and crippled.
Our young were miniature and watery specimens
steeped in a black evil – smelling slime.
You weakened my strain, we became exhausted.
All that is left now are fields of corruption
like some peculiar botanical form of incest
and I behold with sorrow, the waste
of putrefying vegetation.

Now both of us have suffered. At least
for my kind all was over in a few days.
You and your poor nation have many trials
to endure. Your famine will be severe,
continuous, and heavy of heart, afraid,
you will scatter your seeds to the corners
of the earth. Take heed, master, do not
neglect your strain as you did ours,
or they too will grow genetically impure
defective, doomed and diseased.

I served you well – and who knows
who was the exploiter, the exploited.
And does it matter? It is for others to decide.
I leave you to your sorrow, my pitiful cottier,
you will never see our likes again,
your once lusty Irish apple.

This is the Boy

Kenneth C. Steven

The boy came out of hiding and climbed the tree
His face burst into sunlight, the green summer
Budded in the laughter of his mouth.

The boy rainbowed into water, through the pools
That all of August had grown fat with rain—
He felt the cold go deep as daggers down.

The boy ran through the wood and met the moor
Where water colour edges of the stone-age wind
Stood up in cracks and worshipped, old as time.

The boy stood in the forest and stood still
As sunlight dipped the green ink well below
And wrote in curves the spangling of the trees.

The boy came home at night and saw the stars turn pearl
And watched his hands grow white and wither like the leaves
And an autumn wind blew through him and a snow ran from his eyes
For the boy that had run off and was no longer anymore.

Return Journey

M.L. McEwan

'It's a long time since I've travelled by train, you know.'

The old woman slumped into the window seat opposite her, crashing three carrier bags, obviously containing bottles onto the table between them.

Carol lifted her eyes from her newspaper and sniffed with minor irritation, then continued reading her 'Guardian'.

Busily, the woman rummaged in her bags and eventually settled with a bottle of scotch and a plastic cup. She gulped down the drink noisily and sighed with contentment.

'I needed that. I've had such a fraught day.'

The younger woman mumbled behind the newspaper, wishing the silly old woman in the lilac suit that smelt of mothballs would disappear. Why was it that some people had to strike up conversations when travelling? And she always seemed to be stuck with the most garrulous of them, who seemed to be unaware of her body language saying 'get lost'.

She crossed her legs and continued hiding behind her newspaper, pretending to read. But instead she watched the changing landscape: the large hills with the telegraph poles dotted along so symmetrically had vanished, and now the land was flat and marshy and seemed so damp underfoot. Such a sodden miserable country, she thought, full of old miseries like this clump of lilac in front of her.

The old woman fidgeted in her seat, took off her hat and put it onto the table.

'Is it alright if I spread myself out a bit, dear? So many parcels and things you see.'

Her dentures were ill-fitting and seemed to move about in her mouth when she spoke, while the reek of whisky was breathed onto Carol's 'Woman's Page'.

Carol half – wanted to laugh at this grotesque image in front of her. Any other day she would have found her mildly amusing, but not today.

She smiled back at the old woman – or was it more of a snarl?

'That's alright,' she muttered, avoiding her eyes; and wished that the woman would go to sleep or something – and hopefully not snore!

The muscle at the side of her face began to twitch again, faintly at first, and then it jarred and felt like an enormous spasm in her cheek.

'Have you been somewhere nice, dear?'

Oh shit! It had begun. Not only was her face twitching but this stupid woman was going to start up the travel talk she loathed! She obviously could not understand body language. For all to see – enormous quaking, twitching face included – she way saying: 'No language spoken here – English or otherwise!'

Undeterred the woman droned on: a lilac-coated, click-mouthed, moth-balled, whisky-breathed (and now as Carol looked at her) a reptilian-faced creature. She had never seen so many lines on another face, or one so much like darkly-tanned leather.

The woman caught her eyes and tried to hold them fast, but Carol would have none of it and looked fixedly at her lap. The woman's eyes were greenish-grey, very pale, almost like the water she had looked down at again and again when she stood on the canal bridge.

'You look very tired, dear.'

Carol shrugged, holding the newspaper more tightly, willing the woman to look away from her. Watch the scenery or something; go to the buffet car or something, but stop staring at her!

'It must seem strange, seeing me with all those bags. You know, I was at an old friend's funeral today. We'd known each other for oh so many years, were sweet-hearts once. Then he got himself married forty, no nearer fifty years ago. His wife was there today. Never liked her much. She never liked me either, was jealous I suppose. Walter and I had a <u>lovely</u> friendship, for all those years. And then I went shopping, bought a few bottles and decided to have a tiny celebration to see Walter on his way. He would've wanted that – a proper wake so to speak.'

Carol heard her, but could not, did not want to listen. What had a dithery old woman like her have to say that was worthwhile?

She stared out of the window at the specks of sheep clustered upon the grey-green fields, the quagmire fields, and the grey drab sky. Pathetic fallacy indeed, pathetic . . . pathetic Carol. Couldn't even do the deed, couldn't even muster the courage to speak to her. Instead she had walked around the town, being bruised by bustling weekend shoppers; had walked aimlessly, aware of nothing but her unhappiness.

She had stood for God knows how long on the bridge looking down at the grey-green water that stank of sewage, and for a time wanted to jump in. A last dramatic gesture! But instead, she had stood, cold and rigid and alone, until four o'clock and the train back home.

She did not have the guts to knock her door, as she had planned. It had seemed so easy, meticulously timed, as a management assignment. But she could not talk to her, could not bear to look at her again.

'Would you like a little bit of my whisky, dear? Just to keep out the cold.'

Carol nodded and took the perspex glass full of whisky. She bolted it down. The whisky hit her empty stomach and she immediately felt sick. Her face stopped twitching, but her head swirled and the sheep and the cows and the pylons melded into a grey mass of nothingness. . . .

When she opened her eyes again, she realised that she must have been asleep for some time.

The old lady stared at her with a benevolent grin.

'You must've needed your rest, dear. Had a fraught day?'

The woman handed her another glass and Carol quickly gulped it down. She nodded back. Part of her wanted to talk to this old dear, who seemed rather kindly – wise, even.

'Yeh,' she muttered, 'I went to town first thing this morning. Had everything meticulously planned, to the last second. Then missed my chance.'

'Was it the sales, dear? Wanted to buy something special?'

'Somethin' like that.' She gulped down another glass of whisky. 'I wanted to. . . .'

But the words would not come out, and her stomach heaved at the thought of telling this dear, kindly lilac – covered lady the truth. How could she tell her that she went to town wanting to shoot the girl in cold blood, if only she'd had a gun? Strangle the pretty bitch's neck, bruise and suffocate her. She'd wanted to shout at her, curse the tight skirts and high heels. Tell her she was a whore for stealing Michael from her.

But no, she couldn't even knock at her door, couldn't find the courage to stand on the doorstep and speak her thoughts aloud in low measured tones – let alone scream and shout abusively. She didn't dare send a letter of hate and sneak it anonymously through her letter box. Too spine-less to do that.

All she could do was stand on the other side of the street staring at her bedroom window. She wondered if Michael was lying in bed with her, whispering the same words of undying love he had said to her.

Carol opened the 'Guardian', hid behind the Supplement, and let the scotch seep into her brain. She wanted to forget the cruel embarrassment of that day.

The train jerked into High Burnside Station and Carol awoke bleary-eyed. She was aware of tears lying undisturbed on her cheeks and removed them discretely with her hand.

The old woman had already left her seat. Carol watched her stagger down the corridor, her carrier bags clanging against the carriage seats.

She heard someone laugh, then a woman called out in a high-pitched voice, 'Rather too much to drink.'

'Not nice to see,' another remarked.

'Don't expect in a woman of her age!'

Carol heard her own voice respond, far-distant and rather slurred, 'She was a lovely old dear. Has far more character than any of you lot.'

Carol sat back in her seat. The train moved off slowly. The old woman stood uneasily on the platform, looking vaguely at the train she had left. Carol waved to her, but the old lady did not see her. A young man had taken her by the arm as she staggered on the platform. He could have been her grandson, or a porter, or just another stranger.

The train struggled to gather speed and left High Burnside. In the distance Carol could just make out the lilac figure struggling into a taxi. She seemed so frail and vulnerable to her now.

Road to Rannoch

Margaret Gillies Brown

Take the road
From Coshieville to Rannoch.
Schiehallion under cloud in autumn.
Take wilderness and water;
Narrow winding from nowhere to nowhere.

Take colour, colour, colour,
Deepened by wet,
Rich breathing tapestry:
Artist, take blending,
Match it if you can—
Bracken-brown to yellow fern tip
Springing on leaves, shading to gold, orange, red
And its pure essence in rowans hanging earthward.
Miss a beat of colour – jump
To lacquer-black in elderberries.

Take pattern imposed on pattern.
Leaf shape on branch,
Branch angle on trees
Trees against a rising patchwork
To where high-hill-ridges
Are irregular moving shapes
Against flying ragged grey.

Take contrast intricate as the universe.
Bright limned against dark
Yet always making a whole
No falseness anywhere
See these distant sheep,
Pale as river pearls!
Look up at the dark, dying heather
Marked by streaking silver
Like an ageing woman's hair.

Lower, black peat pools
Hide in tawny reeds
And grey sheets of water
Watch cushions of moss
Sphagnum-green as elf-light,
Under the trees the forest carpet
Takes the colour of pheasant's wings.

The cloud is broken,
From the gold pocket
A shaft of sunlight drops—
Glory, glory, glory . . .

I'm thrown above Schiehallion.

Autumn in Weem

Mary Rea

The tree clad Rock transforms
From subtle shades of green
To rowan's leaves of flame
And birch's silvery sheen.
Dark purple bramble lines the path
Contrasting with the purest white
Of snowberry on slender stems
And red rose hips so bright.
The castle's stark grey silhouette
Hides in a misty stole,
And all around are golden fields
Alive with mouse and vole.
While high above on slender branch
The agile squirrel sways,
Seeking out the beech nuts
To gnaw on winter days.

John F. Petrie

Leaves begin to fall—
Catch a few as they flutter by,
Discarded from Septembering frame,
Only to feel them crumple
In over-eager hand.

A boundless prospect—
Strong and full of promise—
Has somehow been encased
In the violet of cloud
As evening approaches.

The tree stands, with arms outstretched,
Of wisdom, kindess, humanity,
The growth of many years,
But pointing to the enclosing
Hollow of the west.

Tehre is time, the wind whispers,
For a last sunburst
Of simple, brilliant fire,
Burning up and up
As if never to set.

The Old House

Jane Higgins

The Old House we call it. Not because it is particularly old, (though it is), but because it's the opposite of our new house – a modern semi occupied only by myself, my parents and my older brother.

It's not often that we speak of the Old House. On the rare occasions when we do, my brother and I talk in muted whispers, as though afraid that THEY might be eavesdropping at the windows or in the hallway. They're not, of course. We left them in the Old House. They couldn't come with us because the Old House is their home, always was and always will be.

I can't tell you when we first saw them, except to say we were very young. Young enough to nod politely at their unexpected arrival and return their gentle smiles, without questioning what right they had to wander through OUR bedrooms in the dead of night. They were adults, you see. They never spoke, of course, but you could tell they were the true occupants and we were, well . . . guests. They didn't mind us being there, or if they did, they never let on. At least their smiles seemed to indicate that we were welcome.

I remember the Lady most of all. Her long black dress swept the floor as she moved soundlessly across the room. Her hair was tied back, though not severely, and on her head she wore a quaint little black bonnet with white lace trim. Most fascinating was the lamp she carried, which flickered and glowed in the darkness, accentuating her soft features and Mona Lisa smile. Night after night, I'd lie awake and watch her gracefully cross the room until she reached the window. There she would stop, hold the lamp aloft and gaze sadly down to the front yard. What was she looking at? Was she waiting for someone? What could be so interesting down there in the middle of the night? She would stay there for hours, never flinching or moving, though sometimes emitting a long sigh as though her very heart was breaking.

One night, curiosity overcame my tiredness and irritability at being woken up yet again and I decided to see for myself what the front yard attraction might be. No sooner had I sat up and touched the covers to pull them back, making a slight rustling noise, when she turned and I was bathed in her wonderful hypnotic gaze. Instantly I was filled with joy that not only could she see me, she had responded! (Before this, despite numerous childish antics to raise a reaction from her and the others, they had totally ignored us. My brother and I, fed up with the lack of response, soon tired of our teasing and retaliated by going tit-for-tat, ignoring them too!)

There was no mistaking that the Lady was acknowledging my existence now, but still she did not say a word. Instead, she began her slow walk across the room. At the foot of my bed, she paused and turned to face me. Helped by the lamplight, I could now see her features clearly. The dark eyes danced and twinkled and laughed. She held the lamp higher, as though inviting me to look closer, and I was pleased to see she was as pretty as her silhouette had suggested; her skin smooth and glowing, her features like porcelain on a china doll. At her throat was the most exquisite cameo brooch I have ever seen, and even as I noticed it, she lifted her left hand and lightly tapped it with her forefinger. Then she smiled as if to say thank-you for complimenting her on it. She could read my mind! She was a wonderful lady! I beamed my admiration.

Suddenly, she frowned and stared at the mussed-up covers, which I promptly straightened, as an over-anxious child might to please a fussy parent.

When I looked again, she was still there, the same loving smile pinned on her lips. Next, she did the strangest thing. She nodded towards the tidied covers as if to say, "That's better." Then she turned and walked across the room to the farthest wall and, ignoring its solid mason built bricks of over a century before, continued straight through it.

The next morning, overcome with excitement, I woke my brother and told him how the Lady had paused to smile and talk. Well, sort of. He wasn't impressed.

"But they don't speak," he retorted angrily, "and they can't even see us. You're a liar!"

My brother can be a bit of a bully, especially if he thinks someone (me) is making up tales to wind him up. So it's hardly surprising that I chose not to continue our conversation. But I desperately needed to tell someone about the Lady. She was so wonderful that I just couldn't keep her a secret.

Dad was in the living-room, relaxing in an armchair, a cup of tea in one hand, a cigar in the other. He stared ashen-faced as I recounted the previous night's events. "You were dreaming, " he spluttered, although I could tell from his panic-stricken manner that he no more believed this than I did.

"No, I wasn't," I answered matter-of-factly. "The Lady woke me up. She's so pretty, Daddy. Who is she?"

"That's enough!" he shouted, bolting upright so that the tea slopped over his white shirt. "Go to your room and don't come downstairs until you can talk sense!"

It was unusual for my father to raise his voice to us children. Even when we interrupted his Saturday afternoon cowboy films by giggling, arguing or fighting with each other, he would simply throw some coins and say, "Here! Away outside and play." The ensuing scramble was over in seconds and, delighted with the bribe, we would run to the corner shop hand in hand, anticipating liquorice sticks and halfpenny chews.

Now, shocked at his manner, I burst into tears before running upstairs and flopping onto my unmade bed. My brother, suddenly an ally, showed some concern.

"No-one believes me! No-one believes me!" I shouted at him through tears. "The Lady did talk to me. She did!"

"I believe you," he replied, "but you shouldn't have told Dad."

I stopped crying. 'Why not?"

"You know why. He's a grown-up."

"Don't grown-ups see them, then?"

He shrugged. "Suppose they must . . . but they don't ever talk about them."

We were not a particularly religious family. The total extent of our bible tuition consisted of packing us children off to Sunday School (conveniently the church was next door) to give Mum an hour's peace on Sunday mornings.

But that evening, just after I had gone to bed, Dad came into my room carrying a huge framed picture of Christ. Jesus' startlingly blue eyes gazed heavenward and red blood oozed from under the crown of thorns. His hands, also dripping blood, were clasped in prayer.

Dad placed the picture upright on the tallboy, where it filled the entire wallspace behind, dominating the room by its very presence.

"There," he said, winking at me. "You won't have any more bother, all right?"

Not quite sure what he meant, but sensing that it had something to do with the Lady. I nodded. At least, he wasn't angry with me any more.

If the Lady did appear that night, she must have been very quiet, because I slept soundly until morning. In fact the next few weeks passed without incident and we decided that the Lady couldn't have been a very good person after all, because it seemed that the picture of Jesus had scared her away.

But one night, I was awakened by my brother shaking me roughly.

"Wake up! Wake up!" he whispered. "They've come back. Come and see."

Sleepily I let him drag me into his bedroom. It was dark in there and I instinctively reached for the electric light switch.

"No, don't!" my brother warned. "Over there, in the corner. D'you see them?

I peered through the darkness. There were two figures, a man and a woman. At first I thought my Lady had returned, for she wore the same long flowing style of dress. But, as I looked closer, I felt disappointment well up inside. It wasn't her! The distinctive hat was gone and this woman was younger, not much more than a girl really. Her blonde hair was tied in ribbons at the back, where it fell in short ringlets. She had her back to us, and so far had not the slightest notion that she was being observed. Her behaviour was far from the serene demeanour of the Lady, for at this moment she was gesticulating wildly at a tall well-dressed gentleman whom she had trapped in the corner of the room. The man raised his arms to defend himself, an unnecessary action because the young lady was not striking him, but flailing in a display of temper for which I would have had to forfeit three weeks pocket money!

The gentleman's lips moved, and although no sound was heard, we surmised that he was begging her to control herself. This seemed to annoy the young lady even more, and he edged around her looking for an escape. He was thin of stature and below his long nose was a spindly moustache which curled slightly at the edges. His dark hair was neatly parted and plastered so tightly to his head that it could have been painted on.

Suddenly he pushed past her. Immediately, she grabbed his arm, only for him to pull it quickly away, whereupon she dropped to the floor. My brother and I pressed our backs to the wall to make room for the gentleman, who strode past us out of the room.

My sympathies lay with the strange lady. Did he push her? Or did she fall? I wasn't sure, but finally decided that it was an accident. If she hadn't been holding on so tightly, he wouldn't have jerked his arm and she wouldn't have got hurt. Now, she lay motionless except for the pretty blonde ringlets which bobbed up and down on her shoulders with each silent sob.

The room flooded with light from the hallway. Footsteps pounded up the stairs. "I'm warning you, get back to bed this minute!" It was Mum.

Forgetting the wretched young women on the floor, we raced back to our respective beds, pulled the covers over our heads and pretended to be asleep.

Thinking back now, I suspect that for most of the time, we slept peacefully through the silent nightly dramas and the apparitions were never visible during the day. But that didn't mean they weren't around.

One wet afternoon, I was playing in my room alone when the huge oak wardrobe suddenly gave a deafening creak. I looked up just in time to see it wobble and then tilt. There was no time to call for help or do anything, except reach out in a futile attempt to stop its massive weight from crushing me. Of course, it was far too heavy for my skinny arms to have much effect and, as its angle to the floor narrowed, I realised my only hope was to race out of the way while it crashed to the floor, or through it as the case might be!

During the split second that I stopped pushing and prepared to run, the wardrobe effortlessly pulled itself back to an upright position – a feat which would have tired at least four strong men because it had been perilously close to the floor.

I breathed a sigh of relief, closely followed by the realisation that I was not alone after all. Someone, or something, was in the room with me. And he, she or it, was infinitely powerful although, at this moment, invisible. I found myself filled with bewilderment and fear. I should be dead, or at the very least should have suffered a broken limb or two. Wardrobes do not spring from an almost prone position to upright by themselves, do they?

Now, on our way to school, my brother and I hurry past the Old House. Often, we get the oddest feeling that we are being watched.

Early Snowfall – Ben Lawers

Judith Young

The burns clown down the slopes,
tumbling and cartwheeling into the glen.
Birches in mustard-yellow uniform
sweep towards the meadows
swaying to the wind's razzmatazz.
Balanced on the sleek black back of the river
equestrienne reflections show off their skills,
as elephantine clouds, with trunk to tail,
process across the sky,
and crow trapezists swing through the gale.

The old mountain ring-masters the performance,
Smooth in a shadowy-purple suit
And sporting a white top hat.

And on the hills below the rutting stags
rise to bellow their applause.

Travelling Home

Rhona Johnstone

Twin beams of light pierce the gentle dark
The last gold slips beneath the hill:
The grey-white wings of suicidal moths
Swoop and flutter their snowflake way
Against the windscreen. Two pairs of eyes
Glow in the roadside woods – the roe deer
Stand fearfully, silently still.
Bare branches hold the remnant of autumn;
Red, gold and russet long gone—
The dead leaves silvered with early frost
Lie damply brown on the forest floor.

Now the pinprick stars appear,
The planets in their courses move
Against the smoothly velvet dark
Of the boundless infinity beyond.
I glimpse the silvery sickle moon
Through the tracery of birch and beech;
The road in front beckons me on,
The lighted windows call me home.

The Tattie Pickers

Grant Cameron

The sun glinted off
the Celtic cross.
October eyes peeping
behind the quiet
quilt of sleep.

Tatties awakened
by rubber-backed youths.
They made a brae
on a hungry bogie.
Wheeled hooves stagger
and stumble on dirty tracks.
Flamboyant hillside watching
the motorised desecration.

Folding filthy field
stretching to the Tay,
they picked on a corner
till teabreak.

The youngsters attacked
each other
with rotten spuds,
tattie baskets as shields.

In the exhausted darkening,
thoughts of a bath and bed.
Twenty hands strangled
bags of Golden Wonder.

The Dull cross distantly still.

Buchanty Spout, October

Margaret Gillies Brown

Nature's tremendous forces,
Swollen water the colour of beer froth
tumbling down cascades,
Silk liquid's might
Against a turmoil of astonishing fish
Determined to reach up-river,
Spring's calm spawning beds.

No dolphin-playtime here
They leap from the boiling pool
Curved, trembling, tail-swishing,
To sidewind, somersault, sunburst back
To where they leapt from.

Thunder backed, roseate bellied—
Colours echoed in wet rock they thrash
Nothing discourages.
Assault after assault
Against the watery garrison,
Leap after glorious leap
Big, small in equal effort.

No code within the blueprint
Says wait till the waters calm.
Spawning calls.
Bruce's spider in the cave
Pales to insignificance.

Above, the Chestnut's yellow fingers stretching down
Spread brilliance from leaf and sun
Below, moss strewn rocks burn green.

Hallowe'en

Kenneth C. Steven

Once upon a time our honeyed lanterns
Went in pendulums along these roads;
Faces were haunted with pondweed green
Heads steepled with wizards' hats,

All October the rivers' drums had beaten
Thick to a flashing white. Now late in autumn
The final fires died out among the trees
And bled the land to broken grey.

That night smelled of chestnuts and cold stars
Breath smoked our whispers, groups of witches
Spooked us at corners and howled our backs—
Clattered behind till our chests caught fire.

We rapped at homes along the straggled roads
Sang jaggedly our songs, remembered bits of verse
Then crumbled, broken down in mirth. Yet still we left
With shiver-green apples, copper hands of coins.

Now televisions murder all night long
Their luminous blue tanks light up each window
And no-one anymore will ghost these roads
For Hallowe'en.

Bridge over the Tracks, Gleneagles Station

Robin Bell

On the bridge today he crossed my mind again,
the local soldier whom I never met.
All I know about him is one thing he's done;
hurrying home, he stumbled with his gun
and blew a round hole in the green parapet
while down below his comrades in the train

laughed and waved at his clumsy coming home.
I first saw his landmark when I was three.
My father held me up and I peeped through
the splintered cladding to the rails below.
One day I grew tall enough to see
without being held. 'You've grown!' 'Of course I've grown.'

Later the bullet hole became chest high
then stayed at the level of my suitcase hand.
To and from London, to and from New York,
between my homes, it was my first landmark.
Last year they stripped the cladding, let the girders stand
criss-crossed and naked. The smallest child can see

the diesels curving smokeless through the trees:
no need to shield Sunday coats from the hot hail
of chugging cinders from the old steam trains.
But, on the open bridge, the hole remains,
fixed more securely than its lost green wall,
measuring its existence against me.

Dust with Everything

Donald Smith

I've had a colour amputated. Does that sound daft? Well, put yourself in my place for a while. The Arabian desert is a colourful place. Forty shades of khaki! In Hindustani, khaki means 'dust coloured'. How right! Those British troops, marching across the deserts of India, South Africa and the Sudan got to know a lot about khaki. They too, probably, felt there was a colour missing from their lives – green!

The wind blows. It doesn't bring coolness. It raises the dust into khaki clouds of grit. It pours through the flap of the tent like a mixed shower of salt and pepper. I shut my eyes and think of the green of the Pentland hills. The curving hill tops. The shades of pasture green melting into the woodlands.

The Arabian sky is blue, when it's not grey with cloud or brown with high-blown dust. The eyes blur with the brightness or squint against the abrasive dust. Nothing here to compare with cloud driven skies and the green sloping farms of Fife running to meet the sea.

The tanks and trucks are painted a bilious khaki-yellow. They churn up dust that sticks to sweaty skin. Never mind, think of driving through the green trees of Glen Isla on a summer's day with cool breezes through the car. Green reeds standing in the trickling burn. Then strolling, with the sound of rushing water all around.

"Water! Hold it. Measure it! Treasure it! You've got to make it last. Pretend you're a small boy again and you don't want to wash or bath! Have a sip to quench your thirst. Then clean your teeth – you'll feel better then. Don't spit it away – use it to shave. You'll have enough left over for a bath – with a damp rag – be quick before it dries hard!"

Think of Dunkeld's Hermitage – roaring water beneath soaring green trees. The Falls of Dochart. The Birks of Aberfeldy. Reekie Lynn. Buchanty Spout where the salmon scud and wriggle over the rocks. Spray, rushing water and trees, green trees.

The Sergeant-Major's stubble head of hair is red. His face is red. It goes even redder when he shouts. He comes from Auchmithie just beyond Arbroath. In spring, he tells us, the green rounded cliff tops are covered with primroses. I often wonder if he thinks of them between his sharp attention to orders.

Small boats come in at Auchmithie's ancient harbour. They take their catches up the hill to a hotel which specialises in marvellous crab salads. And up the road there's a restaurant called the But 'n Ben with home cooked cakes for tea. And all around the green of the fields.

It's 'All Clear' – some of the lads are having fun kicking a ball across a flattened strip of land. Not a blade of grass in sight. One can think of the pitches of Perth, North Inch and South Inch – goal posts standing in the greenest of greens stretching down to the Tay.

A camel train passes. The beasts follow each other, hitched in line. Great bulging sacks of produce hang on either side. On the leading camel the drover peers from the hood of his burnoose, huddling against the dust rising from the line of hoofs. Other animals are attended by small boys who shout obscenities at the troops. Strange how quickly they collect the worst elements of a foreign tongue.

The boys wield long canes – prodding and slashing at the camels as they go. Needful – or just habit? No RSPCA here to limit loads and regulate camel welfare.

Scorpions come in yellow, brown and black. Boots make an excellent overnight hiding place. We bang the heels hard on the ground and give them a shake before venturing to put them on. Hornets come in yellow and black stripes – not my favourite team colours. Flies come by day in hundreds – ravenous for any moisture to be sucked from animal or human eyes or lips. By night, sandflies come in their hordes. Tiny flying electric drills, boring at the skin. Did we really complain about the midges along those damp, green, grassy lochsides when hoping for a fish to rise?

Trudge through yielding sand. Heat and dust. Think of green paths leading through the bracken. Gentle turf, close cropped by black faced sheep. On higher ground the heather preparing its purple glory for the late summer days. Forest plantations following the line of the hills. Are there still song birds, hoody crows, geese and waders crowding inland lochs? How everything revels in those shades of green.

Shovels out. Dig in, dig in! Dig in, to survive. Sand trickles back into the hold. Bunkered on the Old Course at St Andrews? This is one great sandy bunker the size of Scotland! No fairways leading to the greens – greens marked only by the gentle lines of the mower and not a daisy daring to show its head. Sea washed sand alongside the green of the links – clean and fresh. Not like this khaki stuff, waiting for a rare winter downpour to congeal into clinging mud.

Midday. Sun overhead. Hat brim shading the feet. What a scorcher! The eyes are seared. Everything is dust and khaki. Khaki and dust – it's all the same. Brown near at hand. Shading into faded yellowness over the flatness of the miles. Whirling columns of dust race across the desert. Wind stirred by rising heat from roasting rocks. Dust in clothes, dust in boots, dust in eyes, dust in food, dust – dust! Where had it gone, that green?

Then, shimmering, the mirage. Floating above the floor of the desert. The sweep of hills, trees, green slopes, the glint of peaceful lochsides. We know it's just a curved vision of the Euphrates with its date plantations. The mind plays tricks with the eyes. It could be Loch Rannoch. Someone once said – 'There are no atheists in a foxhole.' So please God, in your time, may we come home to 'Scotland the green'.

The Soldier's Grave, Glenderby

Anon

He fell not fair on Flodden's field
With trumpet's tooraloo,
But capercaillie's corn-crake cry
And call of lone curlew.
This shelter'd glen reeks not of men
Nor of their dreadul deeds;
So, better here, with no one near
But God and his vast view.
Long may he rest on Nature's breast;
His spirit need not die.
He gave his life for other's gain
Who knew not how or why.

Goodbye Autumn

Julia Rasmussen

As the wind blew I felt like ice.
I felt miserable.
Mist swirled the sun in a dull sky.
I looked at Maria.
She was breathing mist!
Rain dripped on to a paper bag.
Birds swooped in the sky,
screeching at the mist.
Smoke rose from house chimneys.
They had nice fires
While I froze!
I could only see half of the hills
And I thought
They will soon be covered with snow!

Autumn Versus Winter

Maria Rasmussen

A prowling cloud of mist is settling on the world.
The sun is shut behind the clouds.
I feel the mist dew on my head.
I smell the scent of snow!
I hear the trees whispering
their secrets in the heavy damp air.
They stand almost bare and sad.
The sky and the weather are heavy with mist.
I feel grey and dull.
The King of Mystery has Amulree in his power.
I breathe clouds of smoke.
Birds call to each other in high voices.
Sheep huddle together to keep warm.
Plants are so still as if by a magic spell.
This is King Mystery's fun day.

Eilidh Fearn

In winter the snow falls down,
and the place is all white,
the countryside is covered.
Like your winter coat,
the land has its winter coat,
like icing on cakes.

In winter there's Christmas,
You get your socks out,
for Santa Claus to fill up.
Holly is brought in
From the cold winds outside
With bright red berries.

Some animals hibernate
Others are hunting,
But I'm in my cosy bed,
Waiting for morning.
Soon the snow will melt away.
Winter will be gone.

Siobhan Sewell

People hurrying around doing Christmas shopping.
Earth freezing in the cold bitter wind.
Red yellow and golden leaves falling off the trees
The River Tay cold and choppy.
High hills capped with snow.

Icy roads becoming dangerous.
Numb fingers biting with the cold.

Balloonists balloons bursting with colour.
Lightning strikes the wetness of winter.
Orange leaves being blown in the wood.
On the Tay ripples appear.
Moon and stars light up the sky.

Into The Highlands

David Kennedy

Proud and serene stands the red deer stag
Against the snowy outline of hills.
Head erect, eyes alert,
It looks and listens for movement.

The herd graze peacefully,
hinds with their last year's calves,
But still the stag, antlers held high
Stands and watches and listens.

The herd graze among the heather,
still no sign of young leaves and shoots.
Calves resting safely amongst the bracken,
oblivious to any dangers.

Suddenly, nostrils snorting
the red deer stag senses danger,
the herd takes to their heels,
and disappear over the horizon.

Proud and serene the scene.
Snow covered mountains and an empty glen,
all is quiet again,
no deer to be seen.

Snowflakes On Loch Earn

Andrew Brock

The first snowflakes of winter
kissed the surface of Loch Earn.
Trees trembled, naked, but for a few russet leaves—
an icy blast sent another wave ashore.

Clouds engulfed rusty tinged hillsides.
The silence stirred briefly, by en eerie stag's call.
An isolated boat huddled by its moorings—
as snow, heavy, began to fall.

A female birch shrugged flakes from a branch.
The robin called to shelter
In the empty silence, dusk followed dawn—
A white blanket draped over St. Fillans.

Summer long gone.

The Late Year

Kenneth C. Steven

The day is a long dusk
Geese clamour through heavy air
Thick and breathless mists.

The chestnuts are all down
Boys shuffle the leaves at first light
Find polished mahoganies beneath their feet.

Over the valley
Water lights shine out like cries from farms—
Islands of flood.

The skies are thrashing with gale
Trees far across the fields sweep and flow
Their leaves dancing.

At night the roots of the house creak and sway
Like anchors in deep water—
The moon rushes through fast skies.

In the end trees stand on the hill's rim
Windless and desolate
Like prisoners condemned to death.

Firth of Tay

Joy Hendry

This river spews mist out.
Deep below some demented stoker
fuels the fires
from an eternal furnace of spite . . .
Cold November and the rime
sharp as acid
sets sail down the Tay.
Breathe in and it strikes your lungs
like broken glass;
breathe out and it captures
your warm white gusts
snaps shut the padlock
sweeps your life up and off
down the bend of the river
like lava in spate.

You can do nothing to stop it.
Above, Kinnoull Tower
crumbles,
an indifferent sentinel,
and Perthshire slumbers on.
Yes, souls are in danger here.

Retour

Jean Massie

As I staun here, whar aince ma faither stuid,
Whan wark, for him, was done.
He'd husbanded thae fields ye see,
For fifty years, nie on.

Peesies win on their daft like flicht abune the haugh,
Fae whar he brocht their eggs
Tucked in the front o his bunnet,
Tae be biled as trait for oor tea.

Geese are grazin, as they hae done ilka winter,
Doon aside the loch,
Skreichin an steirin noo,
In readiness for that lang unco journey.

Did he wiss, tae, for ither lans
As he set aboot his darg?
In perfeck rhythm wi his horse
Or broadcastin seeds bi haun.

Tho I hae traivelled far awa
Tae some o thae distant lans,
Like the geese bi some byorner birr retour
Tae staun again, whar aince ma faither stuid.

On the Outside

Carol Burgess

God, they're despicable! Just look at them all sitting there, inside in the warm, laughing and talking as if any of them had anything at all interesting to say. Pretending they can't see me. I can see them looking out of the corners of their eyes.

There's that damn clock chiming again. Ten o'clock this time. Every time I look up at it that tower seems higher. Must be a trick of the light. The moon looks funny tonight too. All sort of fat-bottomed, just hanging there as if it didn't have anything better to do. The old boy up there will be having a good laugh at me down here I bet, thinking to himself, 'What's that daft bugger doing down there, ranting and raving to himself?'

'When one door closes another one opens.' That's what folk say. Just let any fool try saying it to me again and I'll give him doors.

What's happening in there now. It looks so bright and cosy. I like the checked tablecloths and the candles on the tables. Look at all those miserable bastards in there though; what a bunch of happy diners. Stuffing their faces with that 'nouvelle cuisine' crap! I can just hear them; 'Oh Clive, you're so clever. The duck terrine is just divine!" Two spoonfuls of congealed fat and half a tomato, what a treat.

I used to eat in places like that, it was on the expense account. I didn't mind still being starving when I finished because I knew I could get a good blow-out when I got home. Always something tasty in the fridge. Maybe they do that too, go home and pig-out!

Window's getting a bit cloudy. Must be getting warmer in there. Or colder out here. Maybe if I put my hands up to my eyes, and press right up against the glass – there, that's better.

Ho-ho! Wouldn't need to be a lip reader to know what they were saying now! See the look on that one's face. Looks like she stood in dogshite! Oh, the husband's getting Clive over. Bet I know what he's saying.

Thought so; he's pointing at me. "Oh Clive, can't you do something about that unpleasant little man outside? He's scaring Geraldine, and quite frankly he's putting me off my de foi gras!"

Arsehole.

They don't have to worry about me, I'm only looking. What do they think I'm going to do?

That was bad luck earlier. I probably got Fat Charlie into trouble. He's okay, Charlie. Some of the cooks in places like that act like they own the place, but he always gives me good grub. Good parcel tonight. Nice little bit of steak, and the bread was dead fresh. Liked that cheese too, Cambazola I think. Only thing I'd complain about is the apples, wish he'd make it an orange for a change. Still, that's not much to moan about.

Hope I didn't get him into too much trouble. I should have gone when he said, but it was nice and warm by the cooker, and he's good company, a right laugh!

"Go on, eat up and bugger off before Clive gets in." He doesn't like him either, but I suppose a job's a job.

It would have been funny if not for Charlie! That Clive's face when he came in and saw me! Couldn't have looked any more horrified if I'd been the Environmental man!

"Get out of my kitchen you filthy man!" The way he came flapping across at me, shushing at me like that. Like I was a cat peeing on the carpet.

BASTARD! Bastard. Am I filthy? Not filthy. Could do with a shave, but I washed at the Shelter yesterday. I suppose it's the coat. It is manky, but what am I gonna do? Get it drycleaned? And wear what in the meantime?

How dare he push me? I was going to go. Was a bit shocked actually. Sometimes I forget; think I'm just normal. It's always easier when you're with somebody like Charlie that just treats you like anybody else. I think he quite likes me actually. Probably since I told him about Anna. He's always going on about his Dawn, makes out she's a nag, but I think it's just because he doesn't know if it makes me feel bad when he talks about home and stuff. It's funny. Some people get all guilty when they talk to you, as if you hold them personally responsible for them having good luck.

I don't feel like that. Wish I did in a way, it would be good to have someone to blame for all this, but really I don't think any more about their good luck than most of them do about my bad.

Anna and me was just something that happened a long time ago. It was good when it was good. It WAS good. God, I remember that holiday in Cyprus in '74 . . .

No! I'm not starting all that. That's done.

He locked the door after me, the prick! As if I was going to come back in after that! I suppose he's seen all these documentaries about the homeless being mentally ill and deranged, and stabbing people at train stations! Don't suppose Clive could get his poofy little head round people like me once being people like him.

I could tell them how easy it is.

"All right class, tonight's lesson is on negative equity. Negative equity means that, when your marriage breaks up because your wife can't stand the sight of you any more and forces you to sell the house (that you spent every weekend for ten years Doing-it-Yourself in) so that she can make a new start, you actually find that you still owe the Building Society. Then because you fall behind with the re-payments they get your wages arrested, so you can't afford the rent for the poxy little flat you've taken, and the landlord evicts you.

"Next, because you are sleeping on friends couches all the time, you start turning up at work looking like something the cat dragged in, and your boss tells you to get your act together, or get out. Eventually he sacks you and there's nothing you can do about it because you just changed jobs and you haven't been there long enough to do him for unfair dismissal or anything.

And now you're dossing on your friends' couches all day too, and they are beginning to get right pissed off with you. And you don't want to fall out with them because they are good friends, and none of this is their fault, so you say it'll be okay, you'll stay in a bed and breakfast until you get yourself sorted out. They pretend that this is a good idea, and off you go. But the B&B put you out at 9.30 every morning, and you can't cook in your room so you spend all your money going to the afternoon matinee at the movies to keep warm, and eating McDonalds and Burger Kings, and you go to the Library to scour the papers for jobs, which you don't get because you look pretty shabby now that you can't afford to get your hair cut or buy new clothes.

"Then, one day, when you're sitting in the park, you see her with somebody else, and she looks great. You get so angry that you go over and start shouting at her, and the guy she's with whacks you one, and you land on the grass with your nose all bleeding, and you start to cry, and they walk away looking disgusted and she's saying "Drunk I suppose – he didn't used to be like that; I'm sorry, Donald". And you get up and wipe the snot and blood off your face, and think you might as well get drunk then, so you go and buy some whisky from the supermarket, and drink most of it in the park until it gets too dark, and you go back to the B&B. But they won't let you in because the rules say NO DRINKING – so you throw a stone through the window, and they call the police, and you get arrested and charged with breach of the peace, and fined. When you go back to the B&B they throw your stuff at you and tell you to get lost. Now you don't have any money left, or a permanent address, so you have to sign on No Fixed Abode daily, and the social services say it was your own fault and they've no obligation to you.

"That's how you end up on the street. All of a sudden you aren't worth anything anybody, it's hard to remember you used to be worth a lot to everybody."

Clive was yelling at Charlie after he locked the door. I couldn't hear everything, but I caught certain 'key words'. Sorry Charlie; I won't come again.

Better go. If I get to the Salvation Army place before half past I might get a bed. I'm quite tired tonight, it's been a long day.

Listen to me! Been a long day – as if tomorrow will be any shorter. Wonder where I'll get my evening meal now!

What harm was it doing you, Clive? A little bit of meat and a lump of crusty French bread, was that going to put you out of business? Did anyone see me in the kitchen? Was it putting anyone off their food having me sitting beside the cooker getting warm, and having a feed?

Not like it's putting them off now, having me here with my nose glued to the window, it wasn't.

Goodnight happy diners. Bon Appetit!

Winter Evening

Margaret Gillies Brown

In mellow notes
The church tower clock
Strikes seven;
The suppered village stirs.
Savoury smells of frying fish
Seep under the door
Of the corner shop
And herald its opening.
Opposite, under the dim lights
That keep the dark at bay,
A gang of boys and bikes
Gather and discuss
Football, girls, the insides of engines,
Take sudden bursts of energy
And boast on brumming bikes
Up, round the cross and down again
Or breenge across the road
To where Chippie Jean
Dispenses discipline, chips and sound advice
In equal portions.
Lassies saunter up in twos
To lean shoulders against
The cold Co-op wall
Legs out and near enough
To have their saucy sallies
Slung at the boys
Boomerang back.
Youth stands here on the kerb of life
Waiting:
The girls with patient eyes
For "Goodbye Joe – hallo Josephine",
The boys, for their eighteenth year
And walking through the portals
Into the pub and manhood.

At a safe distance from big brothers,
Littler laddies play at 'torchy:
Up black alleys,
In the shadows,
With springing step
On legs
That still would rather run than walk,

Transmit excitement
Electrify the air
With the mysteries
Of childhood and night
Until, from the meeting hut,
A giggle of Brownies
On dancing feet
Quickly trip
To the safety of the nest
The clock strikes ten
And closing time.
From the warm laughter
Of the snug and smokey bar
Old Ted topples.
For a moment
He and the wall collide
And then
On his brave recovery
Weaves widely home
To waiting tight-lipped Morag.
Next dark-haired Don
Steps out
Whistling a cheerful tune:
Right now for him it seems
The World's a glorious place,
The night's his oyster
As he makes with confident gait
For some unsuspecting sonsie Meg.
The half-closed door spits out the rest
In threes, in twos, in ones.
The cop car flashing red and white
Passes, flaunts up and round and down
But doesn't stop.

Rumblings erupt from the village hall;
Rural over for another week.
A gaggle of women bunch out
And stand in small groups
Talking of
Poor Mrs Speedy,
Jane's hacking cough
The wee one's grumbling teeth,

The scandalous price of butter,
Until icy fingers of frost
Cut through coats
And they hurry towards
Warm promise
Of their own firesides.

Soon only the yowling cat
Prowls the empty night
And the houses huddle
As the east wind
Snell and keen
Sweeps down the village street
And brushes it clean for tomorrow.

The Manse Wuid

Jean Massie

Cranreuch seeps intae the very banes
oan this sunless day.
White rimed gress crunches ablo the feet.
The island castle shows its face abune
laich-lyin mist. Cauld
hings i the air; ye maun smell it.
Leafless trees mak up thir ain pictuirs
alangside the burn
rinnin daurk an slow. The wicketie gait
creaks i the stillness. Canny owr the
skytie wuiden brig
noo. Weirdly atmosphere o the Manse
Wuid conjures visions o kelpies i
the boggy places anent
the gang. Holly an yew brainches hiv
tae be fetched fur Yuletide; gaitherin
the Pagan symbols
o a Christian Festival oan
the daurkest day o the year, wi thir
promises o lestin life an new yokins.

John F. Petrie

The road is white with cold dust of settled winter,
And jagged edge of broken wall, dead bush;
With ash despairing in ragged hopeless spears
Beside the bare hummocks of paltry grazings,
Swept by the smell of careless farming decay.

Here – a group of sad, ill-ordered huts
With scrabble door, rusting corrugate and detritus
From the casual care of random hand.

There – the glow of western sky of sea cloud
Making stark the rocks and shore-looped heads
Within the cold shimmer of still sea creek.

Between – in lack-lustre apology for being,
The village dribs and drabs, scurries and scuttles,
In grey, white and dirty wall around the bay.

Bruadairean a'Bhaile Bhriste

Grant Cameron

Fo d'chraiceann ghrànnda
paisgte eadar clachan
tha an nighean leam a'seinn
dhuanagan aosda d'a sinnsir

Cailleach phreasach na crùban
mar leanamh am machlag na h-eaglais.
A briatharan gan labhairt rithe fhèin
a'tilleadh.

Stìobullan, gun truas
a'dìreadh chun nan speuran.
Siridh iad aon neamh,
ligidh iad anail air a'ghealaich.

Calmain a'cogadh 'sa chiaradh
air bonn-uinneig a tha an diugh gun fheum
cùrtairean gan dùnadh mun timcheall
comharra nan coma.

Ach tha a' bhuaidh bheag againne na bhroinn
a chur nar cuimhne an saoghal
anns an robh thu uair
gad bhlianadh anns an t-solus lom.

Tha sinn a'còmhnaidh na bhroinn.
Nar n-ìomhaighean smalaicht'
a'caoineadh ar dearmaid.

Broken City Dream

Grant Cameron

Beneath your decadent skin,
tucked beneath stone,
my daughter sings
odes of old to ancestors.

A woman, wizened, crouches,
foetal in a church.
Her soliloquy rebounds
back to her.

Spires grow, mercilessly,
into the sky.
Searching for a heaven,
resting on the moon.

Pigeons fly in twilight
on an unused window sill,
curtains closing around them
reflecting indifference.

Our little conquests inside
to remind us of the world;
where once you were
bathing in naked light.

We dwell within.
Tarnished statues
weeping with neglect.

Christmas Candle

Irene Gunnion

Flickerin flame – wi yer hauntin shadow
Cast ower holly – an Christmas rose
Light up – like love
An gie me peace
In the quiet comin o this blessèd morn

Mesmerised A am – by ma christmas candle
Filled wi hope – at this solstice o year
Sic a magical moment—
Wi its unspoken words
Catches ma breath—
As it brings forth – a tear

Sculpture

Rosemary Bassett

A rough cool clay is in my hand
I turn it over and observe.
Deep inside it lies my heart,
my soul, my eye.
Totally aware of its potential life
I start to force the energy out.
The heat of hopeful hands,
reveals nothing.

My sticky butterfingers fold and
refold themselves over the softness.
There is a pleasure here,
an unutterable feeling to touch.
With almost a groan, a shiver,
I cut the captive spirit free.
I'm fascinated by the feet –
the sight that lingers in my mind.
The wind blows through the folds.
His cloak has breath at last.
I stand. I see. He's here.
The hermit in the cave.

The Best of Both Worlds

Myrtle Smith

The first sight of 'Order Your Turkey Now' and Christmas trees languishing outside the greengrocers was enough to set me off. I was not prepared for the acute attack of homesickness that clutched at my heart. It attacked the new life we were gradually building up for ourselves in Perth 450 miles away from our old home in England. I had preened myself on the fact that we had settled down pretty well and were beginning to integrate quite nicely. And so we were. But this, our first Scottish Christmas back in the early seventies, brought a sense of loss. We were used to a large gathering of relations and friends, warmed by the remembrance of ancient jokes and experiences of past Christmas Days we had shared. We had only lived in Scotland for three months, and although we had already made some friends, everyone had their own families with them for Christmas and we had no wish to intrude on such parties.

Christmas began when we went to the midnight service on Christmas Eve. The church was crowded. Even the galleries were full. Everybody was smiling, anticipating joys to come. We smiled too. The service brought its own particular magic to the night and as we walked out of the church, with a friendly handclasp from the Rector, Christmas was real and familiar and good.

Our Christmas dinner seemed strange and unreal. All the old familiar things of Christmas were about. The tree, the decorations, the turkey protesting quietly in the oven, the sprouts simmering, the pudding bubbling away. Our little family was all together. The table looked little too. There was no leaf pulled out of it, no extra table at the end, no side table for young ones. Just the four of us. But we were together and many families were not.

The unreality was heightened when, just as we were raising our glasses for a Christmas toast, we were transfixed by the sight of a man coming up the front path, bearing a sack. Father Christmas? No – the dustman. We looked at each other in amazement. On Christmas Day? In the south it would be emergency services only.

In the afternoon we walked in the hill country above Scone. Through the still air we could plainly hear carol tunes played on the church bells. Each leaf, each blade of grass was frosted, separate. A winter wonderland. The distant mountains were white-fringed and lovely. Smoke curled over Perth, the river snaked its way through the valley. A small flicker of pure joy kindled in our hearts. We were no holiday visitors, giving up this beauty to go home; we were home.

Next day, we could hardly believe the sight of shops, offices, banks all ablaze and bustling; the crowds eager to buy Christmas bargains in the sales, which somehow seemed a little earlier this year. Such a contrast to the sleepiness of an English Boxing Day.

The excitement built up towards the New Year. Laden trolleys were pushed round supermarkets as another frenzied round of shopping began. Greetings were exchanged, "See you at Alistair's", "We'll maybe drop in at Jeannie's first", "Dinna get too fou!". Excited children ran about, dodging round the precarious corner displays. Here then was the atmosphere, the good wishes, the excitement which I had felt strangely lacking before. It was Hogmanay which held pride of place to the Scots.

On New Year's Eve, the weather was fine and frosty again and the sun shone warmly in a brilliant blue sky. We had thought such a blue sky was only to be found on the calendars, but here was one. We took soup and sandwiches to Arbroath and walked across the cliffs. We revelled in the noisy drama of the sea boiling and foaming through the long rocky inlets. They were white-fringed too, not with snow this time, but the droppings of the sea-birds, weaving and circling above our heads, swooping down to catch in mid-flight the crusts we threw to them.

In ones and twos small boats were appearing. They were coming into the harbour. Coming home for Hogmanay. It seemed to be the whole fleet of fishing boats. Tomorrow their women would worry only over seeing their men fed; there would be no goodbyes that day. We went down to the quayside and watched the fish unloaded and auctioned straight away. Here we were, not an hour's journey from home, in this marvellous setting of the fishing harbour, quaint old town and the Abbey standing sentinel above. We had come for a short half-day in winter. To anyone having to rise early in order to cross London to reach the south coast on a day's outing, this was reason enough for living far from the old home. The deep flicker of joy burned brighter and more certainly.

We had an invitation for the early part of the evening to the home of some new Scots friends. Drinks, mince pies, shortbread and black bun. Black bun? To soak up the liquor we were told. Just as well, we thought! We saw the New Year in and then walked back home, stepping carefully on the frozen pavement. We met little groups of people out first-footing. They shook hands warmly and wished us a good New Year. It was a good start to our first New Year in Scotland. We too first-footed our neighbours and spent another pleasant couple of hours, getting to know all the people who dropped in on them. When we went to bed, we could still hear people walking about and calling out.

In the morning quietness had descended. We had never known such quietness. Our first Christmas and Hogmanay in Scotland were over. It had been a bitter-sweet time; heartache and happiness mingled, the stimulus and stuff of life. Next year we would know many more friends. Christmas would be real again to us English. Hogmanay would be real to us Scots. Truly we would have the best of both worlds.

Barrels

Rhona Johnstone

Demand must have fallen
At the whisky bottling plant
On the outskirts of town;
The redundant barrels are piled outside
A succession of circles
Set in a large triangle.
When the snow fell this winter
It outlined all the shapes—
Curve upon curve
Elipse upon elipse
Scimitars of white on the dark oak wood.

Taking on Mickey

Yvonne Pirie

An aged man is but a paltry thing,
A tattered coat upon a stick, unless
Soul clap its hands and sing, and louder sing
                    W.B. Yeats 'Sailing to Byzantium'

A cantankerous auld git, that's exactly whit he wis. Well, no' entirely, but for the worst part – almost all of nineteen ninety two – he wis just that; big chieftan o' the anti-smile brigade and him the size o tuppence ha' penny an' aw; a greetin' faced wee get.

It's ironic tae think I wis probably the catalyst o' my misfortune, me bein' his first foot that year. If only I hadnae been in my conscientious 'Florence Nightingale' frame o' mind, that fateful day, when I enthusiastically volounteered for home help emergency duty.

Surely tae god the gloom didnae suddenly descend wi' the new year mist o' that mornin'. It must have been lurkin', bleakly aroond fir the previous eighty six hogmanies, long afore I walked intae his life – ye just had tae visualise that pain cracked face o' his tae realise it.

I went through the 'a' the best fir ninety two' routine, sincerely. I mean he wis an auld man and widnae see many mair miserable years in. I brought a nice bit cake an' shortbread, shook his hand and wished him many mair happy . . . Oh god forbid!, the thought o' spendin' years in his company wis enough tae mak ye no weel. I must hiv been a glutton fir punishment or as short sichted as he wis. However, he assured me – withoot cheer – that he wis on the way oot, didnae want ma cake or shortie, tae tak them and masel hame, pronto, an' no' come back.

Ten minutes I'd been in bleak hoose an' I wis already resigned tae suicidal depression. I lost ma rag, telt the grumpy swine I'd stood fir an hoor in that draughty tenement close waitin' fir him. Frozen tae the bone, almost on the point of hypothermia an aw because he had decided – on the spur o the moment – tae discharge himsel' fae that comfortable geriatric ward; causin aw that bother on a guid new year's day.

The consequences o' his whim had reduced the health and social services budget considerably. An ambulance arranged just fir him!, and draggin' folk oot o' their beds tae service his needs on the mornin' efter the nicht afore! Oh whit a night that wis! Yer head's splittin' jist thinkin' aboot it; a damned nuisance! Whit an attitude . . . could he no' hiv shown some bloody gratitude tae aw the poor souls who hid tae pit up wi' aw that silly nonsense o' his.

He came oot o' that ambulance like a ravin' lunatic, refusin the medics' assistance and swearin' under his laboured breath at the damned contraption they'd gien him tae support his weak malnourished frame. It wis as though he thought the zimmer an' all of us present were mockin' his dependence or somethin' . . . He didnae even say thanks or cheerio tae the crew, jist bellowed a load o' bull at them afore they scurried awa back tae the depot fir a soothin' dram.

The reception I got when I went tae steady him an gie him a hand intae the hoose wis even less polite . . . 'Who the bloody hell are you?' It wis enough tae mak ye greet.

Mind you, the wee tear that fell fae his right eye intae his cup o' tea as he looked lovingly roond that dive o' a kitchen wis heart renderin'. Maybe I could get tae like him in time?. But would ma blood pressure stand the sicht an' soond o' him, daily, fir possibly the length o' time until the telegram arrived. Oh hell no! No, he wis positively on the wey oot. The wee bag o' bones that emerged pitifully fae under the oversized anorak couldnae possible rattle oan much longer . . . Thank god!!!

Come tae think o' it, fae the time I clapped eyes on him till the day his eyes shut fir good, nae other feet but mine crossed that threshold o' despair. Well, the doc popped in once or twice, tried tae persuade him tae tak residence in that nice home on the hillside. 'Lovely place Mickey', he telt him. The reply hid the doc rollin', 'Well tak ma bloody place if ye like it sae much'. It wis embarrassin'.

Once a wuman fae the DSS dropped in, asked if she could re-assess his finances, as their records stated he was being paid three pounds sixty odd pence more weekly than the law approximated for his requirements. Her reply to 'Whit the hell dae ye mean?' – 'You're due the department three hundred and seventy five pounds return of overpayment in pension – blew the balloon right up that day. It hit the ceilin' wi' a thud, defied the gravity o' the accusation an' refused tae come doon again; he wis hyper fir days. She did promise tae re-visit.

Nae bloody wonder naebody came back, once wis mair than enough. Wracked wisnae a sair enough expression tae describe the mental aftermath o' the verbal assaults he inflicted on a'body. He had ye constantly on the rack in that wee den o' a torture chamber. Just when he thought ye were stretched tae the point o' burstin', the wry wee smile would spread thickly o'er his face, like the butter that wouldnae melt in his mooth.

By the end o' the fifth month I'd hid enough, I wis lathered right up tae the eyes; I walked oot. 'Dinnae come back then', he shoutit as I slammed the lobby door, 'Laive an auld blind man tae shave himsel.' See whit I mean . . . he couldnae see past number one . . . I wis half-wey through the painful process o' scrapin' off two weeks growth, the open razor waverin' pointedly o'er the swell o' the distended jugular when he startit. 'Yer takin' the throat off me ya useless bitch.' I wis tempted, sorely, tae pit us baith right oot o' oor shared misery there an' then, but I couldnae dae it. I walked roond the block three times, returned tae, wid ye believe, 'I'm sorry hen, git the bloody denner oan an' hurry up aboot it' . . . God only knows how the last home help stuck it oot fir three years. 'Superwoman' he called her. Maybe she sought asylum in the form of a lobotomy, that would explain it. She couldnae possibly hiv been the full shillin'. No' if she loved him tae bits, like he said.

It wis in the seventh heavenly month that the miracle happened. I'd been prayin' a lot though. Even went tae confession, plucked up the courage tae rid ma conscience o' the guilt. The priest wis one o' thae kind that hid yer knees knockin' – the well on the road tae Rome an' 'winning' type. I telt him everything, the wey I felt aboot Mickey, the lot. 'Dear Lord, that's grave, mortal,' he sighed. Well at least he sympathised wi' me, salved ma soul. I couldnae understand how the penance wis sae heavy. Fifty Our Fathers and fifty Hail Marys! Still, ma knees hid the knock numbed oot o' them by the time I crawled back up the aisle.

It wis either my devout repentance or the Lourdes water that I sprinkled in the basin when I wis gien his feet their weekly steep, that brought on the transformation. It must have been the holy water, 'cause I mind o' tummin the hale bottle in wi a measure o' disenfectant, prayin' the concoction would permeate right doon tae the septic core o' him. The exorcism worked a treat. I walked in that day tae hear him singin' . . . aye, singin'!, like a lintie. Even detected a wee glint in his left eye. The right ane glinted artificially of course, that wis the glass ane. Aye, baith shinin' they were, an him as happy as Larry. There wis nane o' the usual, 'Yer late, whaur the hell hiv ye been, clean the layvie, change ma bed an' cut ma taenails' caper. The first thing he said wis, 'Mak some tea pet an' go doon fur a fish supper tae share atween us, git some mushy peas an aw.' I wis feart tae ask him if he wis feelin a richt, he looked awfy flushed, I wondered if he'd been oan the cough mixture or hid finally went right off his trolley. Maybe it wis acute confusional state due tae faecal impaction or a manic high. That seemed logical 'cause by the time I came back fae the chippie he wis spoutin' oot a load o' wild rhymin' speech. I got the wind up, ran ben tae the bathroom tae get the syrup o' figs, god I had visions o the yellie van cartin' him awa. Shakin', I asked him, 'Are ye aw right Mick?' . . .

'Course I'm aw right. Dae ye like poetry?' . . . Poetry!, an' me thinkin' he'd flipped his lid. Whit a relief! Well, he ranted can fir two hoors, even remembered the first poem he'd learned when he wis only seven. 'The Little Fish'.

By the time the month wis oot he wis glowin' an' playin' the mooth organ like ye wouldnae believe. It wis great! We had take-aways an' sing-songs every day. I even learned aw the poetry an' recited tae him. The tears streamin' when he said, proudly, 'Aye ye arenae half comin' oan.'

When Christmas wis three weeks awa, we pit up decorations in the wee kitchen tae mak it cheerier. He planned the Christmas menu an' asked me tae bring some mistletoe. 'Eh!, wait a minute son, I dinnae love ye that much yet,' I said, jist kiddin' him oan like. We had a trial run o' the Christmas dinner, even got in a quarter bottle o' the best tae see ninety three in.

I wis late . . . really late – mair than half an' hoor. I ran aw the wey up the Auld High Street, fair breathless by the time I got tae the locked door . . . Funny!, he always took the snib off fir me comin'. After five minutes knockin' an' still nae answer, I wis frantic; somethin' wis wrong . . .

He wis a nice young constable, as shaky as I wis under the facade o' steel. Fifteen minutes it took him tae force the lock an' whit seemed like eternity fir me tae walk the few yards tae where Mickey lay on the kitchen flair. He had been lyin' fir sixteen hoors in a pool o' vomit, blue wi' cauld an' barely conscious. His wee palms pure red wi' bangin' oan the concrete flair. Naebody heard him . . .

Two weeks he lay in that hospital bed an' never uttered a soond. The last time I saw him wis Christmas Eve . . . Oh whit a night that wis!!! I read aw his poetry, sang tae him an' brought the mistletoe. I kissed him aw o'er, even on the wee sparrie chist that wis respiratin' frantically. He kent I wis there, I'm sure o' that, 'cause baith eyes were sparklin'. Aye, he wis as happy as Larry . . . but the wee bag o' bones couldnae possibly rattle much longer; so I went through the a' the best fir ninety three routine, sincerely, then . . . I walked oot.

We baith went hame . . . feelin' ten feet tall.

Pink and Little Mouths

Thom Nairn

The dreadful, synthetic inevitable,
    The Scottish dance band,
And the dancers dance on
    The Dashing White Sergeant,
And me, far, far too sober,
    Sitting with a whisky nursing me,
The dancers dance on
    In ugly rings, roughly linked,
Swinging gruff and hairy heads
    As if they were empty,
And the dancers dance on,

Pink and little mouths open.
    All around stark faces sit
With themselves inside, peering out,
    Still dizzying the room spins,
Rings break, reform and spin,
    Heads, legs and tails spin, crash,
Collide, couple, crash and spin,
    Like somebody spilled
The Milky-Way,
    And only this watching
From a neighbouring star.

A New Year

Sheila Fielding

I am crying as I am writing this down. That's all I seem to have done for the last couple of years. I was told today that all these tears are for the first thirty-two years of my life. God, I hope I don't have to cry for the next thirty-two years! It took me a long time to realise what Eve meant when she said I was grieving, but now I know, and it hurts a lot. I think within myself I am pining, pining for something I know I can't have, but it doesn't make it any easier.

I have gone through my life without anybody to give a damn about me. I didn't think it really mattered, who the hell needs someone to give a damn? I convinced myself of this until I wondered exactly what was wrong with me, I was so different from everybody else. With Eve's help, we set about piecing my life together. What a mess! In the beginning it was like a 1000 piece jigsaw puzzle. We've managed to put this together now, apart from one thing – the most important last piece is missing. It would be so nice if that piece could be found, but I know in my heart it never will. I have to accept this, although that is the hardest task of all.

I was climbing the stairs tonight, talking aloud to myself, telling myself 'You are strong, you can do it, just let all that shit go, you're bound to feel better,' but there is a really horrible dark secret lurking that doesn't want to let go. This is secret. This is *the* secret. This is the secret that needs to be left. It's as though there is a sign saying DO NOT DISTURB. But I don't want to keep this secret anymore. I don't know where to put it.

I did a lot of thinking today. I am going back to my old way of thinking, that is, 'I don't need anybody' – if I say it often enough I will begin to believe it again. When you go through life with barriers up, letting no one inside, then all of a sudden they're down – what a weird feeling! Then quick as a flash the barriers have to go up again because you're going to get hurt.

I feel myself getting stronger day by day, after saying all this. I really don't know how much longer I can go about my life with this emptiness and insecurity I have inside. I get so desperate sometimes I could kill myself. I have got Ally, I suppose, but it just isn't the same – I want a mother. Now I bet you never thought you'd hear that from a grown woman. A grown woman! That's what I am. I never really thought about that. Here's me thinking of myself as a lassie. Maybe if I started acting like a woman I might begin to feel better.

I've had a mixed day – a few palpitations in the process. My Health Visitor came this morning to see how the girls were getting along and we had a good long chat about other things. I actually asked her advice about something that was bothering me and she was very helpful and encouraging. She's going to pop in and have a proper chat next week, as it wasn't convenient today, with my Gran in. I seem to be able to open up a bit more about my childhood experiences. It's not been easy, but each time it gets easier.

I have been doing a bit of self-analysis and I think that I have triumphed over these last few days. I don't seem to be needing to phone somebody, not needing to talk to anyone for reassurance. I'm pleased at my progress. Mind you, I'm dying to meet Eve tomorrow and tell her how I'm feeling. She'll probably be glad. I think she might be getting fed up with me. She reckons that I've been getting counselling for more than two years, but I think she forgets that she was away for four months on a course, and that I gave it up for two or three months as well. Sometimes I found myself getting angry at Eve – I used to wonder why, but now I realise that I was looking for something in her that she couldn't give. After all, she is a professional. She has been trained to do her job. I used to think that she was different but now I know she is not. Every client is the same to her. I'm glad I'm writing this down, because it is the way things are going on in my head right now. I feel my dependency on Eve is easing off and I'm glad. I don't think that this is my defences talking – at least I hope not.

Pearl and Bob visited on Monday. They brought a New Year drink with them and I got a little bit drunk. I opened up to them quite a lot through the drink. I don't know if I feel good about it, or bad, as I don't know what they're thinking. Pearl was brilliant that night, but shame is preventing me from getting in touch with them. I felt sorry for Bob though. As he tried to comfort me, I pulled away from him. Hopefully he will understand. He even said "no involvement" but I still couldn't let him near me. That is how much my life has been wrecked by one stupid perverted disgusting bastard and his accomplice – my own mother. That sounds terrible but that is the way it is.

Believe it or not it is showing 2.42am on my clock and my mind is still turning over. My thoughts are again with Larry, who seems to come up every so often with a piece of the puzzle, yet to be put in the proper place. I wish I could pluck up some courage and visit my baby sister's resting place.

I really did not mean what I said about Eve the other night. I really did not mean it the way it sounded, but I seem to think that if I get angry with her, I'll manage to distance myself from her, something I really don't want, but it is for the best, as she isn't going to be there forever – or I should say, I am not going to be there forever.

My thoughts are so mixed up at the moment I don't know which way to turn. I am angry at my mum and I'm angry at him. I just don't know who to hate most. I wish someone would help me, but I know the only person who can help me is myself.

I had a word on the phone with Kathy tonight on the phone. She still has really bad days, which makes me feel better, but Kathy has learned to get on with life. Maybe I'll manage to take a leaf out of her book. It is funny how Kathy remembers a lot of things I'd forgotten and I remember things that Kathy forgot. But the minute something is mentioned, it just hits hard, and we realise we didn't forget, it was just another piece of life that we have managed to block out.

I was in a real angry mood today, I don't know why, but it was poor Ally that got it again. After throwing a full cup of tea across the kitchen I stormed up the stairs and tried to think of the reason I did it – but I couldn't. Ally criticises me a lot, I know he doesn't mean to, but I take it personally. He got on about me not doing any cleaning or anything and I just flipped. The sad thing about it was that the kids were all in the kitchen at the time. I always promised myself that my kids would not be brought up like me and I surely hope that this is not a start – although my anger was not directed at them. Afterwards I wanted to run away someplace. I really wanted to walk out on Ally and the kids and not come back. But I know that is the wrong thing to do. Sometimes I just want some space to set things clear in my mind, sort everything out and learn to live with the hurt and anger. When I first brought all this shit inside me out, I thought for some reason that it would just disappear, never to be seen again. How stupid can you be? The purpose of it is to get it out, deal with it, accept it, then get on with life. So when do I get on with life? Or am I to commit myself to this shit and make myself ill? I have to accept it. I have to get on with life. I have to get on with life. I have to get on with life. How? It sounds like a magic potion – maybe it will work magically. Well, I am trying to do it.

Poor Eve! She got it tonight, me again. I just can't keep my trap shut. I have had a brilliant week, praising myself up, then I go and do a stupid thing like that. Fighting through life is all that I seem to have done, but this is the toughest fight yet. Yet all of a sudden I feel lighter, like there has been a big weight lifted from my shoulders. And it feels good.

I am getting really scared. I know the group is finishing in three weeks and I know that I am nearly finished with Eve. This is the one that really scares me. I am scared of walking out of her office and that's it – bye-bye, bye-bye. I will really miss her a lot. I have got really fond of her. But I know that it is not a dependency. I know that because I can go on without missing her. I know I can go on.

Winter

Louise Moran

Radiant as brides
Tower the opalescent mountains;
Glorious, untouchable,
Sparkling shell-white purity
Beneath the dazzling blue celestial sky.

The buzzard soars
Snatching my soul to Heaven
Cold-cast bronze bathed in light of icy cleanness.
See the gleaming platinum Tay
Binding pearls of rounded hillside
To the emerald forest slopes
Like gods we scan the jewels of the land.
Then, kitten-keening, loud he cries
And swoops to throw me earthwards
Plunging through spreading dark green spruce-sprawl.

Light falls,
Tumble-bumping through the white-furred trees,
Glancing off icicles – sharp as glass—
Splinters into myriad rainbows
And startles a squirrel
(Bleary-eyed, hoard-hungry nut-nibbler).
Then down it shafts in needle-fringed darkness,
Melting into bumpy, stumpy moss and cone-strewn ground
In a mottled, moulten alchemy of wonder.

Beneath my feet
A pale green nose
Pokes through the crusty, frozen earth
Impatient for Glory.

Final Ascent

Sheelagh Heron

After the funeral, (just dust, and a thin wind), I saw
upon an icy summit – upright, flinging wide its sticks—
a figure? Turning, waving, laughing. Leaping out into the snow-filled
   gully.
Screaming out his pain, his joy, his being there.
One once more with the cold, hard hills.

He'd always said that it was good to climb in winter.

John F. Petrie

Snow whirls
In slow butterfly swathes
Gently smashing
The air around and between.

Steel tarn whitens;
Black crag appears,
Hazes, disappears;
Soft grey distance
Focuses eye
On snowing
Blowing in-between;
A corner of peace
Below searing blast.

We are caught
In soft stirring
Of corrie shelter;
And this pause
Of enjoyment
Seems worth
Far more
Than the effort
To get there.

Donald's World

Kenneth C. Steven

Sometimes I went there, in the sleet days after Christmas;
The kitchen hummed, on the black stove
A kettle pluming steam, two collies
Rapping their warning with red mouths.

Inside the old man sat
His same hills in the window,
One side of him gone like a split tree
Withered by strokes.

But out of that sloping mouth
Came foxes, badgers, eagles, stoats—
Years of stories pressed in his mind's pages
Fresh, still alive and strong.

Others came to visit his winter room
With fruit and sympathy and talk,
Sure he was crippled by the savage nights
There in that storm-rocked farm.

I didn't pity him – I envied.
After I'd gone back to the scoured town
I knew his eyes went running into the whole hills
remembering each day.

Gunpowder

Maria McLuckie

I can't stop building
on my version of duty.
Each time I think of them
I don't polish, but gloss;
not wash, nor place in a closet.

I want to spin them
as if they were cobwebs
so I can stare up to
my work of art
when things get in my way.
I'll sweep them under the carpet.
I don't want to pull them
into a vacuum;
I want to watch each layer settle
like dust on a wedding cake.

The Embalmer's Art

Paul Connell

So, as bidden, I went through and had a look. He looked OK. Not much like my dad but OK. This was some guy with a superficial similarity who had led a pampered, well-fed, underworked life, who had died far too early, from no particular ailment and in no apparent pain. It was a fantasy version of my dad – a tribute to the embalmer's art.

Someone once said that as an insult about someone else, didn't they? A politician, I think. Lloyd George? Kind of thing my dad would have known. I'd have to ask him next time I saw him. Oh lookee here he is now!

"So, we're on insults. A tribute to the embalmer's art. Who said it and of whom? Fifteen seconds, I'll have to hurry you."

Silence.

Somewhere in that head there'd been a little electric impulse that would have represented that piece of knowledge, and others for all sorts of nonsense that made him king, or at least duke of all, or at least many of the local pub quizzes till the last few years, another few for the Celtic line-up at Lisbon, and another bunch for now obsolete engineering techniques and a whole 12V battery's worth for the doings and sayings of long dead friends and relatives. And none for birthdays and anniversaries.

Energy can't be destroyed can it? Only transferred. So the force that made those synapses spark must be somewhere. Careering through space perhaps, or coursing in my veins now?

"So then, Life after Death, what's the conclusion, Dad? I think it'd be fair to call you something of an authority on the subject nowadays. You were always telling me to shut up and I might learn something. So?"

Silence.

I learned something. Don't talk to corpses. They're dead rude.

I calculated what would seem a respectable period of paying my respects. A few minutes yet, I think. I checked out the Mass cards piled thick as bills on the sideboard. A limited range of designs, I noted, rather heavy on the doleful Virgin and bleeding heart motifs. I wonder if there's a gap in the market for a more contemporary range? What would they feature, then? If it had to be religious image, which I suppose it had, why not a bold semi-abstract dove in nice primary colours? Or a workers-at-harvest scene, very symbolic. I leafed through the sympathy cards, another pile of muted images of sorrow.

"Who are these people? Bert and Ina? The Mooneys? All at Ladbroke's! I bet their share price has dipped. One question. If any of these folk had gone first, would you have sent a card?"

Silence.

"No I don't think so either, but they'd have got one in your name, wouldn't they?"

Silence.

I opened the curtain a little and gazed out on a scene that had once, when this was my room, been so familiar I didn't see it. Other white-harled terraced houses, the roofs of the railwaymen's cottages now knocked into one. In the distance the hills sweeping up behind the valley where I knew the graveyard waited. On the hills and horizon the scars of the quarrying and mining that had brought my family to this area and then, all seams spent, had sent me elsewhere.

"So, on the whole, and given life's been pretty miserable for you of late, what's it like being dead?"

Silence.

"Keeping an open mind on it? Good idea."

I took another quick peek and went back through.

My mum, attended by a retinue of sisters, aged aunts and village worthies was enthroned amidst a sea of sympathy. I gave her an encouraging smile and, finding it returned, also found a mug of tea and a plate of ham sandwiches in my hand and a soft seat beneath my arse.

Auntie Mary, all bosoms and incense, bore down on me like a stately three-master.

"He looks fine, doesn't he son?"

"Aye, no bad considering."

Her smile congealed as she thought about this. "Did I hear you talking through there?"

"Aye, just a quick decade of the rosary."

She didn't look entirely convinced. "Really? That's good son."

Over in the corner I caught the merest twitch of a grin on my mum's lips, and gave her the merest arch of my eyebrows back. I didn't, after all, get my sense of humour off the wind.

The graveyard. A whipping in off the Pentlands, not fierce but raw enough to have sent most of the mourners scurrying off in the trail of the black limo bearing my mum and the frailest of the aunts up to the club where steak pie and whisky awaited. The workies were already shovelling muck in on top of the coffin, keen to be away out of the cold themselves. I had a wander along the row of stones around the rapidly-filling chasm where I'd just helped to lay my dad.

I recognised the odd name; a guy just a few years above me at school, recently, suicide, years on the dole, in and out of hospital, depression.

Another stone, name meant nothing, had a little round picture of a balding middle aged man. That's new, here at least. I'd seen pictures on gravestones in Italy. In what used to be Yugoslavia, I'd see them on little shrines on bullet-pocked walls where revolution or war had made someone a martyr. Not here. Here gravestones had always been gray, uniform, solid and unadorned. Why stop at photos? Why not videos, holograms, tapes, all to be activated by foot pressure on the nearby path. That'd give the bastards a fright. Till it became normal of course.

"Alright, Jim." A voice at my elbow woke me. It took a second to darken the hair and slim the figure of the overcoat who had spoken. It took another to retrieve twenty years and put a name to the skinny boy within.

"Tommy. How you doin'? Barley recognised you there."

He chuckled. "Aye, catches up with all of us doesn't it. Sorry about your Dad."

"Your fault, was it? I should have guessed."

He laughed again. "Still a sick bugger then. Good."

"Yer'av to laff duncher? Coming up to the club? Mum would want you to. I gave my lift away. Get some air."

He nodded and we stepped out. I took a last look back at the grave as we passed the gates and out into the road, retracing the steps we had all taken half an hour ago. Funny it was always that bit that I anticipated once I knew that he was dying; the short walk round from the chapel behind the hearse, leading a crocodile of friends and family, all part of the drill. In the event I'd been more concerned at dodging the high-tar emissions from the hearse's exhaust which, I noted, had left a gray tide-mark on my trouser leg. Have to get it dry-cleaned. Maybe I need a new suit; the age of peer's weddings had passed but now I knew I faced the early wave of the next generation's and the funerals of the previous.

I'd hardly noticed the scenery on the way round. Now as Tommy brought me up to speed on family, work, mates and football and I skilfully avoided the more sordid details of my own recent history, I had a look around me.

Jesus, what a tip! Past the chapel, a boarded up shop where we'd bought rolls after mass every week, then a wind-charred gap site marked what used to be the picture house, and then what I used to think was the posh bit of town. Now the blank faced 1930s bungalows trying to hide behind privets on either side of the narrow road looked neglected, unloved, undesirable. At the top of the brae we turned in to the street in front of the club joining the stragglers from the cortege that now lay parked haphazardly along the pavement.

I had the key to the visitor's flat in the sheltered housing in my pocket. I could be there in ten minutes, fifteen if I stopped at an off-license. Mum would understand, she always had, always did, but not always would. A mans gotta do. . . .

"After you, Tommy" I nodded, holding the main door open and forming the first platitudinous, empty formality on my lips in preparation for my task within.

The Sorry Sicht

Jean Massie

Ah heard this man oan the wireless say,
"The sorriest sicht ye'll ever see
is weet sheep
in a neep field."

At the tap o Tullybachart oan a
dreich Sabbath day, there they were – a
herd o weet sheep
in a neep field.

Aa clartie an bedraggled, staunin
meeserable i the glaur, puir trauchled
weet sheep
in a neep field.

Luikin fair forfoughen, cooried in
ahent the dyke, they orra shilpit
weet sheep
in a neep field.

Ah heard this man oan the wireless say,
"The sorriest sicht ye'll ever see
is weet sheep
in a neep field."

An ye ken – he wis richt.

Highland Winter

James Adams

Frozen furies
Asset-strip the
Well laid plans
Of hill and glen.

Conjured snowscapes
Migrate from the
Roof of the world,
As monkish clouds
Tear vanities from
Monastic skies.

A triple guitar
Plays morning star
Blues to mollify
Those northern Gods
Of white and gloom,
While a snoring
Sun blows tepid
Then cold over
The whispering land.

Dark Days

Irene Gunnion

Cooried thegither – aroond Castle Balhoosie
Restin in splendour – neath pines trees sweet
Hungry wee birds – some quiet some scurry
Scrapin awa – fur a tasty treat
The days the noo – are dark an frozen
Yet – buds o snaadrap can be seen
Soon tae be graced – in finest regalia
Wi sic style – as befits 'the Guid Folks Queen'

A stand mysel – bit A'm contented
Hushed in peace – though shuir aware
Dark days will pass – aroond Balhoosie
The chillin winds – tae blast nae mair
Tae be born – is the comin springtime
Dancin daffies – wi heids held high
Pray let there be licht – aroond Balhoosie
As sleepy winters – exhales her final sigh

Carrion Living

Alan Jordan

I saw black crows feeding on a roadkill carcass,
squabbling for the last edible remains of
what once held more than flesh and bones.
Now it hugs the tarmac, skin-like surface,
the rain brings a lifelike shine to the lifeless limbs,
an illusory heart beats in sympathy with mechanical drones.

Strange how the eyes smiles, as the birds
leisurely pick the carrion clean. Movement
to life from death. Concentric circular motion,
containing instincts with each passing.
Moving outward, flowing inward, ebbing.
Little ripples in the gaping ocean.

Curious cousins investigate like approaching an open grave.
A rumble warns of another metal shark machine
that sometimes begs forgiveness with pitiful clarion.
Safety stretches away, inversely time quickens
until just before contact, sweet pain, releases
the spirit leaving the casing for carrion.

Time to Remember

Ellen Thompson

Liz sat down, the Word Processor in front of her at the ready, whose wonders never ceased to amaze her, even after four years of constant use. In the desk drawer were sheets of pristine, white paper, lying there passive in its purity, waiting to become alive with the printed word, in that 'oh so neat' way she had never managed to achieve with a succession of typewriters, self taught in the first place. Tippex played an essential part in a would-be writer's existence, making the machine an unsightly mess, more white spots on it than there were black in any 'spotted Dick', rather shamefaced when she took the model of the moment for overhaul, not so regularly as she should have done, due to its customary appalling state.

It was Liz Bennett's grandson who introduced her to this latest acquisition, one of the present-day breed who grew up with computers and possessed enough patience to pass some of his knowledge on. Liz never imagined she would take it in, quite chuffed with her prowess, although that certain kind of wisdom, usually acquired with age, prompted her to absorb only the minimum for her needs. No intention of cramming some of its facets into a head where space was reserved for those flights of fancy, indulged in from time to time and put on paper, next stop for some of them the wastepaper basket, where they rightly belonged.

The learning was a definite challenge, "I'll do it if it kills me," she often muttered when something went wrong, terribly frustrated if her young tutor was not available to sort things out, probably thinking his ageing grandmother a complete idiot. It was left to Liz, always her own sternest critic, to call herself a silly old fool.

At last, she mastered the damned thing whose sole purpose, on occasion, seemed geared towards thwarting her efforts, but had eventually adopted the role of friend and companion, assuming great importance in her life. Strangely bereft, when one serious hiccough meant sending it off for repair, acting if some alien force was in charge, printing nothing but 'gobbledygook', amazed when she finally typed the word and the machine didn't bleep.

So, for a short while, it was back to the typewriter, yesterday's invention, one to which she clung for very sentimental reasons, to treasure until life had no more use for her. After that it would only be another inanimate object, a museum piece someday if it hung around long enough, by which time the fact that someone like herself who spent hours at it, putting thoughts on paper, would have little or no significance. God knows, even the word processor could have been replaced by then by something even more amazing, nothing ever ruled out in this age of technology.

Liz Bennett couldn't remember a time when she didn't have the urge to write, at it one way or another since childhood, scribbling continually in numerous exercise books, much to the chagrin of a very down to earth mother who believed mind and fingers could be put to better use. The books had lines, of course, they usually did in those far off days, and Liz always wrote on the right hand side of the page from front to back, then in reverse back to front, rather confusing to the uninitiated. An idiosyncrasy, no doubt, but most folk have them and this happened to be one of hers. She still scribbled when ideas popped into her head at inopportune moments and it wasn't convenient to use the word-processor, knowing that once seated she would take some shifting, likely to forget that some meal or other had to be on the table at a certain time. Potatoes boiled dry on more than one occasion, the kitchen smelling to high heaven.

There had been many such times during a busy life, stamping around the house to the plaintive cry of "I never can get down to writing when I want to," and Jack, her husband, whose patience their grandson had obviously inherited, took the duster or whatever out of her hand and bundled her upstairs to the box room, converted into a study of sorts, where the typewriter awaited. "Go on love," he would say in a soothing way. "Leave the rest to me," knowing that after half an hour of pounding frustration out of her system, Liz would emerge to rejoin the human race, her grumpiness forgotten, well used to his volatile wife and her eccentricities, wakened more than once during the night to answer a question that couldn't possibly wait until morning.

Nine years, now, since she'd lost her husband, the agonising over for some time but the miss still remained. How could it be otherwise after sharing forty-five years of Jack's allotted span? She was trying hard to recall the last day of his life, to get it all down on paper, hoping to find an answer to so many things. Laying bare the soul never easy but had to be done, in the only way she knew how, by writing, facing up to the bogey men, to what she had chosen to keep locked away in the deepest caverns of her mind. Poetry, an outlet for the emotions, and usually her salvation when life brought unexpected blows, had somehow deserted her that one time she needed its therapy most, her mind a desolate waste. Even now, although determined, Liz doubted her own ability to deal with the situation, perhaps too emotional, the truth of the matter yet to be discovered.

A big sigh escaped her lungs, followed almost immediately by another. This was likely to be much harder than she imagined, going back to recap that one day in her life when the walls came tumbling down. Metaphorically speaking, of course, goodness knows those of their rambling old house had weathered many a storm in over a hundred years of existence. Gazing often out of first floor windows, lounge and dining room, it wasn't hard for an imaginative mind to conjure up some of the scenes it must have witnessed, looking towards the railway station, at the far side of a dual carriageway. So much activity during two world wars, men in different uniforms sent off to fight, some never to set foot on their native soil again, so many comings and goings.

Four years ago they sold the house, said goodbye to Bed and Breakfast, to begin again in a modern bungalow, much more convenient but an enormous wrench, feeling pushed into something she didn't want to do. For the best, actually, no stairs to contend with but a very traumatic transfer, thinking rather irrationally she had left Jack behind, a big bone of contention between her daughter and herself, until sweet reason took over, now quite settled in very different surroundings. Fifteen years since they 'emigrated' to Scotland from Northumberland, with high hopes of a very different sort of existence, back to village life again, limited funds and a barn of a house to redecorate, from top to bottom. And what a task it was, loads of work mixed with both laughter and tears, problems galore, herself at one stage astride two planks in the staircase well, putting wood chip on the walls, husband and daughter hovering, anxiously, on the upstairs landing, their anxiety a tangible thing.

"For God's sake hop it and leave me alone," she snapped, as nervous as they were at her precarious position but taking refuge in bursts of irritation. They all grafted, never thinking such hard work might be too much for a man who always seemed so very fit, an absolute tower of strength in his quiet, unassuming way. Should she have realised and tried to put the brake on his activity? Impossible to answer.

It had been a big decision, making the move at all, but the right one, her roots firmly established in the lovely part of Scotland they had chosen, or which had chosen them, never quite certain which way it was. Not surprised to hear from a relative in Australia that her father's ancestors way back originated in this particular area. It seemed one member of the clan had come back home, full circle.

At twenty four, Jack was graded A.1 and accepted into the Royal Navy. Liz still felt that old familiar sensation when she saw tall, dark young men in bell-bottoms, remembering when she painstakingly pressed a pair with creases down the middle of the legs and Jack's bellow of anguish. "They'll put me on a charge!" he roared at her and spent hours with a hot iron and brown paper restoring them to regulation order.

She spent three and a half years without sight of him in the early part of their marriage and thinking now in terms of lonely Christmases, birthdays and other special occasions, it seemed much longer than it did then, although that was an eternity. Then, at the latter end of the war, nine months separation, the whole time she was carrying their daughter Jane, destined to be an only child. Liz chuckled, softly, seeing herself in a hospital bed, old fashioned earphones on her head, and the excitement of hearing Jack's ship had docked in Portsmouth, no need for secrecy, the war was over. A nurse had breezed in and popped a thermometer into her mouth, then hurried away after a quick look at it, saying as she departed, "My God, woman, I can't put that on your chart, I'll be back when you've calmed down," laughing at the garbled explanation for such an alarming rise temperature.

There were certain periods throughout her life that would fill a book, her long stay in Maternity Hospital, the sixteen years spent as a Children's Nursery Supervisor, and ten seasons of Bed and Breakfast. So much material to draw upon, stored at the back of her mind. Too late now, she sighed, just snippets coming to the fore as she touched the relevant buttons.

The nurses on Maternity were full of fun, threatening to put screens around the bed when the wandering sailor came home from the sea – which they did, much to his embarrassment. Their parting request was that he should bring a packet of tea when next he came, as rationing was still the order of the day and likely to be for some considerable time.

Their reunion, the first time as parents of an infant girl, became a source of amusement for the rest of their lives. After being clasped in his arms and kissed until she was mindless, Liz waited and waited, until at last she gave a broad, teasing smile. "Don't you want to have a look at your daughter?" she inquired, bringing a look of absolute astonishment to his flushed, young face. Jack had actually forgotten, in the joy of just being together, that his wife had recently given birth to his child. "I got plenty of her after that," he countered, whenever she chaffed him about it in years to come, speaking nothing but truth. He'd been a father from the word go.

Now, almost fifty years on, Liz smiled reflectively, thinking how young they all were, so much of their youth taken from them by a cruel war. But she was one of the lucky ones. Jack did survive, for which blessing she was truly grateful – another question swift to mind: would his loss have been any greater then than when it did come, almost four decades later?

How quickly the memories were pouring in, impossible to prevent them, not that she had any inclination to try, the flood gates were open. For nine years she had deliberately suppressed the intrusion of youthful recollections, preferring to dwell in the more immediate past, in which other members of her family could share. Except for the actual day of Jack's death which was more or less blotted out. Only in dreams did they return to plague her, because no matter what, she always remembered he was dead.

Now, her thoughts leapt out of control, taking her back to the first time she set eyes upon the boy who one day would become her husband – fourteen years old, herself somewhere between ten and eleven. A church concert in the local Co-op Hall, the usual venue for this sort of entertainment, in the tiny, colliery village where they lived. He acted the part of a postman and she was the Christmas tree fairy, the idea of which made her laugh out loud. "Me a fairy!" she hooted, now rather well endowed.

Liz didn't find it hard to visualise the dress she wore, made by her mother's aunt, a tailoress, and useful to have around in those poorer days. One of the best dressed girls in the village, everything on her back made from remnants of all descriptions and eventually passed on to those less fortunate than herself. It was like that among them and with no thought of monetary gain, more of a bartering system, one sort of help in willing exchange for another.

The fairy dress was green, as might be expected, falling in soft fullness from waist to ankle, matching tinsel crowning wayward blonde hair, the bane of her mother's life, cut with a fringe because no ribbon or slide ever stayed put for long.

Jack sang a song, 'Letters for you', his postie's bag empty of envelopes before the end of the first chorus, then going through the motions of delivery. A good singer, even then, years of training to follow, developing a fine, baritone voice, sounds of which struck chords of memory, after all this time. Under-confident in many ways, when Jack stood up to sing or conduct a choir he was ten feet tall and she never stopped feeling proud of him.

Liz was at Grammar School, not yet sixteen, when she became aware of him through the eyes of a romantic-minded young lass, soon to blossom into womanhood. He was wont to say that from then on he didn't stand a chance. Not that he saw her in that light, just a kid to his advanced age of nineteen, but they were thrown into one another's company quite a lot at church activities and walking from the larger village nearby. Liz always took the long way round past Jack's house, hoping for sight of him, tall with tightly curled dark hair and a gorgeous smile. He had brown eyes and a smile inherited by their grandson. These often tore at her heart strings. Jack Bennett held great attraction for an impressionable teenager, a feeling that one day would change into love.

God, how she was rambling on, her fingers flying over the keyboard, the words not registering fast enough, as if some force gave her impetus, finding so much to say and still hadn't reached the main part of her story. Exorcism, of a sort, Liz supposed, a cleansing of mind and spirit, long overdue. Better far to let it all out, have a good old Spring clean in the Autumn of her life, well out of season but needing to be done.

Just before she was seventeen, her brother tried to put the cat among the pigeons. The whole family, apart from her father who was at work, assembled around the kitchen table for a meal, her grandparents, mother and the aforementioned brother, more than five years her senior, devilment written all over his good looking, young face. A face that was never meant to grow older, killed in a car crash the following year, when Liz learnt to her sorrow that death is no respecter of age and found herself praying, long afterwards, that she wouldn't die, not when she was just discovering that life can be very sweet.

"Our Liz has got herself a lad," he announced triumphantly, daring her to contradict, which she did most vehemently. "I haven't, I haven't," the hot flush on her cheeks a complete give away. But the news seemed to land like a damp squib. "Has she?" Gran stated in her usual unflappable manner, never one to appear ruffled and nobody else showed much surprise. Liz and her brother had both forgotten the village grapevine. "If that's the case," her Gran went on to say, "she had better bring him home", mother nodding agreement and grandfather not taking the slightest bit of notice, more interested in the food set in front of him.

So Jack was duly introduced to the family, the most surprising thing of all that he didn't demur, normally rather reticent, the pair of them like chalk and cheese, Liz so outgoing. "Full of it" according to her mother, her daughter not quite sure if this was complimentary or otherwise. "Liz is always into everything neck and crop," Mum was fond of saying, which indeed was true, anything she tackled gone into wholeheartedly, no half measures right or wrong, little changed with the passing of the years.

Jack and herself were into a walking-out relationship, nothing terribly serious, her first real boyfriend, who in her youthful insensitivity she discarded every now and again, imagining the grass to be greener on the other side of the street and, finding it wasn't, saying she was sorry and picked up where they left off. Until that one occasion, when she was nearly nineteen and did it once too often, sorry not good enough, the biter bitten.

Liz remembered running home, blinded by tears, the sound of her own voice rang in her ears as if it were only yesterday. "Never mind love," her mother said consolingly, "there are plenty more fish in the sea." And her own reply, right from the heart, "But I love him Mum, I love him." Realisation had struck when it was, apparently, too late.

Memory softened her lips. Whatever else might be said of Liz, she was resilient. She would show him, but how? A how which came quickly to mind, her feminine instincts truly aroused, ready to do battle but no head-on confrontation. That wasn't on the cards. Liz had no intention of saying sorry again, their coming together, if at all, had to be a mutual decision, refusing to accept the possibility of final rejection.

The dress she chose was purple, striking no doubt with her colouring, a shade only worn once since, on another important occasion. They sat directly opposite in the choir, tenors and bass at one side, soprano and alto the other, she was mezzo then, quite a decent voice, a lot of Jack rubbed off on her, unconsciously. Such a pity she had to come down a whole octave nowadays, to sing hymns in church, a real sore point. Jack would never have been sung out, as she was, he knew how to use his voice properly, that wonderful voice. She had it on tape but only unaccompanied, all those years of singing and so little recorded, forgetting life didn't go on forever and the voice would one day be silenced. They had a special song, which became sadder with the passing of time. "Sing 'Friend o' Mine'," she'd requested so often, the words very beautiful, tears brimmed her eyes just thinking of them.

"It was your Gran," Jack confessed, rather sheepishly, as they walked the lanes hand in hand after the service, a natural gravitation towards one another, admitting he couldn't keep his eyes away, just as she intended but didn't say so. "She said it was high time I taught you a lesson," he told her, wondering how someone so volatile would react. But Liz just laughed in the euphoria of a newly discovered happiness, recognising what a wise woman her grandmother was, knowing her better than she did herself, so very sure now that she loved Jack and always would.

Liz sported an engagement ring two weeks before her twentieth birthday, now tucked away in a drawer, too small for swollen fingers. The war was just into its fourth month, a phoney war to those outside the field of battle, a frantic filling of sandbags, telephone kiosks used as makeshift A.R.P. posts, not Civil Defence until later. Jack's age group wasn't yet due for call up and it all seemed so unreal somehow, until news of Dunkirk stirred everyone into reality, tragedy and miracle combined. All those tiny vessels sailing forth to evacuate a retreating army, what was left of it, thousands killed or imprisoned for the rest of the war and the Germans sitting on the cliffs of Calais, poised to invade the British mainland.

Liz could honestly say she never imagined they could do it, learning years afterwards how close it had been. Neville Chamberlain got some stick for waving that meaningless document, declaring 'Peace in our time', but perhaps he was much maligned. War had to come and he did gain a year's grace, in which to make feverish preparation, not nearly enough but the difference perhaps between freedom or occupation, the Battle of Britain proving that the British bulldog still had the incentive to fight and did, in the air most effectively, thanks to many gallant young men in the legendary Spitfires.

With call up imminent, Jack wanted to marry and conquered his innate sense of shyness to approach her father, mother not at all keen on the idea. "She's too young," she insisted, beset by memories of that earlier war, herself not much older than Liz and married only seven months when it began, a son born just over two months later. That same son now in his grave, killed when he was twenty-two, Gran dying that same year. 'The first nail in her coffin,' the old lady said when it happened, which proved to be the sad truth, two members of one family gone in less than three months, setting a pattern for what was to come two years later to so many folk.

But fortunately Dad remembered the comfort it had been, having a wife and baby at home, despite the fact that his own life was on the line, day after day. "Let them" he said and the wedding was arranged, brought forward when Jack received orders to go for a medical, Liz making the trip into town with him. "But you can't swim," she gasped, when he said he was to join the Navy, not discovering until the war was over that non-swimmers were less likely to take risks and usually hung on to whatever they could find, hoping to be picked up before the sea took its toll. A close friend's husband was lost off the Greek island of Cos, a strong swimmer who wrongly thought he could make the shore.

In her present meanderings, Liz reflected on the first days of her married life. To say Jack and herself were as green as grass had to be an understatement, but she remembered in great tenderness how lovely it was to cuddle up to him in bed even if sex at that time was a bit of a disaster. A feeling that never left her in forty-five years of marriage, sorry to think that the last few months before he died, they slept in twin beds, their sleep pattern altered by Jack's illness. Now she was back in a double bed, alone, overcome by a sense of complete desolation.

She shrugged the thoughts aside. No use getting maudlin. Think of pleasant things. When Jack returned home, after a three and a half year absence, sex took on a completely new dimension.

Whether her husband gained knowledge by experience, or hearsay, she was wise enough not to enquire – the latter she hoped, but decided ignorance was bliss. Their daughter was conceived in love, maybe a sense of defiance against fate, so long married and if it came to an end tomorrow, nothing to show for it. "Did the deed and hopped it," became her teasing quip, sorry Jack never saw her with a bump, deprived of that special kind of togetherness between two people awaiting the birth of a child, thankful for the gift of words, always able to express herself in those letters, written day after day. Cheated, maybe, but a small sacrifice when faced with the fact that so many gave their all.

Liz remembered their first home with great affection, never empty of young people, the church drama group, living an unbelievably full life, despite the worry of a mother dying with cancer. What stamina she must have possessed in those days, still did up to a point, downing medication and dismissing aches and pains with contempt, meaning to do just that for as long as possible.

Cancer was a word said in whispers in the early fifties, never once given utterance between her mother and herself, dwelling a while on the relationship they shared. "I'm not afraid of dying," came out of the blue one day, her sick parent going on to say, "but I would like to see my granddaughter grow up. You don't love her the way I do." An astounding claim, or so it seemed at the time, but now as a grandparent she recognised the difference. A special sort of affinity existed with her grandson and that was what her mother resented missing out on. Poor Mum, who bore her pain so well and stayed cheerful under such stressful circumstances.

Why did her mind persist in wandering, no real sequence to its thoughts, so muddled, yet all part of life as she had lived it, to the full. Two years after her mother's inevitable death, Dad expressed a willingness to give up the family home, moving in with them, all living together in amicable circumstances for six years but came to an unexpected end, one Liz never envisaged, compelled in retrospect to think why not.

It happened one lunchtime, Dad just in from the pub, his dinner set aside to keep hot. He seemed rather uneasy, for some reason, just toying with the food on his plate, before the words came tumbling forth. "I'm going to marry again," he said, and if he had struck Liz with a knife he wouldn't have drawn blood, absolutely nonplussed, so much so she dissolved into tears. That did it, Dad got to his feet and vanished upstairs, while she ran to the person who always understood. "Who is he marrying?" Jack queried, the obvious question, one she hadn't thought to ask, reduced to crying like a baby. "I don't know," she stammered amid her tears. "Then you had better find out," was the amazingly calm suggestion and Liz took no further telling, just flew upstairs after her distressed father, wouldn't have hurt him for the world.

Her sixty-eight year old parent was sitting on his bed, very upset, his only daughter, for whom he had great affection, seemed unprepared to accept the one thing upon which his mind was set, which meant dissent, or so he imagined. "She's nice," he faltered, quite out of his depth and, somehow, she became the parent and he the child, a reversal of roles, Liz enormously relieved to discover the lady in question was someone she'd met dozens of times in her own mother's company, when just a girl.

The subsequent marriage, which only ended with her father's death, lasted fourteen years, a happy one, two elderly people who found love and companionship in the latter years of their lives, each with one daughter, who were freed from a certain amount of responsibility for their respective parents and very friendly towards one another. Liz still kept in touch with her stepsister, from time to time, though the two persons who drew them together initially had long gone.

Why couldn't she stop twittering and get down to the nitty gritty of the whole exercise, still somewhat reluctant, rather ridiculous after all. She had already bared her soul quite a lot, may as well go the whole hog. Liz began to think of what her husband had missed by his early demise – not, unfortunately, the break up of Jane's marriage, which in his state of health did him no good. But their daughter and her husband were never right for one another in the first place, Jane still smarting from a broken romance, very vulnerable when they met on a train going to London, where she worked for a year and a half.

"I should have missed that damned train," she was to state rather cynically, thirteen years on, her marriage on the rocks. Who says thirteen isn't an unlucky number? Nothing left between them except their son, the only common ground that remained. Difficult for an older couple, with so many years of marriage behind them, to reconcile themselves to the situation, Jack a sick man when they cried 'finis' and Roy moved out.

"Keep as much of the trauma away from him as you can," their G.P. advised, almost impossible with someone practically housebound, but they succeeded up to a point, most of it passed right over Jack's head, more ill than anyone imagined, including Liz. How could she watch him swallow so many different tablets, day after day, and not know the score? Not stupid by any means, perhaps unconsciously refusing to accept what was staring her in the face, was that it? They had always been able to communicate, so why not then? Better far to have brought their real feelings into the open and discuss what lay ahead. One unwilling to inflict hurt upon the other, what else could it be? A mistaken idea and much regretted now.

"I can't even remember the last words we spoke!" Liz cried from the bottom of her heart, nor could she however hard she tried. There had been conversation on the morning of that fateful day, both at breakfast and lunch, Jack, Jane and herself talking at one stage about holidays. "Take the car and go off somewhere by yourself," Jane was encouraged, but declared it wouldn't be much fun, a woman on her own, "I would rather we all went somewhere." But Liz reckoned there wasn't any hope of that with Jack the way he was. He did seem brighter that particular day, however, and they began to make plans for the afternoon, Liz opting for an hour or two at the typewriter, her Christmas present from Jack, to be the very last – no wonder she still cherished it. Jane offered to walk the dog, then join her Dad in watching a video, 'The Deer Hunter'. Funny remembering that when it wasn't important, a case of the mind latching on to the insignificant and losing what really mattered.

Jane soon returned from her walk, a chilly one, snow on the ground, but Lassie needed to be exercised and do the necessary. She asked where her Dad was, adding, "Not on this floor, I've looked." Liz couldn't recall when she had last seen her husband. "Try upstairs," she suggested, no reason at this stage to be unduly concerned, theirs was a big house and he could be anywhere.

When the search proved futile, Jane was told to look in the wardrobe in her parents' bedroom, "If his anorak is missing, he'll have gone down the garden to chat with Nell." A close neighbour and about as far as he ventured those days.

In the meantime, back to the typewriter, brought sharply out of her dream world by a frantic cry of "*Mum!*", its desperation not to be ignored. Liz burst into the first floor bedroom, where Jane stood transfixed, staring at the floor. "Oh Mum," she agonised, as her mother moved nearer, horrified by what she saw.

Jack lay there, neatly stretched out between the two beds and she knew, with a tightening of the heart, that he was dead, and fell to her knees beside him, feeling for a pulse but there was no sign of life. No tears, just a swift dash to the phone, dialling the doctor's number and dispatching Jane, still weeping profusely, to seek Nell's husband, George. He arrived just before the doctor, who stopped on his way indoors to halt an ambulance, already in the street, the third time he had been called, urgently, in less than two years.

The man who emerged from the bedroom was grave-faced and Liz, perched on the arm of a chair in the big sitting room, knew there was no hope. "Nothing you could have done, it would be very quick, your husband was on a massive dose of drugs."

Liz accepted what he said in a daze, it all seemed so unreal, wondering then as she wondered now why she didn't hear anything. Probably because she was pounding away on that damned typewriter, out of this world, unconscious of everything as usual, while the person she loved most was leaving her forever. But no demonstration of grief, some tears but not a lot, unable to give vent to her feelings, numb almost.

Jane did enough crying for both of them as Liz went through the motions, doing what had to be done, watching Jack being taken out of the house to lie in church until the funeral, yet to be arranged. She touched his face but the man she loved and lived with for forty-five years had gone, only the empty shell remained, the body that is ours for our span on earth – but the spirit had departed, taking her own heart with it.

Someone, she didn't know who, put the typewriter away in its case, the sheet of paper still in it, the words she wrote as her husband was dying. For more than a year afterwards Liz could not bear to touch it and decided the Muse had deserted her, grief the strongest emotion and no relief from it, except in the copious tears shed when alone, her head against the back of a chair, howling like a wounded animal.

She eventually destroyed the sheet of paper, no knowledge of what she had written at the time, not even interested, wishing she could recollect the last words Jack spoke, without success. Only what he said, the previous evening, standing with his back to the coal fire in the lounge, two friends in for supper and a chat. "Whatever life has been with Liz, it has never been dull." Her eye misted over as she remembered the occasion. He had been more like himself that evening, sadly withdrawn of late and looking much older than his years. The memory caught at her throat, hoping she had made him as happy as he did her, recognising in retrospect how often he was right, yet her opinion decided the issue. Just certain times when he dug his toes in and wouldn't be moved. But she had always known when to back down, very few real arguments, only the usual blow ups, Jack quick-tempered but soon subsiding. Jane had inherited this from him, a good daughter and life seemed to be going her way at last. A cancer scare two years ago, a couple of operations, but subsequent X-Rays proved negative. Liz thought of her mother with a sinking heart when it was diagnosed, believing this dreadful scourge had jumped a generation to attack her daughter, praying everything would go smoothly from now on.

"We are having a wedding, Jack," she said, as if he were there in the room beside her, who to say he wasn't. "I believe she has chosen more wisely this time. Do you know what your grandson said when his mother asked him to give her away – with pleasure. A glint of amusement in his brown eyes and a quirk on the lips which reminded me so much of you. I've got the hat, couldn't help thinking of you when I bought it, you always wanted me to wear hats, even when they became less fashionable. It cost me a damned sight more than the last one. Remember when I rang you from town and told you how much I paid for it and you never turned a hair. Sheer extravagance but I guess you knew the Capricorn in me would never get us into the ninth hole, as the saying goes."

The memories began to fade and Liz couldn't help feeling glad, for the time being at least. She was drained, physically and mentally, but it was done, the past given an airing and, no doubt, it would be easier to allow it free rein in future, however long that future might be.

How much pleasure Jack would have found in giving their daughter away for the second time, his pride in her always evident, a good husband and father from the very beginning. She felt like having a damned good cry and why not? Tears and laughter both relieved tension and she had released her fair share of both in her lifetime, no resentment for the former. That is what life is all about, for everyone, no exceptions, and cry she did, as the Word Processor printed out all she had written, beginning with TIME TO REMEMBER in bold capitals at the top of the first page, wishing she had savoured some of the moments more. So much of life spent hastening towards what lay ahead, not realising how quickly it passes. She had regrets, of course, who hasn't, but none of them enough to torment her beyond endurance, as in so many cases. Still 'full of it' as her mother used to say, whatever *it* might be, a zest for living she supposed. She prayed she might keep it right to the very end.

Kindliness Rules OK

T.S. Law

Never has it been in my nature,
  like easie-oasie bothers nane,
to want to bow my knee to someone,
  obeisance like "Thump me upon
the skull if you might wish to do so."

The nowadays, you may imagine,
  such action would be difficult
to do, as once considered like
  anathema abhorrent as
low down among the damned forever.

This morning, though, in Auchterarder,
  while purchasing a loaf of bread,
known as the "staff of life" supportive,
  my unsupported fingers dropped
a fifty-penny piece beside me.

Seeing my hesitation stooping,
  as caunnielyke as "Haud on, noo!"
a dacent wummanbodie by me
  boued doon as gracefulyke as smert,
then haundit me that coin sae kynlie.

Well, I would bow my head to that one
  the any day, for "Kindliness
rules OK", as the street graffiti
  should have it, much more generous
than pride in spirit and in action.

Almost forgot, though, for the halfway
  down the long brae below High Street,
a blackie bird was singing pleasure
  to be alive on such a day,
bonus worth more than fifty pennies!